DATE DUE

OCT 1 5 1990			
NOV 1 5 1990			
30 505 JOSTEN'S			

THE PRINCIPLES AND PROBLEMS OF COACHING

THE PRINCIPLES AND
—— PROBLEMS OF ——
—— COACHING ——

Edited by

JOHN D. MASSENGALE, Ed.D.

Associate Professor and Football Coach
Eastern Washington State College
Cheney, Washington

CHARLES C THOMAS · PUBLISHER
Springfield · Illinois · U.S.A.

Published and Distributed Throughout the World by
CHARLES C THOMAS • PUBLISHER
Bannerstone House
301-327 East Lawrence Avenue, Springfield, Illinois, U.S.A.

© 1975, by CHARLES C THOMAS • PUBLISHER

ISBN 0-398-03258-0 (Cloth)

ISBN 0-398-03259-9 (Paper)

Library of Congress Catalog Card Number: 74 12002

*With THOMAS BOOKS careful attention is given to all details of
manufacturing and design. It is the Publisher's desire to present books
that are satisfactory as to their physical qualities and artistic possibilities
and appropriate for their particular use. THOMAS BOOKS will be true
to those laws of quality that assure a good name and good will.*

Printed in the United States of America
C-1

Library of Congress Cataloging in Publication Data

Massengale, John D.   comp.
    The principles and problems of coaching.

    1. Coaching (Athletics) I. Title.
GV711.M37   796'.077   74-12002
ISBN 0-398-03258-0
ISBN 0-398-03259-9 (pbk.)

CONTRIBUTORS

J. Michael Armer
Gerald Benka
Bob Broughton
Verne Canfield
Philip R. Coppage
John B. Crossley
Wayne E. Dannehl
Robert L. Dodd
Henry F. Donn
Richard J. Donnelly
Harry Edwards
Don B. Emery
Arthur A. Esslinger
Douglas Fessenden
Seth Fessenden
John A. Friedrich
Joseph M. Goldfarb

Paul Governali
Andrew Grieve
Dale Hanks
Harry H. Hoitsma
Warren R. Johnson
Arthur J. Keith
Robert B. Kenig
John D. Lawther
Lawrence F. Locke
John D. Massengale
Wayne C. McKinney
Paul E. Meadows
Evelyn Mitsch
Dale O. Nelson
John E. Nixon
Rod Paige
John Ralston

Jack E. Razor
Henry M. Rice
George H. Sage
Walter E. Schafer
George D. Small
Garry J. Smith
Eldon E. Snyder
Eugene Sobolewski
Barry E. Stern
William F. Stier
Al Tamberelli
Ken Tillman
Don Veller
Mike White
Stanley Wilson
Sherwyn M. Woods

PREFACE

EVERY YEAR COLLEGES AND UNIVERSITIES graduate thousands of students who become teacher/coaches. In general, these teacher/coaches are adequately prepared to teach and coach specific sports, if one considers such items as strategy, rules, drills, techniques and skills. However, it appears that the modern teacher/coach is not adequately prepared for coaching's most difficult problems, the types of problems that occupy the coaches time when he is away from the practice session, the game, meet or match situation. Many experienced coaches feel that coaching at practice or during competition is the easiest part of their job, it is the additional responsibilities of good coaching that makes coaching difficult. This book of selected readings is concerned with those additional coaching responsibilities.

The book *does not* contain readings that are concerned with the specific technical aspects of coaching a sport, such as readings with X's, O's, plays, patterns and diagrams. It *does* contain readings that present contemporary perspectives regarding pertinent problems that confront all coaches of any sport.

This book of selected readings was designed to serve as a basic text, or a supplementary text, for general coaching methods courses that are normally offered at the undergraduate level or occasionally offered at the graduate level. The book can be used for many different courses that are currently required or suggested for physical education majors or minors, coaching minors, or for students and teachers who are attempting to meet coaching certification requirements. For example, the book is useful in any coaching course, regardless of the sport, if the course concerns coaching theory, coaching technique, the principles of coaching, the psychology of coaching, the philosophy of coaching or professional coaching orientation.

In the process of determining the content of this book, hundreds of readings were examined and reviewed, read and reread, with certain standards and criteria being constantly considered. The readings had to present a direct practical application to the occupation of coaching, while making a significant contribution to the understanding of the problems that constantly confront coaches. It was also necessary that the readings pertain to contemporary coaching problems, be readable at the undergraduate level and most of all be thought provoking to the teachers, coaches and students who will use this book.

There is no way that a book of readings can completely cover a field that is as complex and diversified as coaching and this book is no exception. However, the book does include a wide variety of views, including those of professors, public school teachers from several different disciplines, coaches at every level, school administrators, as well as the viewpoint of a concerned mother.

The book has been organized into eight different sections, with each section covering an important general area of concern to most coaches. The first section is entitled *The Coach and Coaching* and serves as an introduction into the profession of coaching. Selections in this section consist of various perspectives regarding the occupation of coaching. Consideration is given to the definition of coaching, the role of the coach and those qualities on which the coach is most often evaluated.

The second section is entitled *The Coach and Teaching* and presents pertinent information describing the coach's role as a teacher and the teacher's role as a coach. The information contained in this section is vital, since most coaches are also employed as teachers, and, in many respects, good coaching is nothing more than good teaching. The areas that are examined are teacher/coach role conflict, the similarity of coaching and teaching procedures, the teacher/coach work load, coaching certification and the coach as a school administrator.

The Coach and School-Community Relations is the title of the third section which presents readings concerning the coach's public relations responsibilities with several different types of individuals as well as interest groups. Some of the topics covered are the public image of the value of athletics, the coach's public relations responsibilities, coach-faculty relations, hints for public speaking and the coach's working relationships with physicians, parents and officials.

The fourth section of the book, *The Coach and the Coaching Staff,* is concerned mostly with the problems that confront coaches of team sports. It is applicable to sports that often have a large coaching staff like football and sometimes basketball. The topics covered in this section are coaching staff rapport, the responsibilities of the assistant coach and the causes and solutions of head coach and assistant coach role conflict.

Section five, *The Coach and Coaching Methods,* include selections that pertain to common coaching methods that are used by coaches of all sports. Among the items considered in this section are training rules, player substitution, facility management, practice scheduling, coaching method analysis, common coaching problems, morale, improving performance, player analysis, practice organization and the coach's professional growth and development.

The Coach and the Athlete is the title of the sixth section, which is concerned entirely with the coach and individual player relationships. The readings in this section describe the athlete as an individual and as a student, while focusing on perspectives like cultural, sociological and educational aspects. The influence of the coach on the athlete is also examined, particularly the coach's influence with regard to academic performance and educational expectations.

The seventh section, *The Coach and the Team,* involves the management of a team and those aspects that develop strong team unity. Aspects like group cohesion, organizational leadership and the team membership of minority group players are considered in this section.

The last section, *The Coach and Psychology,* pertains to the direct application of psychological principles to the act of coaching. The readings in this section present information regarding motivation, learning, practice, transfer, reinforcement and the types of emotional and psychological problems that often confront coaches and players.

Finally, the editor is deeply appreciative of the publishers, editors and authors who granted permission to use the materials that made this book possible.

J. D. M.

CONTENTS

                                                                   Page

Contributors v

Preface vii

Section I

THE COACH AND COACHING

Chapter

1. WHAT IS COACHING?—John Ralston, Mike White and
   Stanley Wilson 5
2. QUALITIES OF A GOOD COACH—Harry M. Rice 10
3. THE ROLE OF THE COACH IN AMERICAN EDUCATION—
   John D. Lawther 14
4. WHAT IS A GOOD COACH?—Wayne C. McKinney 18
5. SCORING THE FACTORS IN SUCCESSFUL HIGH SCHOOL
   COACHING—Don B. Emery 21
6. EVALUATING THE COACH—John A. Friedrich 29
7. GOODBYE, MR. COACH—John B. Crossley 35

Section II

THE COACH AND TEACHING

8. THE PHYSICAL EDUCATOR AS COACH—Paul Governali . . . 43
9. COACHING TECHNIQUES APPLIED TO THE CLASSROOM—
   Gerald Benka 48
10. HOW COACHES TEACH—J. Arthur Keith 50
11. TEACHING LOAD OF THE COLLEGE PHYSICAL EDUCATION
    TEACHER COACH—Ken Tillman 53
12. CERTIFICATION FOR HIGH SCHOOL COACHES—
    Arthur A. Esslinger 64
13. THE PHYSICAL EDUCATOR AND COACH IN PUBLIC SCHOOL
    ADMINISTRATION—Lawrence F. Locke and John E. Nixon . 77

Section III

THE COACH AND SCHOOL-COMMUNITY RELATIONS

Chapter   *Page*

14. THE VALUES OF ATHLETICS—A CRITICAL INQUIRY—Wayne E.
      Dannehl and Jack E. Razor   87
15. THE COACH AS A PUBLIC RELATIONS MAN—Al Tamberelli, Jr.   95
16. COACH-FACULTY STRAIN: SOME OCCUPATIONAL CAUSES AND
      CONSIDERATIONS—John D. Massengale   99
17. RELATIONSHIPS BETWEEN ATHLETIC OFFICIALS AND COACHES—
      Richard J. Donnelly   106
18. ROLE OF COACH, PHYSICIAN IN PROGRAM—Henry F. Donn .   121
19. "UNACCUSTOMED AS I AM . . ."—Douglas Fessenden and
      Seth Fessenden   128
20. LEND HIM YOUR SON—Evelyn Mitsch   134

Section IV

THE COACH AND THE COACHING STAFF

21. HEAD COACH AND ASSISTANT RAPPORT—Don Veller . . .   141
22. SEVEN GUIDELINES FOR THE ASSISTANT COACH—Robert B. Kenig 150
23. THE HEAD COACH AND HIS ASSISTANTS—Harry Edwards . .   154

Section V

THE COACH AND COACHING METHODS

24. COMPENDIUM OF COMMONSENSE PRINCIPLES IN MODERN
      COACHING—Don Veller   159
25. ANALYSIS OF ATHLETIC COACHING FAILURES—Robert L. Dodd   175
26. FACTORS INFLUENCING A COACH'S ABILITY TO ANALYZE—
      Andrew Grieve   183
27. NINE WAYS TO IMPROVE YOUR COACHING—Verńie Canfield .   193
28. IMPROVE PERFORMANCE BY UTILIZING FUNDAMENTAL
      PRINCIPLES OF MOVEMENT—Dale O. Nelson   198
29. GET THE RIGHT BOY IN THE RIGHT JOB—Don Veller . . .   207
30. RECIPE FOR ALL-AMERICANS—Eugene Sobloewshi   222
31. ARE WE REALLY COACHING FUNDAMENTALS?—
      Paul E. Meadows   226
32. THE COACH'S HANDBOOK—Andrew Grieve   231

Section VI

THE COACH AND THE ATHLETE

Chapter *Page*

33. THE VIOLENT WORLD OF THE ATHLETE—Sherwyn M. Woods   241
34. ATHLETES ARE NOT INFERIOR STUDENTS—Walter E. Shafer
    and J. Michael Armer   249
35. THE CULTURAL CRISIS IN AMERICAN SPORTS—Barry E. Stern   266
36. A STUDY OF SELECTED ASPECTS OF THE COACH'S INFLUENCE
    ON HIGH SCHOOL ATHLETES—Eldon E. Snyder   275
37. EVERYTHING THE ATHLETE ALWAYS WANTED TO KNOW ABOUT
    SELECTING A COLLEGE BUT WAS AFRAID TO ASK—
    William F. Stier   282

Section VII

THE COACH AND THE TEAM

38. GROUP COHESION IN ATHLETICS—Garry J. Smith   293
39. THE COACH AS MANAGEMENT: ORGANIZATIONAL LEADERSHIP
    IN AMERICAN SPORT—George H. Sage   299
40. ORGANIZATION BEGINS WITH THE COACH—Dale Hanks . .   309
41. RACIAL EMPATHY AND THE WHITE COACH—Rod Paige . .   315

Section VIII

THE COACH AND PSYCHOLOGY

42. MOTIVATIONAL PSYCHOLOGY IN COACHING—Joseph M. Goldfarb   327
43. THE LEARNING PROCESS AS APPLIED TO COACHING—
    George D. Small   335
44. GET MORE FROM PRACTICE—Philip R. Coppage   347
45. PRAISE OR PUNISHMENT?—Don Veller   354
46. VERBAL CONDITIONING IN SELECTING SKILLS—Bob Broughton
    and Dale O. Nelson   362
47. COACH'S DILEMMA—Harry H. Hoitsma   367
48. EMOTIONAL UPSET AND PSYCHOSOMATIC PROBLEMS IN
    COACHING—Warren R. Johnson   371

THE PRINCIPLES AND PROBLEMS OF COACHING

THE COACH AND COACHING

CHAPTER 1

WHAT IS COACHING?

JOHN RALSTON, MIKE WHITE
AND STANLEY WILSON*

IN THE PAST SIX YEARS, American educational institutions have faced crises of greater magnitude than ever before in history. Militant students and liberal, restless, faculty members have engaged in a variety of activities ranging from peaceful dissent to overt rebellion. Although relatively few in number, the dissident factions have altered, if not changed, the face of American education.

The era has produced a new breed of students and a new breed of athletes. Open hostility and dissension have been manifested by a significant subculture of students. The coach's authority has been questioned in such diverse areas as personal appearance and competitive values. Some high schools and colleges have experienced racial crises, accompanied by demands for admission of more black and other minority athletes. Similar ultimatums have been made in relation to the hiring of coaches from representative ethnic groups.

The academicians have responded in reshaping and modifying curricula. Whole new programs of study have been instituted. Accordingly, the role of the coach has changed significantly. He no longer stands alone as a coach, the entity; his position has become that of teacher first, coach second.

We agree with the necessity and appropriateness of new philosophies and programs embraced by educational institutions. We also agree that coaches must react to new trends. He must not become locked into outdated attitudes, prejudices, or out-

* Reprinted from *Coaching Today's Athlete: A Football Textbook* by John Ralston, Mike White and Stanley Wilson by permission of National Press Books.

moded social structures. As sociological changes emerge, so must the coach be aware of the necessity of altering, modifying, or revamping his long-practiced philosophy of the human and technical aspects of football.

However, notwithstanding concessions on what may appear to be radical changes in response to social requisites, the coach's authoritative and responsible competence must prevail. For the coach to ascertain success, he is tested in nine, ten, or perhaps eleven two-hour sessions on either Friday afternoon, Friday evening, or Saturday during the Fall of the year. His teaching will be put to a test in front of a multitude of judges. He must have the necessary insight and understanding to be able to communicate openly and effectively with the athletes who come under his direction. He must have the athlete totally prepared physically and mentally as he readies himself for the final exam which comes on game day.

The teaching of physical skills relates to the mind more than ever before in sports' history. Today's student-athlete must be motivated to learn with greater efficiency and flexibility primarily because outside pressures and demands never have been greater. He who motivates is a teacher. It is the teacher-coach who captures the essential spirit of an athletic program in a manner that is marked by integrity, imagination and understanding.

All too often in this era of stress and turbulence, the coach does not take the time nor effort to evaluate himself, particularly in terms of the athletes with whom he works. Educators generally agree that coaches should be judged by the same criteria as other members of the faculty. As long as forty-six years ago Knute Rockne recognized the coach's role as a teacher and expressed evaluations succinctly: "The coach has to be a super teacher. He must see to it that the class learns what he has to teach. If he flunks half the class, he flunks with them. It is not what a coach knows, it is what he can teach his boys, what he can make them do" (Knute Rockne, *Coaching*, 1925, p. 209).

Teaching aids and methods of evaluation have improved immeasurably since Coach Rockne's observations. They will continue to improve. Already we rely heavily upon television, sophisticated scouting and recruiting techniques, and refined staff and player personnel procedures. These products of technology contribute to increased efficiency in learning and in freeing coaches to give more individual attention to their players and detailed planning. But they are not the total and final answers.

Perhaps Emerson was looking to this Age of Technology when he advised, "Not he is great who can alter matter, but he who can alter my state of mind." In this context, we are making large and significant demands of the teacher-coach, but we will have a successful program only when we make these demands and when we require him to assume a primary role as an educator.

In a 1959 report by the American Council of Education, it was found in a survey that there was unanimous agreement among students in a variety of institutions that they value far more highly the faculty member who is willing to make known his own commitments. It, therefore, is axiomatic that teachers should understand themselves and their goals as well as their students. We often neglect to consider that the psychology of the teacher is equally as complex as that of the learner. What occurs on the practice or game field is the process of interaction of student and teacher and between the individual athlete and squad as a group. The teacher-coach is a vital element in this process of interaction. Developing an understanding of the athlete or student essentially is a problem of understanding human motivation.

What, then, constitutes and enhances interaction between the teacher-coach and his players? "He [the teacher] must first of all be aflame with interest himself, at least in his own specialty. So aflame, indeed, that it is easy for him to light the torches of youth. If he possesses enthusiasm which grows out of abundant and sound knowledge, he is likely to be successful."[1]

This quality or characteristic in modern sports is not the "do or die" half-time rhetoric that was appropriate and effective forty years ago, or even more recently. Rather, it is a sincere, delib-

---

1. T. H. Briggs, *Secondary Education* (New York, The Macmillan Company, 1933), p. 533.

erate and enthusiastic outcry for something of value. Real enthusiasm, faith and quiet confidence are contagious.

An aware teacher-coach must realize the enormity of the task
before him. He must recognize the tremendous influence he has
on the athletes that come under his direction. The lessons he
teaches on the athletic field will carry over into later life and
will provide guidelines for a young man to accept his responsibility in his chosen profession, his family and the community
in which he lives. We have referred previously to these lessons
as "indelible impressions." They take the form of pursuit of
purpose, teamwork, dedication, perseverance and the vital lesson
that ultimate success in any endeavor comes through the willingness to sacrifice and pay the price to excel.

Coaching is a painfully slow process even under the best of
conditions. It often may appear all the slower because of the
coach's familiarity with his subject. How many times must this
drill be repeated? When will that blocking assignment become
instinctive? There is no miracle for the teacher-coach. A
thoughtful and perceptive teacher-coach knows the limitations
as well as the capabilities of his team members and he does not
unnerve and confuse his players by attempting to force them to
assimilate and digest more rapidly than is possible with their
mental and physical equipment. A successful teacher-coach becomes a living reflection of what he teaches. He must believe in
what he is doing, why he is doing it and the direction in which
he is going. He must exude enthusiasm, dedication, interest and
faith. He must be flexible in what he teaches and the manner in
which he teaches. He must be a winner all the way and strive for
excellence in everything he does. *He must want to win as badly
as a coach as he did as a player.* A coach must possess a pride in
his responsibility which, in turn, will carry over to his players.

Because a coach is such a vital part of a young man's life, he
must always set the proper examples. Not only must we inspire
our athletes to perform their best, but we must inspire their best
behavior. A coach must practice personal integrity, not only in
his associations with the team, but in his personal life both on
and off the football field. At the same time, a coach must de-

velop early in his career the ability to cope with adversity and not to blame his staff or players. If one is to take the bows and applause, he must learn to accept defeat with humility. However, the ability to bounce back from extreme adversity and to hit the practice field with renewed enthusiasm is a constant requisite. A coach must realize that the only way to reverse the tide and get back on the positive side is to work even harder in his teaching, preparation and attention to detail.

Following a discussion of why a young man should or should not seek the coaching profession for his life's work, it only follows that one must determine just what *is* a coach.

Here is at least a partial list of what we consider to be the basic ingredients a coach should have:

1. An inspiration to students and an ability to command faculty respect.
2. Friendly and helpful to team members and students.
3. Tireless worker.
4. Colorful and imaginative—ability to operate under the public's eye with dignity, gentlemanly appearance and sportsmanlike conduct.
5. Good disciplinarian—helpful attitude but respectful control.
6. Capacity for organizing recruiting program if coaching at the college level.
7. Commitment to operate program within the rules of his league or conference.
8. Ability to fit into the athletic department organization and cooperate in overall program.
9. Understanding of the role of students and respect for students in nonathletic activities.
10. A good organizer and administrator. Must have executive ability to get the most out of those employed by him.
11. Flexibility in his coaching methods, techniques and system.

CHAPTER 2

QUALITIES OF A GOOD COACH

HARRY M. RICE*

THE FIRST QUALITY that I look for in a coach is his professional ability as a teacher on the staff. He is a teacher first and then a coach. Teaching is of primary importance whether it is in the classroom or in an athletic sport. This does not mean that coaching is of lesser importance than classroom teaching or that classroom teaching is of secondary importance to coaching. It means that the school curriculum encompasses both academic learning in the classroom and athletic learning in the various sports.

The athletic program is part of the educational program; it may be considered as a subject taught and one from which educational experiences are derived by participants, both contestants and spectators. *More precisely, the athletic program is part of the physical education program.* The objectives of the athletic program must be in harmony with the objectives of physical education just as the objectives of physical education must be in harmony with the objectives of secondary education. The athletic program then is as much the responsibility of the principal as is the instruction of any other subject. The relationship then of the coach with the staff should be consonant with the highest level of the teaching profession. He is a teacher first and then a coach.

The next quality that I look for in a coach—does he know his subject sport for which he is an applicant to coach? What participation has he had in high school, college, or professional? Experience as a player, although not always a requisite for success-

* Harry M. Rice, "Qualities of a Good Coach," *The Bulletin of the National Association of Secondary School Principals,* Vol. 43 (December 1959), pp. 152-154.

ful coaching, establishes confidence of professional colleagues, the students and the community that the coach knows his subject. To have played the sport with reasonable success, to have experienced being coached as a participant in the sport and to have earned the praise and recommendation of his coach as a worthy candidate for a position of leadership in coaching, is a first step of primary importance in being considered for a coaching position on my staff. Knowing your subject sport by being an outstanding player will not of itself insure success as a coach. Just as a teacher may know his subject well, but flounder in putting it across to his pupils, so may a successful college star in athletics be out of field in coaching unless he can adjust from the player role to the role of the teacher. This then leads me to the priceless talent of all human beings. Some of us have attempted to describe it, but few of us are able to define it completely. It is known as *personality.*

The personality of the teacher determines in a large measure the quality of a good teacher. The personable coach has qualities that attract boys to respect his personality, to be loyal and seek his approbation in doing their best. They have faith, confidence and abiding loyalty in his teaching. There are various ways that coaches may build up *esprit de corps* in the boys they coach. Scholastic eligibility, physical conditioning, training rules, rules of the sport, moral and spiritual values, code of dress and pupil conduct, and loyalty to the team and the school are all primary in the teaching of a successful coach. He may win athletic contests, but if he fails in these fundamentals of teaching, the true and proper perspective of values in life are lost indeed.

The rules of training and standards of conduct should be drawn up and explained by the coach to his boys. A personal letter from the coach to the boys and a letter to the parents are ways to get across understanding of what the coach expects in his sport. A more personal approach is for the coach to visit the homes of his boys and meet the parents face-to-face. He can answer the parents' questions about the policy and organization of the sport. Reassurance to the parents that the best interests of their son is first in the coach's mission goes a long way to projecting the personality of both the coach and the school and community he serves. All this takes time, effort and faith. But the person in the coach, just as the person in the teacher, can only be known by such demonstrations of personality.

Finally, a basic quality that I look for in a coach is *character*. It is of first importance in the profession of teaching. "Character is what we are; reputation, what people think we are." A *coach is in a position to have a stronger influence for good in the lives of his boys than any other staff member*. The first test of character in athletics is that rules of eligibility for participants shall be strictly adhered to. The participant in the sport must meet all requirements to enter the sport. The coach will not compromise with rules and regulations, such as smoking, drinking, gambling, *et al.*, in clearing players for his sport. Players who are in danger or risk of a physical injury being aggravated are not permitted to participate in the sport unless cleared by the team physician. Conduct unbecoming a player, foul and abusive language by a player are not permitted. A coach should never tolerate insubordination in relations with his players. A coach never argues with officials or demonstrates uncontrolled emotions in the crises of winning or losing an athletic contest. Calmness in victory or defeat is a necessary virtue for a coach to pursue for its everlasting effect upon the character of the teams and the individual learning experiences it provides for the players and the spectators.

How shall we evaluate our coaches? I believe in the principle of healthy competition in athletics, as I believe in a free and competitive enterprise system. But we must not evaluate the coach solely on his won-lost record, any more than we would (or should) evaluate a teacher of an academic subject solely on the number of 500-plus scores his students in any one year received in the College Board Examinations. If we conceive the work of the coach as being that of *education*, then winning athletic contests is only one criterion of success.

Other criteria might well be the coach's pervading influence in maintaining standards of morality, decency, honor and courage; in his building self-confidence (with a leavening of humility); the teaching of cooperation, good will and understanding. As a former social studies teacher, who loved his work, I can see with clarity too the unique opportunity, even the inescapable responsibility of the coach to practice and teach good sportsmanship, which is an essential ingredient in good citizenship. I must face up to my responsibility in the teaching of good sportsmanship, but I owe it to plain candor to submit that the coach is the one on the firing line. It is he, primarily, who determines the tenor of sportsmanship in his players—and the spectators. When the coach walks out on the field, or the basketball court with his boys, he is *the school.* When he sits on the bench, and lives through a decision which he believes is incorrect, he is *the school.* None of us in the schools stands so often in the white floodlight of publicity as the coach. It's good to win, *but it is what the coach is, that is important.* You all remember with me, "Your actions speak so loud that I cannot hear what you say."

In conclusion then, these four qualities are attributes that I look for in a coach:

1. He is first a teacher, then a coach.
2. He knows his coaching sport; his experience as a player and a coach is demonstrated by his leadership.
3. His personality pervades the sport he coaches and sustains an abiding interest by the staff, the students and the community.
4. His character is subscribed to in both playing the sport he coaches and the faculty he is a part of by the students, both contestants and spectators.

The philosophy of a good coach should be, *"A game worth playing is worth winning fairly."*

CHAPTER 3

THE ROLE OF THE COACH IN AMERICAN EDUCATION

John D. Lawther*

THE LATE ARNOLD GESELL once said that it was through play and games that the child gets the "opportunity for effort, and failure and success, for judicious risks and thrills and a store of experiences which build up his morale, his capacity to endure and stand the gaff, his early learnings in sportsmanship."

Before the present generation, only England of the great civilized nations based its physical, moral and leadership training on the lessons from the sports and games of the athletic fields. In the so-called "great public schools" of England in which the aristocracy of Great Britain were educated, the schoolmasters as well as the students spent their afternoons together on the play fields. This aspect of English education was considered an essential part of the training of Great Britain's future statesmen and military officers. The Duke of Wellington's statement that the battle of Waterloo had been won on the playing fields of Eton and Harrow has been quoted many times.

Let me quote somewhat similar opinions expressed by Thomas Wood and Clark Hetherington at the beginning of the present century. Wood said:

> Very little profitable instruction in theoretical ethics can be given the elementary or even in the high school. Children and youth get most of their moral instruction in relation to action, and many important ethical principles may be instilled in connection with the large primitive types of conduct involved in personal health problems, and in games and sports. The playground, gymnasium, and athletic

---

* John D. Lawther, "The Role of the Coach in American Education," *Journal of Health, Physical Education, and Research,* Vol. 36 (May 1965), pp. 65-66.

field afford the best opportunity for the learning of moral lessons, sometimes even by college students.[1]

In the same year Hetherington wrote:

> The fundamental character education through the guidance of conduct in play is not completed in childhood. It continues through youth, and long after moral education by intellectual inspiration may be well begun. The athletic field of the late adolescent years is as truly a laboratory of conduct as is the playfield of the child. This is the last chance age for intensive moral training by direct personal guidance and discipline. Fourteen to twenty is the critical period in which all the fundamental social traits and moral habits are formed, and they are formed in a large measure on the play side of life. . . .[2]

The athletic sports in our educational system can well be a form of recreational therapy from the grind of the academic classroom and from the anxiety neuroses of adolescence. Athletic competition motivates many youngsters to achieve undeveloped potentialities in skill, in emotional control under stress, in social development, and in strength and endurance. Athletic skills provide our youth with means for escape from the boredom and monotony of inactivity or, what is worse, from spending their energy in socially disapproved directions. Our youth use their athletic skills for social group participation in areas which they enjoy and in which they have greater confidence in their abilities to do their part acceptably. They learn to escape from emotional upsets by physical self-expression in sports.

You, as a coach of boys' or girls' athletic teams, must remember that highly competitive activities arouse much emotional excitement and deep feeling. In this heated atmosphere your players are going to be molded in some way. Their abilities and shortcomings, their emotional reactions, their drive, energy, determination, or lack of it—in short, their personality quirks and eccentricities—will be revealed. Behavior codes and attitudes are learned rapidly under group social pressures and emotional con-

1. Thomas C. Wood, "Physical Education," *Health and Education*, Ninth Yearbook, Part I, National Society for the Study of Education. (Bloomington, Ill., Public School Publishing, 1910), pp. 89-90.
2. Clark W. Hetherington, "Fundamental Education," *American Physical Education Review*, Vol. 15 (December 1910), p. 633.

ditioning. Under such emotional arousal youngsters are more impressionable, more subject to change. Herein, of course lies the absolute necessity for careful guidance. If these youngsters cannot achieve a certain amount of recognition, approval, success in activity, and therefore status, they may resort to abnormal or antisocial behavior. Unsportsmanlike conduct, breaking rules, fits of anger to cover up failure, may be expected to crop out and need correction. These youngsters' lapses from proper social codes, from complete fairness, are due to lack of understanding of how to secure success, group approval and prestige.

You, the coach, have a closer relationship and a great influence on youngsters than almost any other teacher. In your content area (athletics) in which physical, moral and social behavior are of vital importance, you will have a great influence on these youngsters. Your influence is inescapable in spite of the fact that it thrusts upon you an almost fearful responsibility for directing character formation. The competitive world—in children's play, in athletics, in life—is neither gentle nor kind. You, the coach, must be both kind and firm. The youngsters *need* understanding and *want* firm guidance by one they trust. They want the firm guidance to help them over their uncertainties and insecurities. They want to be respected adults and they appreciate regimens requiring adoption of mature, responsible behavior.

You, the coach, can hardly help becoming a community personality, an important member of the faculty and a focus of attention of many students. Your personal behavior will be under considerable scrutiny, hence you will have to be constantly aware of the example you set. To succeed you must be energetic, dynamic and forceful. Sports skills are the means through which you teach, so you must become an excellent sports teacher. However, you will find the direction of interschool sports a highly interesting and unusually exciting profession. I know of no other occupation which is more rewarding in human satisfactions. All down through the ages of history, competitive sports have fulfilled such a felt need of man that neither religious edict nor royal decree has been successful in abolishing them. Cozens and Stumpf once stated:

The exercise of physical skill, mental acumen, and spiritual courage in the field of sports and games is as old and as integral a part of the culture of mankind as the expression of these same human capacities in the fields of music and art. The rich and colorful heritage in this area of human experience is as much a part of the birthright of the children of earth as the songs that have been sung and the pictures that have been painted. . . .

Common interests, common loyalties, common enthusiasms, those are the great integrating factors in any culture. In America, sports have provided this common denominator in as great a degree as any other factor.[3]

---

3. Frederick W. Cozens and Florence Stumpf, "American Sports from the Side-lines." *Journal of Health, Physical Education, and Recreation,* Vol. 23 (November 1952), p. 12.

CHAPTER 4

WHAT IS A GOOD COACH?

WAYNE C. McKINNEY*

A GOOD COACH has a sound technical knowledge of sport and an insight into athletes, which he incorporates into a highly organized twelve-month coaching plan. The *mediocre coach* has a superficial knowledge of sport, but he thinks he knows it all. According to the German philosopher, Johann Wolfgang Goethe, "There is nothing more dangerous than an active ignorance."

A *good coach* is capable of helping the student achieve his athletic potential. The *mediocre coach* cannot gauge the student's athletic potential because he lacks evaluative ability.

A *good coach* builds his team on a foundation of individual skill teaching. The *mediocre coach* frequently becomes so obsessed with the overall team goal that he ignores the basics.

A *good coach* keeps abreast of technical and scientific advances by being actively involved in the physical education profession. A *mediocre coach* has no scientific curiosity and continues using antiquated ideas for the sake of expediency.

A *good coach* is capable of adjusting his game to fit his players' intellectual and neuromuscular skill levels. The *mediocre coach* continues using offenses, defenses and strategies which have worked for him in the past, regardless of the specific abilities of his personnel.

A *good coach* applies scientific principles of conditioning on a twelve-month basis. He knows that the extra strength, endurance, flexibility and skill developed in the off-season and preseason can spell the difference between a winner and a loser. The *mediocre coach* conditions his team pragmatically—"like my old

* Wayne C. McKinney, "What Is a Good Coach?" *Scholastic Coach*, Vol. 39 (March 1970), p. 86.

coach did it"—during the season only. He is the type of coach who still believes that weight training causes "muscle-boundness."

A *good coach* emphasized education first and athletics second. The *mediocre coach* places athletics ahead of education. On the college level, he may advise an immature athlete to take "snap courses" in order to remain eligible. And when the athlete's eligibility runs out while he's still a year or more shy of his degree, the mediocre coach will rationalize, "Well, a little college is better than none at all"—and go looking for other immature athletes to con.

A *good coach* hates to lose, but he will not try to win at any cost. The *mediocre coach* hates to lose, and will not be too circumspect about how he wins—disregarding the cost to his student-athletes and himself.

A *good coach* teaches the long-range values of athletic participation. The *mediocre coach* pays little attention to axiologic considerations. The pursuit of excellence with its many related and potential values are of no concern to him, because he cannot conceptualize the relationship between the abstractions within value theory and winning ball games. A good coach is aware of this relationship and uses it to motivate the student-athlete.

A *good coach* does not let his ego distort his professional motives for coaching young men and women. The *mediocre coach* is highly ego-involved: in fact, self-promotion is one of his major motivational forces for coaching—"the big-time syndrome." This type of coach psychologically needs the "reflective glory" gained through the achievements of his team or individual athletes. In other words, the mediocre coach may need the athletes more than they need him!

A *good coach* plays up his team to the communications media. The *mediocre coach* usually discusses *his efforts* to develop *his* team for *his* school.

A *good coach* gives ample credit to faculty and student assistants at all times. The *mediocre coach* takes all the personal credit he can during winning efforts and mentions assistants in a negative manner during losing efforts.

A *good coach* is respected by students, student-athletes and peers on the faculty. A *mediocre coach* DEMANDS this sort of respect but seldom gets it. (He frequently confuses fear for respect.)

A *good coach* is a physical educator who is dedicated to the totality of his profession. He has developed a professional attitude that makes teaching a physical education class at 9:00 a.m. as challenging as coaching a varsity program at 4:30 p.m. He knows that the basic process of teaching and coaching is the same. The main differences lie in the skill and motivational levels of the students. The good coach accepts the fact that the 9:00 a.m. student is even more of a challenge to teach-coach than the varsity athlete.

The *mediocre coach* is too preoccupied with drawing "X's" and "O's" on blackboards and viewing films to do anything more than roll out balls in the physical education classes. The "ball roller" does very little *real* teaching or coaching during a twenty-four-hour day.

SCORING THE FACTORS IN SUCCESSFUL HIGH SCHOOL COACHING

Don B. Emery*

L ETTERS OF RECOMMENDATION are apt to read: "I think he will make a successful coach." What does this really mean? What is a successful coach? Who is a successful coach?

Starting with a survey of the recent articles and books on successful coaching, the author set down each item mentioned in the form of a score card. Four headings were used, divided as follows:

  I. Coaching Methods and Techniques
    A. Methods of practice and coaching
    B. Team morale
    C. Physical condition and welfare of players
  II. Personal Characteristics, Education and Training
    A. Personal characteristics
    B. Education, training and background
    C. Self-improvement
 III. Organization and Administration
 IV. Public Relations
    A. General practices
    B. Within the school
    C. Within the community

Next, a five-man jury was chosen, consisting of two staff members from the Indiana University School of Health, Physical Education and Recreation, and three doctoral candidates in the physical education division.

All jury members had had a minimum of ten years of experi-

* Don B. Emery, "Scoring the Factors in Successful High School Coaching," *Scholastic Coach*, Vol. 31 (March 1962), pp. 60-65.

21

ence in coaching and physical education, with the average being twenty-three years. Four of the five members were currently engaged in college physical education work involving direction of majors in the field.

Instructions to this jury read as follows:

Rating Scale: Indispensable factor for successful tenure (5 pts.), Desirable and valuable factor (3 pts.), Some value but not always essential (1 pt.), No value and should be deleted (0 pts.).

Instruction: (1) Apply the rating scale to each of the items under the four general areas. (2) Feel free to add items to any of the four areas or items under any of the subareas.

After the jury's evaluation, items with less than fifteen points were discarded, leaving a final total of 114 items for the revised scorecard. Points were set up to total one thousand.

A second jury was then selected to evaluate the items on this revised card. These members included:

1. Public school administrators from small, medium and large school systems, with all but one having had previous experience in coaching and all directly associated with the athletic program.

2. College and university personnel engaged in the professional preparation of majors in physical education, selected again from the small, medium and large institution, and all with a rich background in athletics.

3. Directors of physical education in the public schools, all of whom had coached or were still coaching, with one to four high schools under supervision.

4. Active coaches from single high schools, each of whom had served an average of fifteen years.

Purposes

1. To aid the athletic director in evaluating his coaching staff.
2. To set up desirable standards for coaches to attain.
3. To appraise the personal status of the coach in attaining these standards.
4. To reveal the areas of strength and weakness of a coach.
5. To provide a specific basis for personal improvement.

Directions

1. Evaluate each area and assign points so that the sum of points scored in the four areas combined will be one thousand.

2. Assign points to each subarea so that the total points of all the subareas will equal the points assigned in that area.

3. Assign points to each item under each subarea so that the total points earned for the items under that subarea will equal the points assigned for the subarea.

4. Avoid using any fractions of points earned for areas, subarea or items.

Following is the way the highly competent jury of twenty educators evaluated the 114 factors influencing success in high school coaching (the numbers in parenthesis after each item refer to the points it received):

I. Coaching Methods and Techniques (365 pts.)

A. METHODS OF PRACTICE AND COACHING (153 pts.): The high school coach should:

1. Use professionally sound coaching methods (11).

2. Utilize basic laws of learning and psychology of good teaching in his coaching (10).

3. Carefully explain and demonstrate fundamentals and diligently strive for perfection of execution (10).

4. Teach at level players are able to understand and be able to explain reason for doing certain things (10).

5. Be straightforward and truthful in talks with players (10).

6. Have ability to analyze and correct mistakes of players (10).

7. Be well-acquainted with physical, mental, social and psychological make-up of player (9).

8. Consider individual differences in both ability to learn and to perform (9).

9. Adequately emphasize every aspect of sport needed by players for their caliber of competition (9).

10. Show patience in all coaching details (9).

11. Have ability to teach players what he knows himself (9).

12. Strive to keep injuries at a minimum without sacrifice of player aggressiveness (9).

13. Consciously strive to enhance concomitant learnings (8).

14. Use originality and imagination in coaching (8).

15. Use a positive approach in coaching (8).

16. Play as many boys as possible in each game (8).

17. Place emphasis upon performance rather than form (6).

B. TEAM MORALE (110 pts.): The high school coach should:

1. Create a good feeling of team loyalty among players (12).

2. Maintain good discipline and treat disciplinary cases in accordance with infraction and individual (11).

3. Offer encouragement and constructive criticism when team is losing and accept responsibility for team (11).

4. Be fair in treatment of all players (10).

5. Give credit to players when team wins (10).

6. Back up team at all times, making criticism of them only in their presence (10).

7. Prohibit swearing, gambling and other unsocial acts (9).

8. Be friendly toward all players (8).

9. Talk frequently to young and inexperienced players to prevent discouragement and to bolster morale (8).

10. Provide a pleasant atmosphere and efficient service in dressing and training rooms (8).

11. Encourage players to participate in other school activities (7).

12. Do not become too familiar with players (6).

C. PHYSICAL CONDITION AND WELFARE OF PLAYERS (102 pts.): The high school coach should:

1. Maintain good physical condition among his players throughout season (10).

2. Unhesitantly remove a player from any contest whenever an injury may be serious (10).

3. Be concerned with physical and mental welfare of players and take precautions to guard against ill health and injuries (9).

4. Conduct a graduated conditioning program at beginning of season (9).

5. Demand a high standard of maintenance in all areas of participation, including showering and dressing facilities (9).

6. Allow players to participate in setting up and enforcing training rules (8).

7. Supervise training room and obtain adequate help (8).

8. Be thoughtful of injured players and seek to keep up their morale (8).

9. Acquire a doctor's permission for an injured or ill player to return to practice (8).

10. Seek to provide a good emotional climate for players (8).

11. Make provision for services of a doctor at all home games or make certain one is on-call (8).

12. Consult with players on preseason conditioning (6).

II. Personal Characteristics, Education and Training (314 pts.)

A. PERSONAL CHARACTERISTICS (156 pts.): The high school coach should:

1. Essentially desire to coach (10).

2. Have ability to motivate staff and players toward desired goals (10).

3. Never criticize an assistant before players or in public (10).

4. Practice good human relations with players, students, faculty and community citizens (9).

5. Possess a good philosophy of life (9).

6. Be emotionally stable and self-controlled during excitement and competition (9).

7. Exhibit sound judgment in making decisions (9).

8. Have a liking for and understanding of age group he coaches (9).

9. Possess a highly competitive spirit and a great desire to win (9).

10. Exhibit and tolerate some humor in coaching and daily living (9).

11. Give credit to staff for commendable work (9).

12. Have good rapport with players he coaches (8).

13. Possess a pleasant, outgoing personality and be of high moral character (8).

14. Be available for consultation on any personal or scholastic problems players might have (7).

15. Refrain from seeking all forms of subsidization (7).

16. Encourage boys to participate in sports other than one he coaches (7).

17. Develop and maintain an immunity to criticism (6).

18. Manage his personal finances well (6).

19. Encourage players to seek his advice on matters pertaining to sports (5).

B. EDUCATION (65 pts.): The high school coach should:

1. Be considered highly competent in sport he coaches—rules, techniques, strategies and skills (13).

2. Have undergraduate major in P.E. (8).

3. Have participated in sport he coaches on high school level (8).

4. Have participated in college sport he coaches (7).

5. Be a head coach in only one major sport (7).

6. Have received graduate training from a reputable school in P.E. (6).

7. Have B average or better in his physical education courses (5).

8. Have graduated from school with a good area reputation in its physical education program (5).

9. Have master's degree in P.E. or plans to obtain one (5).

C. SELF-IMPROVEMENT (95 pts.): The school coach should:

1. Study and analyze his coaching system (10).

2. Be willing and able to devote abundance of time and energy to coaching duties (10).

3. Maintain good health and physical condition (10).

4. Study weaknesses and strengths of his players (9).

5. Attend coaching schools and clinics (9).

6. Be willing to accept new and proven techniques relating to coaching (9).

7. Read current books and periodicals pertaining to sports he coaches (8).

8. Seek expert advice on improvement of his coaching techniques (8).

9. Assemble an up-to-date library of professional literature (7).

10. Participate actively in professional organizations (7).

11. Consider criticisms directed at his coaching and weigh and appraise such comments for what they may be worth (7).

III. *Organization and Administration* (142 pts.)

The high school coach should:

1. Have a well-organized plan for entire season (15).

2. Have a good, detailed lesson plan for each practice (15).

3. Possess ability to recognize atheltic skill and potentiality of success in participants (14).

4. Ensure adequate development of a junior varsity team (13).

5. Make adequate provision for adequate care and maintenance of equipment & facilities (12).

6. Ably administer game details both at home and on trips (12).

7. Plan, prepare, present and administer his budget well (12).

8. Be economical in purchasing of equipment and order through regular school procedure, yet never compromise quality (12).

9. Treat opponents as guests at home contests (11).

10. Be aware of his legal responsibilities as a coach and take precautions against any negligence (11).

11. Encourage development of fundamental skills throughout elementary school program (11).

12. Move cautiously in dissolving old school and community traditions (9).

IV. *Public Relations* (179 pts.)

A. GENERAL PRACTICES (45 pts.): The high school coach should:

1. Be mannerly on and off field (11).

2. Cooperate with press, radio and T.V. (9).

3. Maintain good relationships with opposing coaches (9).

4. Dress appropriately (8).

5. Not publicly criticize game officials (8).

B. WITHIN THE SCHOOL (63 pts.): The high school coach should:

1. Cooperate with school officials and fellow faculty personnel (10).

2. Understand administrative organization of school (9).

3. Recognize educational purposes of school (9).

4. Take cognizance of and follow school policies (9).

5. Avoid criticizing school officials and faculty members (9).

6. Not ask faculty members for special privileges for players or for himself (9).

7. Maintain good relations with student body (8).

C. WITHIN THE COMMUNITY (71 pts.): The high school coach should:

1. Keep athletic philosophy compatible with educational philosophy of community (9).

2. Interpret his program to community as part of complete educational program (7).

3. Cooperate with parents regarding development of proper attitudes toward diet, sleep, rest and regular school attendance (8).

4. Be available for and willingly accept speaking engagements (7).

5. Avoid criticism of community projects, groups, and individuals (7).

6. Be acquainted with community environment, customs, ideals, economic conditions and attitudes (7).

7. Know leaders of community (6).

8. Belong to community organizations (6).

9. Choose his friends carefully (6).

10. Take part in community activities (6).

CHAPTER 6

EVALUATING THE COACH

JOHN A. FRIEDRICH*

E VERY COACH IS INTERESTED in improving himself and doing a
better job. Although many coaches are quite capable of ap-
praising their own individual qualities and abilities, it frequently happens that they tend to overlook certain important factors.

In order to overcome this difficulty, a form of an evaluation
sheet for coaches is suggested. This evaluation form has been designed primarily for the players to use in evaluating the coach;
however, it may be used by others also, provided they know the
coach well. Although some school authorities may object to having players pass judgment on their coach, the fact remains that
a great deal of beneficial knowledge can be gained through such
a process.

Often, the tendency exists to evaluate the coach almost entirely on the won and lost record in his sport. Since much more goes
into coaching, it is truly a pity that the coach has such a limited
and inadequate criteria by which to be evaluated. An evaluation
form, as suggested here, can provide an excellent means for the
coach to obtain reactions to the many other factors involved in
coaching besides winning games.

It is hoped that this evaluation form may be helpful to those
coaches interested in finding out in what ways they can most adequately improve their effectiveness. To be of the most value, the
results as indicated by the forms, should be used in actually attempting to make improvements where needed.

To be significantly high, average or low, a trait should be
marked accordingly by at least half of the group. A numerical

---

* John A. Friedrich, "Evaluating the Coach," *Athletic Journal*, Vol. 33
(January 1953), pp. 42-45.

interpretation may be made by averaging the numbers checked for each trait by the players making the rating.

A total score may be computed; however, each individual item must be considered separately in making a final interpretation of the evaluation.

In having players fill in the forms, it is suggested that they be asked to take as much time as needed, circle their choice, and feel free to respond frankly.

The form to be used follows.

COACH EVALUATION SHEET

Name of coach   Date
Team or teams for which he has coached you   Your Age

Your coach is trying to do as good a job of coaching as possible. You can help him to improve his effectiveness as a coach by filling out this evaluation sheet as completely as possible. Since you are not required to sign the sheet, please feel free to give frank and honest responses.

Instructions

Circle the number which you feel best applies to your coach with respect to the traits and characteristics listed. The following scale designates what the numbers mean.

In order to save space we are not repeating the chart each time, but instead are including the reading marked (a), (b) and (c). (a) Appears under ten at the left-hand side of the scale. (b) Appears at the center of the scale under five and (c) appears at the right-hand side of the scale under zero.

Scale

Excellent	Good				Average			Poor		Very deficient
10	9	8	7	6	5	4	3	2	1	0

(Circle only one number for each trait listed)

COACH'S PERSONAL QUALITIES

1. *Cheerfulness.* (a) Always cheerful, pleasant, and happy. (b) Cheerful about half of the time. (c) Never cheerful, always glum and sad.

2. *Common Sense.* (a) Always uses good common sense and judgment. (b) About average in common sense. (c) Never uses common sense.

3. *Co-operativeness.* (a) Co-operates very well with players and others at all times. (b) Co-operation is about average. (c) Very unco-operative.

4. *Courage.* (a) A great deal of courage at all times. (b) Average courage. (c) Lacks courage to a great extent.

5. *Courteousness.* (a) Good manners, respectful and courteous at all times. (b) Average courtesy. (c) Very discourteous, disrespectful and uncouth.

6. *Demanding of Respect.* (a) Coach demands and receives a great deal of respect from players at all times. (b) Receives about average respect. (c) Receives little or no respect.

7. *Efficiency.* (a) Coach makes excellent use of time, material and equipment at all times. (b) About average in making use of time, etc. (c) Very inefficient.

8. *Emotional Control.* (a) Well able to control his feelings at all times. (b) Average ability to control his feelings. (c) Loses temper easily, gets upset easily, flies off the handle much of the time.

9. *Friendliness.* (a) Friendly and likable at all times. (b) Friendly about an average amount of the time. (c) Never friendly or likable.

10. *Industriousness.* (a) A very hard worker, always on the job and doing his best. (b) Works hard and does his best about an average amount of the time. (c) Never does work, neglects duties and responsibilities.

11. *Initiative.* (a) Has a great deal of drive and vigor at all times. (b) Often has an average amount of drive. (c) Little or no drive.

12. *Judgment.* (a) Excellent judgment used at all times. (b) About average judgment ability. (c) Little or no judgment ability at all.

13. *Originality.* (a) Has many new and original ideas and suggestions. (b) Has an average amount of original ideas. (c) No new or original ideas at all.

14. *Physical Appearance.* (a) Always well-dressed and neat appearing. (b) About average in appearance. (c) Very slovenly and untidy in appearance at all times.

15. *Pride in Work.* (a) Takes great pride in doing his work

well and accomplishing his job. (b) Average pride in his work.
(c) No pride in his work.

16. *Reasonableness.* (a) Very reasonable and understanding
at all times. (b) Reasonable average amount of the time. (c)
Complete unreasonableness in demands and attitude always.

1. *Sense of Humor.* (a) Excellent sense of humor at all
times. Witty and able to joke about many things. (b) Average
sense of humor. (c) No sense of humor. Very serious and cynical.

18. *Self-Confidence.* (a) Very confident of what he can do.
(b) Average confidence. (c) No confidence in himself.

19. *Sympathy.* (a) Very sympathetic at all times. (b) Shows
average amount of sympathy. (c) Hard-hearted. Shows no mercy
or sympathy.

20. *Unselfishness.* (a) Very unselfish. Always thinking of the
welfare of others. (b) Unselfish to an average degree. (c) Extremely selfish. Thinks only of himself.

21. *Voice.* Coach's speaking skill concentrates my attention
very well. (b) Speech about average in effectiveness. (c) Speech
is ineffective and distracting, making concentration difficult.

In what ways do you think the coach could improve himself
personally so that he could do a more effective job of coaching?

COACHING SKILLS AND TECHNIQUES

1. *Ability to Teach Fundamentals.* (a) Does an excellent job
of teaching. (b) Does an average job. (c) Very inferior.

2. *Ability to Demonstrate Skills for Most Effective Learning.*
(a) Demonstrations very clear and instructive. (b) Average demonstrations. (c) Very inferior.

3. *Ability to See and Analyze Players' Mistakes.* (a) Sees practically all mistakes and knows how to correct them. (b) Sees and
corrects about half the mistakes. (c) Sees no mistakes and corrects none.

4. *Ability to Correct Mistakes.* (a) Excellent. (b) Average.
(c) Very inferior.

5. *Ability to Get the Best Out of Players.* (a) Able to get all
players to do their best at all times. (b) Able to get half of the

players to do their best about half the time. (c) Never able to get any players to do their best.

6. *Ability to Work Democratically with Players.* (a) Very democratic. Group makes decisions whenever possible and carries them out. (b) Uses about half and half autocratic and democratic methods. (c) Completely autocratic.

7. *Ability to Explain Things to Players.* (a) Explanations very clear and concise. (b) Average explanations. (c) Explains things very poorly.

8. *Ability to Stimulate Good Sportsmanship.* (a) Excellent. (b) Average. (c) Very inferior.

9. *Ability to Develop Good Team Spirit.* (a) Excellent. (b) Average. (c) Very poor.

10. *Ability to Develop Leadership in Players.* (a) Develops a great deal of leadership. (b) Develops an average amount of leadership. (c) Develops no leadership.

11. *Ability to Make Players Feel They Belong.* (a) Players all have a strong feeling of belonging to the team. (b) Players have an average feeling of belonging. (c) Many players feel left out and rejected.

12. *Ability to Make Players Feel Important.* (a) Able to give practically all players a sense of importance. (b) Gives some of the players some sense of importance. (c) Gives no player a proper sense of importance. Never praises—always criticizes.

13. *Ability to Provide and Maintain Equipment.* (a) Has excellent equipment and keeps it in excellent shape. (b) Has average equipment and keeps it in average shape. (c) Poor equipment—poorly kept up.

14. *Ability to Instill Self-Confidence.* (a) Gives players a great deal of confidence in themselves. (b) Gives players an average amount of self-confidence. (c) Gives players no self-confidence.

15. *Ability to Instill Determination.* (a) Makes players very determined to do well. (b) Gives players average determination. (c) Gives players no feeling of determination.

16. *Ability to Maintain Discipline.* (a) Always has the situation well under control in a friendly manner. (b) Average amount of control of the group. (c) Has no control of the group.

17. *Ability to Keep Players Interested.* (a) Interest always at a high level. (b) Maintains an average amount of interest. (c) Players uninterested and bored.

18. *Ability to Evaluate Different Types of Play.* (a) Understands and knows how to use many systems. (b) Average understanding and knowledge. (c) Very deficient.

19. *Tries to Help Players Develop Values and Morals.* (a) Tries to develop high ideals in the players. (b) Develops average ideals and values. (c) Develops low and poor ideals and values.

20. *Helps With Personal Problems.* (a) Helps a great deal with the personal problems of players. (b) Gives average help to players with problems. (c) Gives no help with personal problems.

21. *Skill in Judging Ability of Players.* (a) Judges ability of the players very well. (b) Average. (c) Very interior.

22. *Gives Players Personal Attention.* (a) Gives special attention to individual players very often. (b) Gives average personal attention. (c) Gives no personal attention.

23. *Guards Physical Welfare of Players.* (a) Gives excellent care to injuries. (b) Gives average attention to injuries of players. (c) Does not even consider the welfare of the players—neglects injuries, etc.

24. *Accepts Suggestions and Constructive Criticisms.* (a) Very receptive and open to suggestions. (b) Accepts average amount of suggestions. (c) Will not accept any suggestions—rejects them.

In what ways could the coach improve his coaching skills so that he could do a more effective job of coaching?

Some of the things I dislike about the coach are:

Some of the things I like about the coach are:

In general, I think the coach has done his job
(a) Excellently ....
(b) Good ....
(c) Average ....
(d) Poorly ....
List below any other comments you may have.

CHAPTER 7

GOODBYE, MR. COACH
How to Fire the Mentor of a Winning Team

JOHN B. CROSSLEY*

EDITOR'S NOTE

It has been said that three individuals occupy impregnable positions in the school: the secretary, custodian and coach. Let us take the coach, for example. The time may come in the life of every administrator when he must face the facts, gird himself with courage and fire the coach—a winner at that. What a horrible thought! Yet the author says that this can be done and offers a practical approach to those who find themselves in this sticky situation. He is chairman of the Department of Educational Administration at the University of Hawaii in Honolulu.

MR. PRINCIPAL, why and how do you fire a coach? Gives you the shudders to think about it, doesn't it? Haven't you known administrators who were fired themselves because they fired or tried to fire a coach?

The purposes of this article are:

(1) to suggest a framework upon which evaluation of the coaching staff may be based,

(2) to suggest evaluative procedures and

(3) to "story-tell" or role-play the case of reemploying one coach, dismissing another.

Fortunately there is an ever increasing number of school administrators who see and make known to the athletic department, the student body and the community that the athletic program is an integral part of the educational program of the school, a part of the curriculum—not "extra" curricular. These administrators have already provided criteria upon which to eval-

---

* John B. Crossley, "Goodbye, Mr. Coach," *The Clearing House*, Vol. 42 (November 1967), pp. 152-155.

uate the athletic program and teachers (coaches) of the program.

Any institution must have a reason for its being. Certainly those responsible for the administration of a school have either helped to develop or have inherited a philosophy of education for that institution plus stated objectives of the educational program. In general, a statement of purposes is in written form for most high schools in the country. These purposes or objectives of the educational program are quite clear and concise.

Whatever the educational philosophy of the institution may be, whatever the stated objectives of the program may be, since the athletic program is a part of the curriculum developed to carry out the objectives, these then become the evaluative criteria used in determining the contribution each course, each experience, provides in attaining these goals and the criteria upon which the evaluation of each staff member rests. In other words, how effectively does this course, this activity, this teacher, this coach contribute to the purposes of the educational program?

How does the administrator evaluate the athletic program?

First: He is responsible for interpreting to members of the athletic department and the coaching staff the overall purposes of the educational program of the school. In employing coaches, he shares with them his expectations for the athletic program—that it will provide every participant opportunities to achieve to his maximum the values and objectives of the school's educational program. He points out that in a broad sense the coach is a "teacher" first, a coach second.

Second: With every justification, he may look for high standards of contributions by coaches to these goals, for the direct and indirect influence of the coaching staff upon team members and upon the entire student body in many instances is greater than that of members of any other teaching department of the school.

Third: Recognizing and relating the importance of coaching and athletics in the life of students, it becomes clear that he is a firm believer in athletics and will provide support and assistance for each activity.

Fourth: He reminds the coaching staff that, as chief administrator of the school, he has the responsibility of evaluating and reporting his evaluation of both the program and the staff to his superiors and to the community. To be as objective as possible in his evaluation, he must observe at first hand each aspect of the program, including the effectiveness of each teacher. He makes it clear that by such observation he not only becomes more objective in his evaluation but also is more competent to be of assistance in providing all means for teaching to be effective—such as, better equipment, better learning conditions. He also can from firsthand observation report to the community the superior work of teaching and coaching he is sure he will see.

Thus he reports the necessity of his seeing the athletic program at work—by observing practice sessions, dropping into dressing rooms, being on the bench at games. He reports that on such visits he will be only an observer, will not interfere with coaching; if he has any suggestion, it will be made privately to the coach. Hopefully, he can truthfully say that he anticipates that such visits will be due to his deep interest in athletics. By the expression of such interest, he also notes that it enables the administration to be identified by teams and student body as supporters of the athletic program.

Given a situation where the suggestions above have been carried out with agreement and understanding, let us "pretend" a case of reemployment of one coach, a request for a resignation (or if necessary, dismissal) of another.

The football and basketball seasons are over. The time has come for final evaluation of all members of the teaching staff, including coaches. While the conferences between the two coaches in our story are, of course, independent of each other and private, for the sake of comparison, they are reported together item by item.

PRINCIPAL: "*Mr. Football Coach—Mr. Basketball Coach,* as you know, these last two weeks I have been having conferences with all members of our faculty, making our evaluations for the year. I have your file with me which has reports of my other conferences with you during the year, the reports of my observations at practices, games, etc. Of course you also have copies of all these and so nothing new will probably come up today; rather, we will try to put the whole story together.

"*Mr. Football Coach,* you know how pleased I have been with the way you have handled the fellows on your team. I am glad I could get you the extra money to get additional team equipment so you could keep even the poorer players on the squad all year. Even though they got to play little, they gained a great deal both in physical development and in self-esteem by being members of the squad. I was glad to see you got each of them in at least one game—glad that you used your less able players in some games rather than win by a big score.

"*Mr. Basketball Coach,* I certainly can say you won some games by astronomical scores. I know that pleased the boosters' club, but as I urged you early in the season, I wish you had kept a larger squad and given more fellows a chance to play. You had the equipment, it would have cost no more in transportation and I offered you a second assistant if you felt you needed one.

"*Mr. Football Coach,* I am not sure you know, but both Bill and Ed, the two fellows who were just able to stay eligible during the season, both now are 'out of the woods' and are going to have nearly a B average in all subjects this semester. I appreciate how much you did to encourage them in their school work. You not only made good players out of them, but, through your efforts, they are benefiting from their entire school program for the first time.

"*Mr. Basketball Coach,* do you know that I am still having a rough time with Miss Smith and Mrs. Jones regarding their attitude toward our athletic program? They complain bitterly each time one of our tennis or baseball players has to be excused from their classes for an away game and are constantly 'digging' at the athletic program in the faculty lounge. I think they are winning some converts to their point of view. As you know, for we talked about it at the time, this is due primarily to your harsh criticism of them because they would not change grades in their courses and keep two of your players eligible. I am afraid you have not helped us in our efforts to raise the respect of our student body for quality academic work.

"*Mr. Football Coach,* I want to tell you again how much I appreciated that letter a few months ago from Mr. and Mrs. Brown, expressing their appreciation of how you had helped Jim get himself straightened out in his attitude toward girls. Thanks to you, all is O.K. now. An example of how a coach can help a kid have not only a clean body, but a clean mind.

"*Mr. Basketball Coach,* perhaps you have not heard, but two fellows who played for you this year were suspended from school last week for having and passing around at school obscene pictures. I guess you were not very successful in ruling out the smut and foul language your gang was using in the dressing room so frequently.

"*Mr. Football Coach,* only this morning I saw the final results of the election for student body officers for next year. You will be pleased to know that that big tackle of yours will be student body president and your second-string center will be treasurer. I think this is primarily a result of your work with the Letterman's Club. I know that you and the club members helped them develop their platforms and plan their campaigns which were both dignified and astute. Those fellows will help us have a better school next year.

"*Mr. Basketball Coach,* I am sorry you could not find the time to assist in any of our student body activities this year. You coaches have a lot of influence on our students and we could have used you in any number of ways.

"*Mr. Football Coach,* I want to thank you again for your contribution in building up good sportsmanship on the part of our students and our patrons who come to our games. Your behavior on the bench, your attitude toward game officials, your pep talks to your squad, your talks at our pep rallies, all contributed to our school and community having an enviable reputation in regard to good sportsmanship.

"*Mr. Basketball Coach,* you know how disappointed I was regarding your behavior at our games. I think I talked with you after each game, doing all I could to help you gain better self-control. But I certainly failed, for in our play-off game for the conference title you behaved worse than at any time during the season. If I had been the referee, I would have ousted you from the bench. Your worst offense was the very evident use of sarcasm on Sam when he missed those two foul shots and you pulled him out of the game.

"*Mr. Football Coach,* well, that is it. I am glad you are on our faculty. You have contributed much to the purposes of our total program. I am glad you turned down the offer to go to X Community College next year. We need men like you at the high school level where perhaps you can do more for boys and the entire student body than at the collegiate level. I know you wish you had won that last game and third place in the league, but maybe we will hit next year. Anyhow, keep giving us the full benefit of your total ability as a 'teacher'; we will not demand championships.

"*Mr. Basketball Coach,* I am sorry all of my summaries today have to be negative—except one—of course, we did win the league championship and the southern-conference title. However, you will recall our conference when you were assigned as head basketball coach and the description, which you have in writing, as to how we see sports contributing to all aspects of our objectives of an educational program for boys and girls. I admire your 'coaching' ability, but am sorry I cannot recommend that you continue with us due to your failure as a 'teacher.' I will be glad to recommend you as a coach for a professional team."

In summary, it is suggested that if the philosophy and objectives of education are known and accepted by the teaching staff, are explained to parents and the community, if the coaching staff is made aware of its responsibilities and its unique opportunity to assist each player to profit from attaining—to the best of his ability—all the established goals of the educational program, and if cooperative and meaningful techniques for evaluation of each coach's contribution to these purposes are established and carried out, then the administrator is professionally obligated and equipped to make and stand behind his evaluative decisions. He *can* fire a "winning" coach!

THE COACH AND TEACHING

THE PHYSICAL EDUCATOR AS COACH

PAUL GOVERNALI*

IN NO SINGLE ASPECT of the job do some physical educators wrestle with conscience more than when fulfilling their roles as college coaches. These coaches live in a materialistic society in which success, power and money are end results in themselves; but, they work in essentially an idealistic setting where the fullest intellectual, moral and social development of young adults is professedly the purpose of education. In this total environment wherein values contravene each other, these instructors find themselves torn between the human desire to do what they *ought* to do as teachers and the equally human desire to do what they *must* to survive as coaches. For some coaches aware of conscience and sensitive to personal, ethical standards of behavior, the conflict between what *ought* to be done for students and what *must* be done for victory sometimes creates an anxiety too great to bear. Such physical educators leave coaching at their earliest convenience. Some coaches with relatively little conscience or sensitivity, the clams living within themselves, still function without anxiety and, while doing so, consciously or unconsciously erode the moral core of the very students entrusted them by the community.

The physical educator as coach is subject to both external and internal pressures. The external forces are applied by students, parents, alumni, the business community and the press. In their misguided judgment, some people tend to rate colleges and universities not so much by their faculties, libraries and students as by their coaches, stadiums and athletes. The pressure to create a

---

* Paul Governali, "The Physical Educator as Coach," *Quest*, Vol. 7 (December 1966), pp. 30-33.

favorable public image through winning college teams is exerted not only by student bodies credulous that job potential will thereby be enhanced, but also by parents who need egos refurbished (their sons and daughters attend), a provincial alumni (I went to a better college than you), a business community bent on progress, a euphemism for profit (big games attract big crowds that spend) and a press intent on increasing readership (more advertising space at higher rates).

In short, successful college teams make everyone happy except, perhaps, some coaches, faculty and administrators with enough conscience to be troubled by the half-truths sometimes necessary to recruit good athletes. Worse yet, malpractice *does* breed easily in surroundings where unsaid lies are considered *de rigeur:* admission of athletes who fail to meet regular requirements; irregular methods of dispensing financial assistance, particularly by booster clubs; needless jobs conceived and created for sports competitors only; lightened academic loads for athletes, thereby extending an ordinary four year college term to five or six; clandestine out-of-season workouts to stay abreast of opponents doing the same; and red-shirting, withholding athletes from competition during the sophomore year to insure a steady flow of more mature, experienced players during their years of eligibility.

In the United States, intercollegiate sport and its conduct is a reflection of an individualistic, competitive and acquisitive society traceable in general to a predominantly British and Northern European heritage. This legacy also includes the thinking of philosophers like the Englishman John Locke, whose writings influenced those who drafted the Declaration of Independence, and the ideas of economists like the Scotsman Adam Smith, a champion of "Laissez-Faire Capitalism." In a social order which exalts profit making, encourages sharp dealings in economic transactions, glorifies commerce and extols competition, it is no wonder that the business tycoon epitomizes the ideal man and is looked to for leadership by the community.

To most American businessmen success is equated with profit. To make money is to be successful; to lose money is to be unsuccessful. Because most businessmen do not understand education, its ideals and principles, purposes and methods, because they do not comprehend the slow process of personality development in students, they can only understand and judge intercollegiate sports by applying business criteria to determine what success is. Thus, they equate winning with profit and losing with loss. If the business makes money, retain the store manager; if the business loses, fire him and hire another. Most communities are geared to this impulsive "American Way" of solving problems and not inclined to concede that occasionally no *one* person is responsible for failure—that a set of circumstances may conceivably be involved. Most coaches, through hard experience, have learned to live with the idea that circumstances—the injury factor, parity in budget and scheduling—can easily alter lifetime won and lost records. Losing coaches without tenure, those who, in particular, teach the so-called major sports or those sports from which revenues are derived, know they are vulnerable because of community pressures for change exerted on administration, or because losing teams make no money, in itself a pressure on administration. The following platitude, well known in coaching circles is cynical yet appropriate. "When you're winning, you don't need any friends. When you're losing, your friends can't help you anyhow." An athletics environment in which this cynicism flourishes is hardly conducive to the best learning situation for students.

If external forces *can* be controlled, the coach still must cope with his own internal pressures caused by personal actions not in accord with his feelings. Man is a product of his past, of all he has experienced in his political, social, economic and ethnic environment. To act contrary to belief may cause disaster for some. Physical educators willing to search their souls and be candid will readily admit that the purposes, methods and objectives of physical education often have no relationship with those in intercollegiate athletics, particularly at schools which support high-powered sports programs.

Briefly, the general purpose of physical education is to contribute to the students' total development, while that of intercollegiate athletics is, frankly, entertainment for the public and student body, personal glory for players and coaches and profit when possible. (Otherwise, why recruit and charge admission?) Methods in physical education are usually informal and based on beliefs in the worth of an individual, flexibility of procedure, and individual differences. In athletics, methods tend to be formal; that is, procedure is arbitrary and predetermined and the coach is a dictator. The objectives of physical education, from a personal standpoint, are total health, and esthetic expression and appreciation. The goal in athletics is to win.

As a pertinent digression, to win is good. But in *educational* sport, to *want* to win is a greater good. The outcomes attributable to this *desire* to win last longer. For example, winning gives one pleasure, satisfaction, joy, all positive feelings but soon dissipated in time—an hour, day, week or month. Losing makes one sad, frustrated, regretful, all negative emotions, but also soon dispersed in time. What is important in educational sport is the *desire* to win, because it brings young people together and makes discipline in training and competition intrinsically a good experience. In this controlled learning environment itself, the mental, moral and physical qualities deemed admirable in our culture (integrity, perseverance, respect, *et al.*) are developed by instruction and exercise. What is nurtured in a directed learning situation lasts a lifetime, whether the game is won or lost.

At any rate, many colleges *pretend* that the purposes, methods and objectives of athletics are one and the same with those of physical education. In these schools, some coaches accept ambivalence as part of the job, part of the real world. However, there are some whose conscience makes it impossible for them to be untrue to themselves. Internal pressure forces these teachers to give up coaching.

To continue with the effects of internal pressure, most coaches are hired knowing their primary duty—to coach their specialties and to win. Many coaches have competed half a lifetime or more in their sport, sometimes professionally, and they coach because they love the game. But coaching is a hazardous profession, even with tenure. The awareness of potential spotty won and lost records can be haunting—too many losses induce neither prestige nor applause, but rather, deflation of ego, loss of self-esteem and a threat to survival.

To stay in coaching, a physical educator with or without tenure *knows* he must win his portion of games or more. It is at this point that the sensitive coach must wrestle with conscience. The question is, should he emulate the sharks of the business world who maneuver in a shadowy sea of half-truths, the business leaders who cut corners, deal in sharp practices and ultimately achieve success the "American Way"? What if in so doing he fails to meet the personal standards he has unconsciously set for himself? Should he act in accordance with principles based on a lifetime of experience? What happens if his actions are not in harmony with his beliefs? Will the feeling of anxiety be too strong to bear?

Many coaches with conscience, those who *should* be teaching young people the way they *ought* to be are ultimately forced out of coaching because of external or internal pressures. Many coaches relatively without conscience, those who *use* athletes for self-aggrandizement and personal prestige, remain in coaching and continue, consciously and/or unconsciously, to contribute to the moral degeneration of these students and a skepticism incongruous with youth. Innocent and naive students may well consider themselves betrayed; they deserve better in the fundamentally idealistic atmosphere of the university. What must students with awareness think—young men, who know that what is preached and practiced has no interrelationship. In this environment, is it no wonder these people leave college with a cynicism more appropriate for veteran politicians than young adults?

Intercollegiate athletics and its conduct in the United States is more Roman than Greek in spirit. Instead of individual excellence, we pursue the favorable won and lost record (life and death); instead of beauty, power (the better to run off-tackle with); instead of moral excellence, an easy amorality. What is necessary in educational sport today is a return to the early Athenian concept which accentuated the ideals of beauty, harmony, excellence, versatility, moderation and virtue.

In our social order, this return to old ideals seems highly improbable.

CHAPTER 9

COACHING TECHNIQUES APPLIED TO THE CLASSROOM

GERALD BENKA[*]

RECENTLY, I SAT DOWN AND READ from several sources about "good" teaching, jotting down some of my own ideas as I went along. The more I read and thought, the more apparent it became that my years as basketball coach and the hours spent each day in the gymnasium with my student athletes were really my most organized time. Couldn't this organization be carried over into the classroom? As I visit classrooms and supervise teachers, it is obvious to me that many of the coaching techniques I learned and used are employed in the class regularly by the competent teachers.

Think of the following techniques in reference to the classroom and pupils instead of the gym and players. I am sure you will agree that these ideas and methods can easily be transferred.

(1) The squad is studied. What kind of material do I have this year? Are there any past records or performances to check?

(2) Fundamentals are reviewed. What do we know? What must we know? Nothing should be taken for granted.

(3) Weak points must be strengthened. Extra time and drills possibly are spent with certain individuals before or after practice.

(4) Long-range plans are reviewed. What is our schedule? What are the strong points of the opponents? What are the season's goals?

* Gerald Benka, "Coaching Techniques Applied to the Classroom," *The Clearing House,* Vol. 43 (December 1968), p. 212.

(5) Short-range plans are reviewed. What must we stress the first few weeks?

(6) Each day, each practice is planned, organized. Before we step onto the floor we know what we will attempt to accomplish that day. Time is budgeted. Not too much time is spent on any one phase.

(7) Everything we do has a reason and is explained to the members of the squad. If they understand the reasons behind our actions, they work more diligently and meaningfully.

(8) Practices vary in order to keep interest, to motivate, to stimulate. We know when to work and when to relax.

(9) Each day's and each week's work is reviewed. What did we do? What did we accomplish?

(10) We work with the materials and room we have. Wishing for a new gym, more balls, more baskets is not going to help us now. We make do with what is there.

(11) Everyone is aware of policy and procedure. Proper behavior, promptness, courtesy, fair play and respect is expected and taught.

Such teaching devices as the film, the chalkboard, charts, illustrations, demonstrations, individual and group conferences, and special help are used throughout the year. Exchange of ideas with colleagues, attendance at many contests and perusal of literature goes on regularly.

Aren't the above ideas and techniques the ones which your better teachers have been doing for years and will continue to do?

CHAPTER 10

HOW COACHES TEACH

J. ARTHUR KEITH[*]

TODAY, THE ATHLETIC COACH is an outstanding teacher who uses the most modern teaching methods. Coaches have been leading the educational profession in the speed of adoption of educational innovations and the extent of individual instruction used in the teaching-learning situation.

VISUAL AIDS

Audio-visual materials are used extensively in coaching athletics. Movies are important to the instructional program of the coach. Athletes have an opportunity to observe themselves in action. Errors are visible to the boy himself; the importance of teamwork is dramatically portrayed; examples to follow are shown. Teacher education specialists advocate the use of video tape to analyze teaching performance: this principle (seeing one's performance on film) has been used for years by coaches to encourage a higher level of performance by athletes.

Other instructional uses of movies include watching performances of experts in order to learn from their example. Inspiration is provided through observing movies of championship contests or professional games.

Improvement through audio-visual aids is encouraged by several other devices. Electronic timing devices for track, such as the lap timer at the University of Oregon showing elapsed time to the tenth of a second, are an aid to learning to pace oneself. This is a modern, albeit expensive, improvement of the stop watch.

Polaroid cameras are excellent for immediate reinforcement

---

[*] J. Arthur Keith, "How Coaches Teach," *The Physical Educator*, Vol. 24 (December 1967), p. 162.

of learning skills. The athlete performs the technique while his coach takes a snapshot. Analysis of the picture is followed by another performance of the skill. The recent development of the variable speed sequence polaroid camera offers extended opportunity for improvement of this teaching technique. A boy may now perform the skill while his coach films a sequence of the technique. The eight picture analysis is then ready for examination.

Wall charts have long been used on bulletin boards and locker room walls for demonstration purposes.

Loop films have been in use in athletics for some time; however, they have not been convenient to use. The 8 mm cartridge film loop has overcome this handicap. The athlete may now select the cartridge demonstrating the skill he wishes to view, slip it into the projector, view the technique as many times as desired, and then practice the skill. More cartridge films are available in athletics than any other subject.

OTHER TECHNIQUES

Large and small group instruction, cooperative staff planning and use of teacheraids are trademarks of the coaching profession. The general teaching staff has just recently begun to adopt some of these methods.

Every athletic program of any merit is characterized by cooperation among the learners. Older boys help younger boys; more skilled performers demonstrate their technique; assistance is readily available to the slow learner. Varsity team members take a great deal of pride in adopting a beginner and helping him blossom into next year's varsity performer.

Another teaching technique skillfully used by the athletic coach is individual instruction. Every possible opportunity is utilized to demonstrate to a single boy the correct technique. Individual encouragement, praise and correction are fundamental to the teaching success demonstrated by coaches.

CLINICS

Part of the reason for this utilization of modern techniques and equipment might be explained by the "separate" budget of the athletic staff. The coach has some freedom to make decisions regarding the equipment he should have.

The coach attends many in-service clinics to learn to improve his skill in using new techniques and equipment. Most of these in-service clinics are organized around a "how to do" theme. There is a place for subject matter, but the emphasis of most clinics is on technique. Coaches are eager to share ideas and to adopt the best of techniques they observe.

Instead of criticizing the athletic coach and assuming that he is "just a coach" who also teaches, educators might well observe the many positive teaching techniques used by coaches. Team teaching, individual instruction, learner cooperation and utilization of audio-visual materials and self-improvement through in-service education are in more evidence in teaching athletic skills than in many other areas.

CHAPTER 11

TEACHING LOAD OF THE COLLEGE PHYSICAL EDUCATION TEACHER COACH

KEN TILLMAN*

IT IS AXIOMATIC in any field of endeavor that qualified, enthusiastic personnel is a prerequisite for successful operation. That education subscribes to this belief can be evidenced by the fierce competition for the talented teacher and the continuous search for individuals who will bolster a specific department or area of instruction.

THE TEACHER

The caliber of the physical education programs in the United States is determined, to a large extent, by the type of physical educator who does the teaching. We know that finances, facilities and administrative support influence any educational program, but the worth of a program is ultimately determined by the personal qualities of the individuals who teach and direct the program.

The teaching load of the physical education teacher is closely related to the problem of obtaining teaching excellence in physical education. It is a simple matter to say that the load of the physical education teacher should be the same as the load of teachers in other fields. Adherence to this principle is important and it can be strictly followed when the physical education teacher is involved only with teaching of professional classes and research as most colleges and universities have stated policies in regard to load responsibilities in these areas.

---

* Ken Tillman, "Teaching Load of the College Physical Education Teacher Coach," *The Physical Educator*, Vol. 25 (October 1968), pp. 131-134.

SOME PROBLEMS

However, there are two distinct areas that complicate the teaching load situation for most physical education administrators. The first is the problem of equating the teaching of laboratory (activity) classes with the teaching of professional (theory) courses. The second trouble spot is the load adjustment that must be made for nonteaching departmental duties. A major problem is the physical education teacher who also has coaching responsibilities.

Other academic areas have similar load adjustment problems, but they are not of the same magnitude as those in physical education. Speech departments have load adjustments to make for the teacher who coaches the debate team or directs plays. Some science departments give varying load credit for teaching laboratory classes. When situations are similar it is desirable that colleges and universities develop uniformity in policy which will go across departmental lines. The physical education administrator should work toward this end. He should also strive to develop a workable teaching load formula, within the school policy framework, which is directly applicable to his department.

COACHING PLUS TEACHING

The comment has been made by many physical education administrators when discussing the coaching-teaching combination of responsibility that it is impossible to do justice to both jobs. This is not an accurate statement. There appears to be a twofold reason why this type of dual responsibility is unsatisfactory from a physical education director's viewpoint in many situations. *First* of all, frequently a person with dual responsibility is hired primarily for his coaching prowess, potential or proven. He may have little or no interest in physical education in the first place and it is no wonder that the dual responsibility in this instance is not desirable for the physical education department! Unfortunately for our field, this is the same person who is given tenure in the physical education department; and then when he is fired as a coach the department has a very disinterested and many times unqualified full-time staff member. Ironically enough, the press release when this situation develops will frequently read, "Mr. ...... was relieved of his coaching responsibilities so he can devote full time to his physical education duties."

Second, why many men who coach and teach physical education simultaneously fail to adequately fulfill their teaching responsibilities is the unrealistic teaching-coaching load. This phase of the problem is the basis for this article. Although the college situation is the area under consideration, there are many implications for the high school situation also.

EXCEPTIONS

It is heartening that many coaches are also good physical education people. Unfortunately, too many administrators have had the idea that coaching is something that can be done in addition to handling teaching responsibilities. It is inevitable that some phase of responsibility must be slighted and the very nature of the activities involved usually means it will be the teaching that does not receive the needed amount of time. Although there are admittedly those nonprofessional individuals who will use coaching as an excuse for poor teaching, it is frequently the case that an unrealistic work load makes it impossible for even the most conscientious person to do his best in both areas over a long period of time.

OVERLOAD?

Frequently the administrator does not realize how the demands of coaching have changed during the last twenty years. The coaching staff at Southeast Missouri State was asked to make a job analysis of their coaching responsibilities and to compute the hours spent on each task. It was found that the fewest hours spent during the school year by a coach for a specific sport was 215 hours and the largest number of hours involved in coaching a sport was 1,462. Naturally, the amount of time will vary from school to school depending on the emphasis placed on each sport, the personality and experience of the coach, conference rules and regulations as far as number of contests that are permitted and amount and type of recruiting allowed. It is no wonder that many coaches are unable to spend sufficient time on their teaching duties when the time demands of coaching are considered. It was with this thought in mind that a questionnaire study was undertaken to determine the teaching-coaching load policies at various state schools in the United States.

A STUDY PLAN

Southeast Missouri State College was using a teaching load formula which was in use when the school had less than 4,000 students enrolled. Its enrollment at the time of the study was 4,800, and its projected enrollment is 7,500 students by 1975. It was decided to use two size categories in analyzing the questionnaire data. One group was composed of schools with less than 4,000 students and the other group had 4,000-7,500 students. One hundred and sixty-two questionnaires were mailed. One hundred eleven returns were received for a return percentage of 68 percent. There were forty-three questionnaires returned from schools of less than 4,000 enrollment and forty-eight from schools in the 4,000-7,500. Twenty returns were also received from schools that had more than 7,500 students. These questionnaires were not used in this study.

Each enrollment category was analyzed by determining the median, mean and range of teaching load reduction for various working responsibilities. It was also necessary to distinguish between schools on a semester system and those on a quarter system.

Sports "fit" into the quarter system more efficiently than they do in the semester system. A coach who coaches a fall sport will be able to devote more time to his teaching responsibilities during the winter quarter. This same principle applies to the coach of a winter or spring sport. The overlapping of sport seasons during a semester causes the administrator an additional headache. This is particularly true in colleges or universities where a sport receives only seasonal emphasis. Wrestling and swimming seasons are part of both semesters. The wrestling or swimming coach might have just as much of a time demand on him during his season as does a football coach.

However, the administrator is going to find it difficult to provide sufficient reduced time on a two semester basis. Usually a compromise is made and a partially reduced load is given for both semesters. This results in too light a load part of the year and too heavy a load during the rest of the year. Tennis and golf coaches have the same situation present in areas where weather limits these sports to six or eight weeks during the spring semester, and indoor practice is not feasible. The amount of out of season time that is required of a coach is another factor that must be considered in both the semester and quarter systems. This is very difficult to evaluate because coaches vary considerably in the amount of effort they expend out of season.

THE RESULTS

The policies of some schools that returned their questionnaires were not applicable to the format of the questionnaire. Among the policies used in institutions that do not provide a percentage reduction for coaching responsibilities are the following.

1. The athletic director tells how many hours the coaches will be available and they are paid by the physical education department according to the percent of total time spent teaching physical education.
2. The coaches and athletic director do not teach.
3. Athletic and physical education departments are separate. Extra pay is given to coaches for teaching coaching courses. In one school any coach who does teach must have a teaching load of twelve hours.
4. All coaches except football coaches teach twelve hours a week. Football coaches, trainer and athletic director do not teach.
5. Physical education department pays for percent of full load a coach teaches and athletic department pays the rest.
6. Coaches come from other departments. At some schools they are paid and at others they are not.
7. One college has a formula to give credit for travel time, serving on committees and advertising as well as credit for time spent coaching.
8. Some colleges indicated the coaches teach a specified num-

ber of courses or have their load reduced by one or more courses. It was impossible to use this information in this survey since total hours were not indicated.

9. All coaches teach one-half time and coach one-half time.
10. Major sport coaches do not teach. Minor sport coaches teach full time and coach as a "labor of love."
11. The athletic department teaches a specified number of hours. Coaches are assigned hours to teach by the athletic director.

The survey indicated that there is a wide variance in the load reduction policies of colleges and universities. It was also obvious that there is a relationship between the size of the school and the amount of load reduction. The larger the school, more load reduction permitted. This would seem to be logical. The larger the school becomes, the more time is demanded for carrying out coaching responsibilities. For example, recruiting frequently becomes more time-consuming, there is a greater need to attract crowds and more off-season time is required. Numerous exceptions were noted in this survey. Some large schools do not emphasize their athletic program or at least some parts of it. These schools frequently allow a minimal teaching load reduction. On the other hand, some small colleges have very high-powered athletic programs and they allow as much as 100 percent reduction for coaching responsibilities.

The mean load reduction of head football coaches at schools with fewer than 4,000 students was 50 percent during the football season. At the schools with 4,000 to 7,500 students, the mean reduction was 72 percent. A similar increase in the amount of load reduction was noted for head coaches in other sports and for assistant coaches as the size of the school became larger.

In the colleges with fewer than 4,000 students, head coaches in sports such as basketball, baseball, and track were receiving from 31 percent to 40 percent reduction for their coaching responsibilities on the average. Assistant coaches in football had an average reduction of 35 percent and basketball assistants 26 percent in their seasons when schools were under the semester plan. Coaches in golf, wrestling, swimming, cross country and tennis had their mean load reduced from 14 percent to 20 percent. The intramural directors at this size of school received a teaching load reduction which averaged 23 percent.

In the 4,000-7,500 student range, the mean load reduction increased for coaches of all sports. Basketball, track, and baseball coaches had reductions of 64 percent, 59 percent and 52 percent respectively during their seasons. Assistant football coaches had 49 percent reduced load and assistant basketball coaches 48 percent. Reduction for head coaches in golf, wrestling, swimming, cross country, and tennis had mean load reductions that ranged from 26 percent to 46 percent in their seasons. The load reduction for the intramural director increased to 48 percent.

LOAD FORMULA OUTDATED?

The survey indicated that many physical education teachers are being given inadequate load reduction for their nonteaching responsibilities. This is probably more prevalent now due to rapidly growing enrollments. Many schools are trying to operate on the load reduction formula that was used ten or fifteen years ago when enrollments were half of what they are today. It is easy for the physical education administrator to view teaching loads from the perspective of what was demanded of him as a teacher-coach. Whether we like it or not the demands on the physical education teacher are also greater if he is to stay abreast of space age philosophy and techniques.

It is unfortunate when physical education and athletics are separated in a college or university. However, unless proper load reductions are permitted for coaching responsibilities it seems that the only solution for physical education is to separate it from the athletic program. This survey indicated that a number of institutions are requiring unrealistic teaching loads of their coaches. It is obvious that either teaching or coaching is going to suffer or the competent individual will drive himself to the point where he will find it necessary to leave the teaching profession. The physical education profession can use the talented individual who is also interested in coaching. Let us not drive him away.

A physical education teacher's work load is affected by the same factors that determine the load of teachers in other disciplines. Teaching too much, tasks such as service on campus committees, insufficient clerical help, counseling duties and public relations demands are examples of college staff requirements that can place an excessive burden on all teachers. Factors such as type of course, amount of preparation needed, degree of evaluation needed, number of students taught, preparation of instructor to teach the course, energy levels of the instructor and number of different preparations also must be considered in determining the teacher's work load in any area of the college or university curriculum.

COMPLICATIONS

Unfortunately, the work load of the physical education teacher-coach is complicated by many other things. A major consideration is the weight that is given to the teaching of activity classes. The survey indicated that colleges have a wide range in their policies. Some use a 1:1 professional to activity course ratio whereas others use a 2:1 ratio. There was much variance within these extremes. The survey indicated that most colleges and universities use a 3:2 ratio or some ratio that approximates this one. It was also noted that the activity contact hours an instructor would teach ranged from twelve hours to thirty-two hours. Two colleges had a twelve hour load, three were in the twenty-seven to thirty-two hour range. All of the remaining schools had an activity course teaching requirement of fifteen to twenty-four contact hours for a full load. Comments indicated that school policy in this area was not acceptable to many physical education administrators.

The answer indicated that many colleges and universities still require their physical education staff members to be responsible for equipment issue and equipment and facility maintenance. Lockers, locks and uniform issue are the responsibility of staff members at some schools. Physical education staff members are also expected to supervise locker rooms, towel rooms and school laundry operations. Additional duties as athletic trainers, or concessionaires during athletic contests were also mentioned as non-teaching duties of some staff members. It should be noted that these duties are seldom considered when computing the work load of physical education staff members. Several schools indicated that student labor was used as often as possible to relieve staff members of many menial tasks. However, staff members then have supervisory responsibilities.

Physical education administrators are struggling to find a work load formula that will be applicable to their situation. Answers also indicated that many schools do not currently have a satisfactory work load formula for the teacher-coach. It is obvious that a nationwide work load formula would not be feasible nor even desirable. There are variables unique to each situation that must be considered by the physical education administrators. Some of these factors have been discussed. Time required of the staff member to carry out nonteaching and noncoaching duties must be considered. School policy on number of hours that constitute a full teaching load will influence the teaching load formula for the physical education teacher-coach.

Other teaching load variables were pointed out by the administrators. In some institutions additional credit is given for graduate teaching. Some schools vary teaching load with professorial rank. The overlap of coaching responsibility must also be considered. For example, the swimming coach who also coaches golf would probably not get a load reduction for both sports during the second semester. Dual coaching responsibilities make it very difficult to follow a rigid teaching load formula with a definite reduction for each sport that is coached. The way graduate assistants are utilized will also affect teaching load reduction that will be permitted for coaching duties.

Every administrator must have some type of a formula to follow when determining staff load. Several of the administrators were emphatic in pointing out that such a formula should not be used as a "straight jacket." Adjustments must be made after considering the situation and the individual involved.

Policies and procedures used at other colleges and universities are also helpful in arriving at a workable formula.[1]

RECOMMENDATIONS

The following guidelines may assist the administrator who is interested in developing a teaching load formula for his department.

1. Use your own college teaching load as a starting point. Determine the total number of work hours that are considered to constitute a full teaching work load.
2. Find out how much time is involved in nonteaching and noncoaching responsibilities that are in addition to those duties of all faculty members.
3. Compute the approximate time involved in carrying out coaching responsibilities.
4. Strive for an equitable ratio between professional course and activity course teaching. A 2:1 ratio is totally unrealistic if you are to have quality teaching in your activity program. A 3:2 ratio would be an acceptable starting point.
5. Examine teaching load formulas from other colleges and universities that are comparable to your institution.
6. Choose a work load formula that seems most appropriate to your situation and make adjustments in it on the basis of points 1, 2, 3 and 4 above. Provide a percentage reduction for the various nonteaching responsibilities.
7. Give your formula a trial run with your present staff to see whether or not it is defensible and workable.

---

1. Keith Bowen, "Work Load Formula at Eastern Michigan University," *Proceedings, National College Physical Education for Men* (December 27-29, 1965), pp. 19-20.

Richard C. Havel, "Compensation and Load Relief for Athletic Coaching—Some General Observations," *Proceedings, National College Physical Education Association for Men* (December 27-29, 1965), pp. 14-17.

Tom Leaming, "Teacher-Coach Work-load Survey" (Unpublished Study, West Georgia College, Carrollton, Georgia), 1967.

S. Marshall, *op. cit.*, "Work Load for the Teacher-Coach," pp. 17-19.

Richard K. Morton, "The Teacher's Job Load," *Improving College and University Teaching*, Vol. XII: No. 3 (Summer 1965), p. 155.

S. C. Staley, "A Work Load Formula" *The Physical Educator*, Vol. XVII: No. 3 (October 1960), pp. 95-97.

8. Make adjustments in your formula as they are needed due to departmental growth, changing emphasis in your department, or other changes in demands placed on your staff.

It is important that an administrator continually evaluate the formula that he is using.

Remember that a teaching load formula should be used only as a guide. The capable administrator must make assignment adjustments on the basis of individual capabilities and his ever-changing departmental situation.

CHAPTER 12

CERTIFICATION FOR HIGH SCHOOL COACHES

ARTHUR A. ESSLINGER[*]

THE MAJOR PROBLEM confronting interscholastic athletics in the United States is the fact that approximately one-fourth of all head coaches of junior and senior high school teams have had no professional preparation for such a responsibility. Their sole qualification is their participation on a college or university team in the sport concerned. While such participation experience is advantageous, it does not begin to constitute an adequate preparation for coaching a secondary school athletic team.

It has been generally conceded that the best preparation for the position of head coach of a high school athletic team includes the combination of a physical education major plus participating experience as a member of the varsity team of the sport to be coached. Participating experience plus preparation as a physical education minor has been considered the minimum acceptable background. Yet nearly one out of four of our head coaches does not meet this standard.

The implications of this situation are serious. It has long been recognized that competitive athletics have exceptional educational potentialities. Their inclusion in our secondary schools has been justified on the basis of their significant contributions to educational goals. It is erroneous to assume, however, that untrained leadership can elicit the potential educational values which are inherent in athletics. Optimum results cannot be obtained by the coach whose only qualification is that he was a letter-winner in college. If we are to have quality education then

[*] Arthur A. Esslinger, "Certification for High School Coaches," *Journal of Health, Physical Education, and Recreation,* Vol. 39 (October 1968), pp. 42-45.

we must have quality leadership. Our entire educational system is predicated upon the concept that educational outcomes depend upon professionally prepared leadership.

The coaches who lack professional preparation are handicapped in obtaining the social, moral, ethical, mental and physical values inherent in interschool sport, and they are also not capable of protecting the health and well-being of the participants. They do not understand the dangers of violent body contact sports upon the human organism. Their lack of background in the structure and function of the human body is a serious liability which keeps them from knowing how to prevent injuries and other damage, to recognize and to evaluate injuries, and to follow the proper course of action when they occur.

It is regrettable that all coaches are not physical education majors who have competed in intercollegiate athletics. This represents the ideal which, unfortunately, cannot be attained. In most secondary schools it is not practical to man all head coaching positions with physical education majors. The reason is that most secondary schools compete in from seven to ten sports and field junior-varsity and freshmen as well as varsity teams in most, if not all, of them. The number of physical education staff members which are needed to handle the physical education program is not adequate to provide head coaches for each of these squads. In this situation the principal must call upon academic teachers to coach some of the teams.

Another problem is that some letter-winners on college teams want to enter a teaching career and to coach but they do not want to major and teach in physical education. They prefer to prepare themselves as teachers in other subject matter areas. The solution to this problem is to provide such teachers with the minimum essentials which all coaches should have.

The AAHPER Division of Men's Athletics has long been aware that many coaches were not adequately prepared for coaching assignments. To attack this problem, a Task Force on Certification of High School Coaches was appointed. The members are:

Ted Abel, Pittsburgh, Pennsylvania, Public Schools.
Milton Diehl, Madison East School, Madison, Wisconsin.

Jack George, Roslyn, New York, Public Schools.
Robert Jamieson, Grimsley High School, Greensboro, North Carolina.
M. G. Maetozo, Lock Haven State College, Lock Haven, Pennsylvania.
Don Veller, Florida State University, Tallahassee, Florida.
Arthur Esslinger, University of Oregon, Eugene, *chairman*.
Roswell Merrick, AAHPER consultant.

The Task Force came to the conclusion that the best way to "liquidate" unqualified coaches is for each state to establish certification standards for teachers of academic subjects who desire to coach. Such standards should be designed only for coaching—not for teaching physical education. The standards should represent the basic understandings and competencies without which no individual should coach. It is not intended that these standards apply to coaches now in service; rather, the recommendations are designed for future coaches.

Out of its deliberations the Task Force has developed a program which includes the minimum essentials which every secondary school head coach should possess. If such a program were required in every state for certification of coaches, interscholastic athletics would be appreciably improved over what they are today. The courses and course outlines follow.[1]

	Semester Hours
Medical Aspects of Athletic Coaching	3
Principles and Problems of Coaching	3
Theory and Techniques of Coaching	6
Kinesiological Foundations of Coaching	2
Physiological Foundations of Coaching	2

MEDICAL ASPECTS OF ATHLETIC COACHING

The athletic program can never be termed educational unless the health of the participant is a primary objective. Medical and safety aspects are the heart of good athletic administration. Consideration of the individual's well-being must involve related safety factors.

1. In the development of these courses and course outlines, many competent, experienced authorities in the various areas were consulted. After completion, they were submitted to eleven leading physical education departments for review, criticisms and suggestions. The replies received from these sources were incorporated in the final draft.

In order to give the health and safety aspects proper emphasis in the preparation of a coach, the following areas are recommended.

I. Medical Aspects—
The medical aspects of the athletic program must be under the direct supervision of physicians.
   A. Preparation of the athlete for participation
   Physical examination
      1. "Team" approach—physicians, school nurses, coaches and athletic director; dentists, when needed
      2. Importance of administering an efficient and well-planned examination
   B. Prevention of injury and illness
   C. Perception—early recognition of injury
II. Protective Equipment and Facilities—
   A. When the participant has been medically approved, proper fitting of the best equipment is necessary. Eliminate "hand-me-down" system
   B. Facilities—
   Use of padded walls, sponge rubber for jumping pits, proper mats, turfed areas, proper maintenance
III. Training—
   A. General measures relating to health
   B. Use of tape or bandaging and other protective equipment
   C. Emergency care of injuries
   D. Physical therapy
   E. Prevention of overtraining
   F. Psychological counseling
IV. Injuries—
   A. Injury prevention
   B. Procedures when injury occurs
   C. Post-injury care
V. Medical and Safety Problems—
   A. Sources of information
   B. Importance of the coach having proper knowledge of sleep and rest, vitamins, drugs, smoking, drinking, teta-

nus immunization, hot weather training rules, fads and
fallacies
  VI. In-Service Training—Care of the Athlete—
      A. Arrangements for seminars and in-service courses for
         coaches
      B. County and state clinics
 VII. Medical Research Related to Athletics—
      A. Organizations—information
      B. Conference proceedings
      C. Journals

PRINCIPLES AND PROBLEMS OF COACHING

Because of the immensity of this area, some pertinent items
may not have been included. The individual instructor is encouraged to develop any additional items deemed necessary.
   I. Personal Relationships—
      A. Qualities of the Coach
         1. Positive attitude
         2. Pride in players
         3. Concern for interests of other people
         4. Firm but pleasant
         5. Golden Rule
      B. Influencing and Controlling Behavior in Athletes
         1. Be yourself
         2. The private talk
         3. The grapevine method
         4. Setting the example
         5. Handling individual differences
      C. Creating and Maintaining Discipline and Desire
         1. Necessity for hard work
         2. Goal setting
         3. Traditions
         4. Spreading enthusiasm
         5. Use of captains
      D. Vital Relationships
         1. The principal
         2. Teaching colleagues
         3. Parents

4. The janitor
5. Community—booster clubs, PTA, churches, etc.
E. The Coach and His Assistants
  1. Choosing assistants
  2. Loyalty
  3. Delegation of responsibility
  4. Delegation of authority
  5. Bilateral relationship
F. Athletes and Their Emotional Problems
  1. Problems in the home
  2. School problems
  3. Girl problems
  4. Jealousies
  5. The extrovert
  6. The introvert
  7. The status seeker
  8. The "psyche" case
  9. The prima donna
  10. Case histories
II. Organization—
  A. Organizing and Planning for Practice
    1. Season objectives
    2. Weekly objectives
    3. Daily plans
    4. Time
    5. Weather
    6. Staff
    7. Equipment and facilities
    8. Helpful hints
  B. Athletic Contest Management
    1. Importance of efficient management
    2. Before-game preparation
    3. Game responsibilities
    4. Post-game responsibilities
    5. Preparation for out-of-town contests
    6. General management duties and policies
  C. Athletic Equipment
    1. Purchase of equipment

2. Marking of equipment
3. Issuing of equipment
4. General care of equipment
5. The equipment inventory
   D. Athletic Finances and Budgets
1. Finances and athletic programs
2. Methods of raising funds
3. Ticket selling problems
4. Purpose of an athletic budget
5. Preparing the budget
III. Important Considerations—
   A. Training Rules and How to Enforce Them
1. Good training—a must
2. The policeman-type
3. No-rules-at-all type
4. The scapegoat approach
5. Squad-oriented type
   B. Selection and Evaluation of Personnel
1. Comparison to industry
2. Individual sports
3. Team sports
4. Being objective
5. Types of evaluation
6. Past performances
7. Getting the right man in the right job
   C. Motivation and Special Inducements to Athletes
1. Awards (letters, trophies, etc.)
2. Publicity
3. Championships
4. Scholarships
5. Special "gimmicks"
   D. Coaching Ethics
1. Players
2. Opponents
3. Officials
4. School colleagues
5. Coaching colleagues

6. Public
7. News media

THEORY AND TECHNIQUES OF COACHING

I. Educational Implications of the Sport—
   A. Role in education
   B. Role in physical education
   C. Philosophy
   D. Objectives
      1. Of the sport
      2. Of the coach
      3. Of the player
      4. Of the spectator
   E. History
II. Fundamentals Detailed—
   A. Teaching methods in performing skills
   B. Drills for developing basic skills
      1. Offensive
      2. Defensive
III. Technical Information—
   A. Offensive tactics
   B. Defensive tactics
   C. Strategy
   D. Use of teaching aids
IV. Scouting—
   A. Film analysis
   B. Prescouting check list
   C. Game scouting check list
   D. Post-game scouting check list
   E. Individuals
   F. Team
   G. Player performance rating systems
V. Conditioning for a Specific Sport—
   A. Developing
   B. Training
   C. Conditioning
   D. Emotional aspects

E. Educating (conceptual content)
VI. Organization and Management—
  A. Pregame preparation
  B. During event
  C. Post-game aspects
  D. Outline of duties for team managers
VII. Practice Sessions—
  A. Daily
  B. Weekly
  C. Seasonal
VIII. Safety Aspects of Particular Sport—
  A. Rules and regulations
  B. Facilities, grounds
  C. Officiating
  D. Supplies and equipment
  E. Prevention of injury
  F. Legal aspects
IX. Rules and Regulations—
  A. Of the sport
  B. Penalties
  C. Local
  D. State
  E. National
X. Evaluation—
  A. Season in retrospect
  B. Collection of appropriate materials
  C. Plans for following year
  D. Preparation of reports to administration

KINESIOLOGICAL FOUNDATIONS OF COACHING

I. Anatomical Factors—
  A. The coach must have sufficient knowledge of human anatomy to:
    1. Recognize any symptoms of ailments or deviations from normal health in order to provide first aid when such care is indicated and to secure the services of a physician when they are needed
    2. Select equipment which will fit best and offer maximum protection

3. Conduct an adequate physical conditioning program for the squad as well as for the individual players needs
4. Establish a program for the prevention of injuries (By being aware of the parts of the body which are most subject to injury such as the knee, shoulder, and ankle and the parts of the body subject to the most serious injuries such as the head and spine, the coach can more intelligently take measures which will reduce injuries)
5. More effectively tape and bandage his players

II. Mechanics of Movement—
   A. A knowledge of the mechanics of movement is indispensable to the coach and such information helps him to:
   1. Recognize more readily individual differences in the performance of a particular motor skill
   2. Develop more fully the individual student's potential in performing a motor skill
   3. Recognize more readily typical body alignments and their influence on motor performance
   4. Eliminate much "trial and error" in giving correct "coaching tips," producing more effective results in a shorter period of time
   5. Teach his students to use good and efficient body mechanics in all movement, thus reducing the number of injuries and the amount of fatigue
   6. Make more efficient use of coaching time
   7. Understand better the problems of efficiency and economy of movement
   8. Analyze performance more scientifically and base recommendations for improvement on sound anatomical and mechanical principles

PHYSIOLOGICAL FOUNDATIONS OF COACHING

I. Physiological Factors—
   A. The following areas of physiology are essential to the coach in order to provide him with an understanding of how the human organism functions.

      1. Central nervous system: motor functions
      2. Nervous system: sensory functions
      3. Properties and constituents of the blood
      4. Physiological mechanisms involved in the circulation of the blood and lymph
      5. Respiration
      6. Body fluids and kidney
      7. Metabolism and nutrition
      8. Endocrine system
      9. Growth and development

II. Exercise Physiology Factors—
  A. Circulatory and respiratory adjustments
      1. The heart
      2. Heart rate and exercise
      3. Circulation of the blood
      4. Circulatory adjustments during exercise
      5. Body fluid changes in exercise
      6. Pulmonary ventilation
      7. Gas exchange and transport
  B. Environment aspects
      1. Environmental and body temperatures
      2. Cooling power of the environment
      3. Effects of external heat
      4. Effect of cold
      5. Effect of altitude
      6. Effect of humidity
  C. Metabolism and exercise
      1. Oxygen requirement and oxygen intake
      2. Aerobic and anaerobic metabolism
      3. The steady state
      4. Oxygen debt
      5. Influence of training on oxygen intake and debt
  D. Nutrition
      1. Elements of adequate nutrition
      2. Planning the athlete's diet
      3. Fluids
      4. Distribution of meals

5. The pregame meal
6. Half-time feeding
7. Making weight
8. Weight loss in athletics
E. Drugs
  1. Drugs affecting the autonomic nervous system
  2. Drugs affecting the central nervous system
  3. Drugs affecting the circulatory system
  4. Drugs affecting metabolism and nutrition
  5. Hormones
F. Conditioning
  1. Chronic effects of athletic training
  2. Warming up
  3. Practice schedule
  4. Maximum training capacity
  5. Recuperative ability
  6. Preseason
  7. Early season
  8. League competition
G. Strength training
  1. Factors in strength
  2. Physiological basis of strength training
  3. Weight training exercises
  4. Weight training regimen
  5. Isometric training
  6. Circuit training
  7. Weight training hazards and benefits
H. Endurance training
  1. Physiological training
    (a) Anaerobic training
    (b) Aerobic training
    (c) Heat training
    (d) Rhythm training
  2. Pace
  3. Training programs
    (a) Over and under training
    (b) *Fartlek* training

(c) Interval training

(d) Repetition training

(e) Circuit training

SUGGESTED READINGS

1. American Medical Association: *Protecting the Health of the High School Athlete*. Chicago, Ill.: AMA. n.d.
2. Bender, James B.: *How to Be a Successful Coach*. Englewood Cliffs, N. J., Prentice-Hall, Inc., 1958.
3. Forsythe, Charles E.: *Administration of High School Athletics*. Englewood Cliffs, N. J., Prentice-Hall, Inc., 1962.
4. George, Jack F. and Lehmann, Harry A.: *School Athletic Administration*. New York, Harper & Row, 1966.
5. Lawther, John D.: *Psychology of Coaching*. Englewood Cliffs, N. J., Prentice-Hall, Inc., 1965.
6. Ryan, Allan J.: *Medical Care of the Athlete*. New York, McGraw-Hill, 1962.

CHAPTER 13

THE PHYSICAL EDUCATOR AND COACH IN PUBLIC SCHOOL ADMINISTRATION

LAWRENCE F. LOCKE AND JOHN E. NIXON*

School administrators, contrary to common belief, are not all former coaches—but the daily working experiences of the coach and physical educator make him a most appropriate candidate for positions in school administration.

THERE IS A MYTH of long standing and high reputation among teachers that physical education and athletic coaching are the yellow brick roads leading to public school administration. The term "myth" is advisable because there is considerable doubt as to the facts of the matter. A 1960 survey of the school superintendency by the American Association of School Administrators[1] thoroughly debunked the notion that there was any nationwide trend to promote physical educators and coaches to positions of administrative leadership at the local school district level.

Even if it were found that physical educators and coaches were represented in public school administration only in proportion to their numbers in the teacher population, there would be two clearly divided groups of opinion as to the propriety of the situation. A number of persons concerned about the quality of education in American schools believe that the so-called academic background is the best for superintendents and principals, and that altogether too many physical educators and other non-

---

* Lawrence F. Locke and John E. Nixon, "The Physical Educator and Coach in Public School Administration," *Journal of Health, Physical Education, and Recreation*, Vol. 37 (May 1966), pp. 36-37.

1. American Association of School Administrators, *Thirty-Eighth Yearbook: Professional Administrators for America's Schools*, Washington, D.C., National Education Association, 1960.

academic majors are infiltrating these positions. This view is reinforced by the general image of the coach as a nonintellectual, although it has not been indicated how many constitute "too many," nor has any acceptable evidence been presented to show that the subjects of concern, as a group, are any less successful in administration than appointees from other teaching areas.

A second body of opinion is held by persons who feel that physical educators and coaches are at least as likely to make good candidates for administrative positions as are other teachers. This position is reinforced by the fact that many outstanding school administrators have been coaches, or hold formal college degrees in physical education, or, as often happens, have backgrounds in both areas.

In an issue of the *Teachers College Record,*[2] Joel Hildebrand, a long-time "private guerilla fighter in the battle of basic education," took occasion to note approvingly the passage of California Senate Bill 57, with its prescription of an academic major for certification as a school administrator. Hildebrand indicates directly that this legislation takes particular pertinence from the situation delineated by Eugene W. Dils' study concerning the school experience background of California's superintendents.[3] The finding fastened upon with grim satisfaction was Dils' revelation that within his sample of district high school superintendents, fifty-eight listed "high school teacher" as their prior school experience, while seventy-nine listed "teacher-coach" with an additional thirty-six indicating "physical education." Hildebrand makes clear that he considers these appointments to be risky, if not outright irresponsible, choices by the school boards concerned.

> "There are ex-coaches who, by virtue of personal qualities and self-education, have become satisfactory principals and superintendents, but such *exceptions* do not justify a widespread practice of employing principals who are *less well educated* than their teachers."[4] [Italics ours]

2. Joel H. Hildebrand, "The Battle for Basic Education," *Teachers College Record* (October 1962), pp. 51-69.
3. Eugene W. Dils, *Position Sequences of California School Superintendents.* Unpublished Ed.D. dissertation, Stanford University, 1953.
4. Hildebrand, *op. cit.,* p. 55.

This statement reveals obvious and perhaps understandable confusion concerning the appropriate interpretation of Dils' findings and the perennial difficulty for the layman in distinguishing adequately between coach, teacher-coach and physical educator. By general educational usage, "coaching" is a function of the after-school interscholastic sports program, while physical education is a subject matter area within the required daily program. Many coaches are classroom teachers who have had little or no training in physical education. It is difficult to know in precisely what sense Hildebrand uses the term "coach" but it seems likely that it is intended in the generic sense—"all those associated with sports and games."

Hildebrand's statement contains an explicit sequence of logic: (1) those associated with sports and physical activities are not "educated men" when compared with teachers of academic subjects, (2) only "educated" men make suitable school administrators, and (3) barring exceptional cases of "self-education," men associated with physical activity and sports should not be considered for administrative positions in the public schools.

There are several apparent premises that could have permitted this line of reasoning. The most obvious is the supposition that the education obtained by the individual coach or physical educator is inferior to that of the so-called academic major. Several facts having the stubbornness of particulars seem to preclude any such conclusion. The phrase "teacher-coach," as commonly used in public schools (and by Dils) means just that—a classroom teacher who also coaches in the after-school program. Surely, it cannot be seriously maintained that the practice of employing history, English and mathematics teachers for coaching tasks has a deleterious retroactive influence upon their professional preparation!

By almost universal usage the term "teacher-coach" explicitly excludes "physical educator-coaches." If it is actually the physical educators whom Hildebrand wishes to cut from the herd, he then acts against both law and custom. In most states the great majority of teachers are given a substantial portion of their professional preparation in classes that cut across field areas. Courses such as Educational Psychology, History of American

Education, Philosophy of Education, and Classroom Pedagogy are shared by future teachers from many subject matter areas. This is true not only of the so-called methods courses but of all general education at the undergraduate level. To this point at least the core of common background has been powerfully reinforced by state certification requirements. In the area of preparation most directly relevant to Dr. Hildebrand's concern, courses in public school administration, classes are never segregated by subject background and hence no claim for inferiority of preparation can be admissible.

The second possible premise for Hildebrand's reasoning is the less obvious and perhaps covert assumption that the coach or physical educator is likely to be basically inferior to other teachers on one or more of the factors (presumably intellectual) that he chooses to include under the rubric "educated." It is upon this latter point that some comment seems appropriate.

Many people respond to the public school physical educator in such a manner as to suggest the operation of a well-defined stereotype. In the idiom of contemporary social science this is a "public image." Such an image is the sum of the widely shared expectations and perceptual sets that occur in regard to a group or role within a culture.

The image of the physical educator is at times neither prestigious nor positive. It is anticipated that he will be different from other teachers and that the differences will follow certain well-established prejudices. For example, among the most frequently encountered stereotypic expectation is low verbal ability and the consequent impoverishment of intellectual capacity.

Actually, it seems reasonable to maintain that the physical educator, because of his unique role, does stand somewhat apart from his fellow faculty members in the academic community of the public school. Such diverse matters as the location of his classroom, his teaching uniform, his relationship to the students, the content of his subject matter, his acquaintance volume in the community and his own interests all serve to make the physical educator highly visible within a typical faculty group.

Surely people are shaped by their occupations. We internalize the demands of our role until they become a permanent part of our personality. The only real question is in regard to the functional significance of these patterns.

Aside from the purely personal level this matter remains largely academic until such time as individuals are called upon to make decisions that involve, in an overt or covert way, their image of the physical educator. The choosing of public school administrators is one of the operations into which the public image of this segment of the teaching profession can be projected. In many school districts the stereotype is translated into acts of policy that are negatively or positively oriented toward the applicant with training and background in physical education. As some school board members can ruefully testify, there may be a substantial difference of opinion among teachers, administrators and parents in regard to the wisdom of either course. As Robert Havighurst once wryly remarked:

> "The subtle rankings that go on among teachers themselves may not coincide with the ranks accorded teachers by the wider community. Thus it may be the teacher of agriculture or the athletic coach who may enjoy the highest esteem in the community but who, in the eyes of fellow-teachers, occupies a position of low prestige in the teacher hierarchy."[5]

Some factual information in regard to this question was gathered in a recent study supported by the Kellogg Foundation and conducted through the Stanford Project for Leadership Development in Public School Administration.[6] In this analysis of performance on a battery of psychological tests by 129 physical education teachers who were candidates for positions in public school administration in several states, a number of interesting results were revealed.

Differences, statistically significant at the 1 percent level, emerged when the performances of the physical educators on a test of abstract verbal ability were compared to the performances of a group of teachers from other subject matter areas.

---

5. Robert Havighurst and Neugarten, Bernice, *Society and Education* (Boston, Allyn and Bacon, Inc., 1962), pp. 164-65.

6. Lawrence F. Locke, *The Performance of Administration Oriented Physical Educators on Selected Psychological Tests* (Unpublished Ph.D. dissertation, Stanford University, 1961).

These differences were precisely in the direction predicted on the basis of the public image. The physical education teachers scored lower on verbal ability. Additional results, however, indicate critical reservations in the interpretation of this difference.

Despite significant statistical differences between the test performances of physical educators and other teachers, the distributions of the scores remained surprisingly congruent. For example, 42 percent of the secondary school physical educators tested scored as high or higher than the median performance of academic teachers on the test of abstract verbal ability.

It was further revealed that the classification "physical educator" includes a number of surprisingly heterogeneous subclasses. To say that physical educators have "less verbal ability" than other teacher groups would be a useful generalization provided it were both true and relevant to some decision-making operation. When it is discovered that apparently this is not true of active, degree holding physical educators at the secondary school level, and that other subgroups must also be treated as separate cases, then the effectiveness of the generalization declines. An operating rule that offers barely better than a fifty/fifty chance of being correct in a particular instance is likely to prove more of a burden than a useful way of stating a hypothesis.

If the capacity of abstract verbal manipulation is accepted as one reasonable reflection of intellectual quality, then the best available evidence indicates that the concern implicit in Hildebrand's statement is misplaced. Our analysis of test data from over one hundred applicants in twenty-two school districts in several states indicated that the physical education candidate for public school administration is, for any practical purpose, the intellectual peer of other teachers. Any wholesale rejection of physical educators as candidates for school administration on the basis of supposed intellectual difference is not supported, indeed it is substantially contraindicated.

Those persons interested in discovering, training and appointing the most promising kinds of school administrators must address themselves first not to the nature of the candidate group, but to the requirements of the job. What must the administrator do? What are his major roles within the school context? What kinds of working relationships must he establish with teachers, students, parents and the community? Armed with answers to questions like these a selection committee seems more likely to make wise decisions than when armed with a set of a priori assumptions about which groups of teachers are, or are not, "educated men."

While it is not our purpose to debate the point here, we would maintain that given the commonly accepted definition of the role requirements for the public school administrator it is possible that the *day-to-day working experiences of the coach and physical educator make him more rather than less appropriate as an administrative candidate.*

If we are to act upon present evidence, every candidate for a position in public school administration must be considered on his own individual, unique merits. There is no place for the operation of a stereotype that does disservice to the needs of the school and discredit to those who choose its leaders.

THE COACH AND SCHOOL-COMMUNITY RELATIONS

CHAPTER 14

THE VALUES OF ATHLETICS
—A CRITICAL INQUIRY

Wayne E. Dannehl* and Jack E. Razor

An over-emphasis on winning has resulted in the exploitation of athletics for other than educational purposes. As a result, the values of school sports have been attacked. School and community have a responsibility to examine their attitudes toward competition and to deemphasize victory as the only goal of sports.

WITHIN THE PAST DECADE, the productivity of America's public schools has been scrutinized. Many traditional practices and goals have been questioned. As a result, numerous changes have been made to alter the curriculum, the physical plant, the size and racial and economic composition of the school population, the organizational structure, and the duration and frequency of the day-to-day school operation.

With the cost of education today rising at fantastic rates, many phases of the school program are being reevaluated to determine whether the expenditure for their continuation is justified on the basis of their educational value. In addition to program evaluations by school boards, administrators, faculty and citizens groups, student bodies on both the college and high school levels have shown that they, too, question the values of established education patterns and desire to be involved in developing new and meaningful educational goals.

Invariably, one of the first programs to be reviewed, and often attacked, is the interscholastic athletic program. The reason for this is twofold: 1) Its value in terms of educational con-

* Wayne E. Dannehl and Jack E. Razor, "The Values of Athletics—A Critical Inquiry," *The Bulletin of the National Association of Secondary School Principals,* Vol. 55 (September 1971), pp. 59-65.

tributions and economic expenditure is questioned by members of school boards, and 2) It serves as a focal point for bringing a financial crisis to the attention of a sometimes apathetic public. Most communities are strongly in favor of interscholastic athletics and the idea of their possible elimination generates the popular as well as financial support necessary for their continuation.

That athletics do have educational value has been accepted by both educators and the public; however, educators close to athletic programs have long been aware of serious abuses and their deleterious effects. Athletics in many schools are so exploited that they become highly suspect and open to the attacks of their critics. A discussion of values associated with athletics and the exploitation of them may give some insight, therefore, into the dangers which can befall this part of a school's activities program.

ATHLETICS ARE FUN

One of the most important and often cited values of athletics is that they can be a source of fun and enjoyment for the participants. Also they are excellent, acceptable forms of energy release. A most enjoyable aspect of sports and games is the thrill of competition with others or with an established criterion. However, too often the game takes on such importance that enjoyment is secondary and winning is primary.

Some coaches practice teams hour after hour, day after day, and on Sundays and holidays. Practice periods become so competitive and laborious that the participant no longer enjoys the game. Since high levels of excellence are expected and demanded, coaches often push players to the point that they find it difficult as students to function adequately in academic school activities. The underlying motive in operation is, of course, winning. It has become so important to win in our society that the fun of the game is lost to the daily drudgery of practice. Some coaches preach that the only thing that is fun is winning. Posters such as "Winning isn't everything; it's the only thing" are common in many locker rooms.

Further, high school athletics have become so competitive that students are expected (and sometimes forced) to practice and compete in only one sport the year around, especially in such sports as gymnastics, swimming, track and field, and wrestling. Participants also are often sold the idea that if they want to excel they *must* participate in a high level, off-season program, even if it means foregoing participation in other sports.

While this restriction is most likely to be imposed in schools of considerable size, the overzealous desire for excellence is manifest in most schools, regardless of their size. For example, in many schools, the coach forces students to participate in the activities the coach chooses: a basketball coach will not permit a boy to play football because he may be injured and thus be unable to play basketball; football coaches insist boys work at weight training all winter; swimming coaches do not want "their" swimmers running track.

Another abuse is that coaches who have sports that run concurrently sometimes argue over the "services" of a certain boy. Situations occur where a six foot six inch boy is not allowed to wrestle because he has the makings of a basketball player. The basketball program is a money maker, and therefore anyone with potential must play basketball. All of these practices detract from the fun of sports. While the value of fun in athletics is widely recognized, it is seldom realized.

ATHLETICS CONTRIBUTE TO PHYSICAL FITNESS

Physical fitness has always been one of the values and goals of athletic participation. Few would argue that a sound body does not contribute to a happy life. Although coaches verbalize the value of fitness for athletes, many of them do little to teach an understanding of the underlying concepts. Usually, athletes do not participate in carry-over activities after their competitive days. In fact many leave the competition of high school or college sports with a distaste for both activity and competition. Invariably, coaches stress strength and skill activities at the expense of cardiovascular and flexibility development. While most coaches recognize that the cardiovascular system is the base upon which all activity is built, including daily living, few stress this beyond its contribution to a "winning" effort.

If fitness is really one of the values of competing in athletics, it must be taught in such a way that participants do not learn to hate the means to the end. Yet, some coaches and physical educators use exercise as a form of *punishment*. The practice of making students do push-ups, sit-ups or laps for some misconduct is common. The logic of such a practice, if fitness is truly a value and not just an important factor in winning, escapes reason. Such an approach only reinforces any dislike a student or athlete has for exercise. Since most high school sports cannot be considered lifetime activities, a football player or wrestler, for example, should depart from his competitive experience with a basic understanding of the values and procedures for maintaining fitness during his later life. Perhaps a good beginning might be for coaches to show by example how a truly fit person lives. Obviously, coaches cannot and should not train for competition, but they can exercise and maintain a level of fitness that is exemplary of appropriate physical fitness for adult living.

ATHLETICS TEACH SELF-DISCIPLINE

The basis of an orderly life is self-discipline. It is axiomatic that an individual must be able to use his time wisely if he is to achieve established goals. Athletics can teach young people how to discipline themselves, requiring them to organize their schedules in order to complete each day's activities. Many studies have shown that athletes do better scholastically during seasons of competition than during off seasons. This is one indication that athletics are valuable and help the student become organized. However, this value of discipline is often abused by overly exacting coaches. *Self*-discipline should be the goal—without the coach's complete and absolute control.

ATHLETICS TEACH SPORTSMANSHIP

This is one of the most often cited values and, unfortunately, the one most often abused. Athletes are supposed to learn to be humble in victory and gracious in defeat, but the behavior of contestants, coaches and fans is often so antithetical to the stated value as to make our critics laugh.

The ever increasing problem of crowd control, reflective of

the exploitation and demise of sportsmanship, has caused many schools to abandon night games and close contests to spectators. Although this is a social phenomenon resulting from many complex factors, the bad sportsmanship of coaches and game participants often sets the example for the crowds to follow. It is mandatory, therefore, in terms of practicality as well as philosophy that the behavior of both coach and team be above reproach. Coaches must never encourage antisocial behavior through their own actions; they must exert leadership, accept decisions and display appreciation for skilled and courageous play. When coaches display unsportsmanlike behavior, they are bringing into question their ability to teach some of the values of athletics. This problem, like others we have mentioned, seems to originate from the overwhelming desire to win.

ATHLETICS GENERATE SCHOOL SPIRIT

Another value of athletics is that they unify a school by providing common, concrete goals, involving all students and creating a feeling of common purpose. The anticipation of an athletic event is frequently the stimulus to a student's feeling that school is an exciting place to be. But this value, too, can be abused by overemphasizing the importance of such an event. For example, pep assemblies every week during a football or basketball season can result in the loss of hundreds of class hours. Or sometimes students (and *faculty*) not caught by the enthusiasm and "esprit de corps" are subjected to ostracism by the more ardent enthusiasts. Thus, school spirit can generate such a high level of emotion that learning and the normal social amenities are all but suspended. Undue pressure often has a negative effect on the participants, too, when school spirit runs at very high levels, resulting in their becoming ineffective in the sport as well as negligent in class responsibilities.

ATHLETICS KEEP SOME STUDENTS IN SCHOOL

It has been stated that many boys finish school only because they want to participate in athletics. If this is true, then athletics are surely valuable. But there is danger here, also. Directing athletes into easy courses must be minimized. Rather, they should be guided to find subjects that really interest them.

Another abuse which must be eliminated is that of placing pressure on teachers to keep students eligible. Teachers should never be expected to give athletes any extra consideration simply because they are athletes or because they need a grade to remain eligible.

ATHLETICS TEACH SELF-RELIANCE AND COOPERATION

Participation in athletics teaches the importance of each individual on the team as well as the importance of team work. One of the greatest abuses, then, comes when coaches force student athletes to conform to rigid standards of conduct and dress. Standards should never be so rigid as to deprive the individual of his right to be a singularly different person. It seems incongruous to speak of teaching self-reliance on one hand and then to demand a prescribed dress code for all on the other.

Coaches must also be very careful in their public descriptions of players. The press has many times been guilty of overemphasizing the importance of a certain player. Public acclaim should always stress the team and not the prowess of a selected few. It is natural to notice outstanding individual performances, but the stress should be on the team effort. Where individual sports are concerned, there must be a conscious effort on the part of the coach to teach the athlete the compatibility of self-discipline, self-reliance and cooperation.

ATHLETICS CAN PROVIDE COLLEGE SCHOLARSHIPS TO STUDENTS

Many coaches point to the number of scholarships earned by athletes as a "practical" value of sports. Their presence and utility cannot be denied, but neither can their associated problems. For example, in some places coaches *tell* student athletes where to attend college. How many times have the words, "I'll never send an athlete to University X," been spoken by coaches? Scholarships should be considered, at best, as a bonus for participation; they should never be the *reason* for participation.

When scholarships are emphasized by the coach, he is subjecting the potential recipient, the team and himself to a multifaceted problem.

A particularly important problem in this area is college recruiting: Outstanding athletes are sought by so many college recruiters that it sometimes becomes difficult for the student to attend class, practice or play. Too much school time is often taken by these "scouts" in their talks with students. Colleges are under such pressure to have winning teams that they have stooped to such unethical practices as altering high school athletes' class rankings and college board scores in order to qualify them for entrance into college. While the benefits of scholarships are many and obvious, their value can be exploited and abused unless carefully conceived guidelines are established and enforced.

SUMMARY

The fact that athletics are an important part of our American culture is difficult to deny, but it is also important for students to realize that society rewards a winning effort whether it be in athletics, business or education. Athletics can be of great value to the educational, psychological and social growth of students, but moderation is the key to that value. Competition on the athletic field tends to lose its educational value when victory is the ultimate goal.

The solution to the problem of exploiting athletics and thus not realizing their educational potential lies in the attitude of the school community. Many communities take so much pride in the winning record of their teams that coaches must win or be dismissed. A coach in this situation is, of course, likely to submit his players to many of the abuses mentioned earlier. It is the function, therefore, of the school board, school administrators and the community, as well as the athletic staff to ensure that the educational values inherent in athletics are not perverted by an over-emphasis on winning.

Like all educational programs, athletics can be defended only to the extent to which they contribute to established goals. When school people, especially coaches, consider winning a concomitant result of athletic competition and not the basis for such activity, athletics will have an excellent opportunity to achieve desired outcomes.

The values of athletics are many and inherent within the activity, but exploitation through ill-conceived goals and improper administration is common and on the increase. Only through careful philosophical inquiry and practical application can the values be realized.

CHAPTER 15

THE COACH AS A
PUBLIC RELATIONS MAN

AL TAMBERELLI, JR.*

THE COACH'S JOB does not begin and end with his team. To be a successful coach, one must be able to deal successfully with the press, community, parents, teachers, coaching staff and student body.

THE COMMUNITY

It takes full-time living with a community and its people for the coach to understand the community. It is very important for a coach to know the socioeconomic status of the community, its religious feelings, its feelings toward interscholastic athletics, social tensions and customs. Once these are known, only a foolish coach will try drastic changes or outline programs that will be in conflict with these policies.

The coach should try to become involved in the community; attend the church of his choice; become active in civic organizations such as the Lions, Kiwanis or Rotary. This will help him to solidify his position and show the community that he has a sincere interest in its betterment. He should patronize the local merchants, especially sporting goods dealers.

TIP: In so dealing with sporting goods dealers, check on their "service" (costs, emergency service, and can they get what you want when you want it).

THE PRESS

The press, more than anything else, can make or break a coach. Do not use the press as a crying towel or as a spotlight for

---

* Al Tamberelli, "The Coach as a Public Relations Man," *The Coaching Clinic,* Vol. 9 (December 1971), pp. 21-22.

yourself. The following are a few suggestions you might keep in mind in dealing with the press:

1. Get acquainted with the sportswriter.

2. Do not give him false information.

3. Do not confuse his article by giving him names and numbers for the game and then changing them.

4. Explain why you may want to have a closed locker room for fifteen minutes after a game.

5. Set up a picture day.

6. Have statistics available for him.

7. Explain your strategy to the reporter so he can write an intelligent article.

8. Extend to him game passes.

9. If you as a coach feel an answer to a specific question will be detrimental to your team, be ethical and just say "no comment."

10. Do not use the paper to degrade your team or an opponent or another coach, or even school policy.

11. Set up times when you will be available, so you are not bothered at practice or while in preparation for a game.

12. You must strive for a mutual trust and a cooperative relationship.

If these suggestions are followed, your relationship with the press will be trustful and cooperative. The reporter will know you will give him a story (and remember—that's his job), and he will not be forced to write "off-the-record statements" to fill his column.

PARENTS

In dealing with parents, you must try to find out their feelings toward athletics. Have they had a boy in sports? What were the results? Are they athletic, overprotective or complacent toward their son? How do they feel about their son being out for sports?

Parents will support you if they believe you are working for the best interest of their boy and not at his expense. Remember, most parents see sports activities through the eyes of their son and not the team, whereas, you are concerned with all the boys.

Suggestions in dealing with parents:

1. Your appearance and morals are of prime concern.

2. Meet with the parents before the season. Explain your philosophy and the high ideals you will encourage.

3. Maintain personal contact during the season to tell them of the success of their boy and his fine character.

4. Stage a Mom and Dad night at a game.

5. Send a letter out after every game explaining it. Be careful not to boast of one boy or degrade any boy or boys.

6. Try and explain the basics of the game to the parents, about equipment and what to look for at games.

7. Make the parents feel important.

OTHER TEACHERS AND ADMINISTRATORS

Remember, you are a professional person; you are a teacher and you are expected to be cooperative with the principal of your school as well as with other teachers and coaches. You cannot force your sport on these people.

Suggestions for dealing with the professional staff:

1. Explain your program to these people and listen to suggestions.

2. Make it very clear that you see these boys out for your sport as students and you expect no special treatment.

3. Back the academic program and teachers to your team.

4. Make yourself available to assist teachers with disciplinary problems whenever possible, or any other problems.

5. Express the need for cooperation if a successful academic and athletic career is to be experienced by the student athlete.

DEALING WITH THE NONATHLETE

Remember you are a teacher and the same determination, dedication, and interest you show towards your team you should display toward the rest of the student body. Good student body support and enthusiasm has won more than one game for a coach.

CUSTODIANS

These people can be a very big help in your programs as far as laundry facilities and equipment care are concerned. Give them season tickets and acknowledge them at your awards dinner or assembly.

I have tried to deal with the coach in his relationships with people who will help to insure him of a successful career. I feel to discuss his relationship with his players and coaches would be another article. I will say one thing concerning this relation— there are not too many successful or long-lasting dictatorships to- day; nor are there any "jellyfish" running successful operations.

COACH-FACULTY STRAIN: SOME OCCUPATIONAL CAUSES AND CONSIDERATIONS

JOHN D. MASSENGALE*

INTRODUCTION

IN HIGH SCHOOLS, colleges and universities there often exists an atmosphere of strain or alienation between coaches and the remainder of the faculty, including the administration. In order to minimize this strain, for it probably cannot be eliminated, the probable causes of the strain must be identified. The strain may be in the form of constant underground grumbling, or it can sometimes be brought out into the open in the form of active hostility. Regardless of the openness of the strain at any given point in time, the potential tension between coaches and faculty persists.

The purpose of this brief paper is to identify some of the possible causes of coach-faculty strain and illustrate how the unique aspects of the occupational role of the coach can cause the creation and perpetuation of the strain.

THE OCCUPATIONAL ROLE

The first consideration, and perhaps the most important, is the fact that modern coaches are the product of the American athletic system. The American athletic system, through the public schools, has a tremendous and unmeasurable socialization effect on the athlete, who may eventually enter the field of coaching. In all probability, this socialization is partially responsible for

---

* John D. Massengale, "Coach-Faculty Strain: Some Occupational Causes and Considerations," *Scholastic Coach* (in press).

some of the general personality traits that appear to be characteristic of the mass of American coaches.

According to Ogilvie and Tutko, when an athlete enters the
field of coaching he brings with him some personality traits that
are characteristic of athletes and coaches and not necessarily
characteristic of other members of the faculty. Coaches as a
group are aggressive, highly organized, inflexible and seldom pay
attention to what others say. They have an unusually high
amount of psychological endurance, which others often see as
either persistence or stubbornness, depending upon their point
of view. Coaches also appear in general to be extremely conservative, politically, socially and attitudinally. They plainly dislike
change.[1]

These personality traits may well be the foundation material
for coach-faculty strain. In addition, these traits are often
viewed out of proportion and then compounded by the unique-
ly complex occupational role of the coach.

Along with the socialization of the American athletic system,
the coach more often than not, is formally educated in the field
of physical education. Edwards summarized the work of others
and presented the view that physical education majors actually
have more in common with students who are not planning to
teach, than students who plan to enter the field of education. He
suggested that physical education majors, as compared to other
prospective teachers, have a more traditional philosophy of education, a slightly lower social class background, tend to be more
dogmatic and appear to have different social values.[2]

These factors may also influence coach-faculty strain by creating barriers of nonacceptance or partial acceptance. The result
can be the exclusion of the coach from the type of educational
hierarchy that is open to the other faculty members.

Another consideration is the stereotype of the coach often
held by other members of the faculty. They often agree with
critics like Scott, generally viewing men in the occupation of

1. B. C. Ogilvie and T. A. Tutko, Self-Perception as Compared with Measured
Personality of Male Physical Educators. Paper presented at Second International
Congress of Sports Psychologists (Washington, D. C., October 1968).

2. H. Edwards, *Sociology of Sport* (Homewood, Ill., Dorsey Press, 1973).

coaching as dehumanizing, autocratic and insensitive to the individuality of the young men they coach. Faculty, as critics of the coach, often emphasize that coaches employ leadership behavior that is unduly authoritarian and provide examples such as rigid rules, an overemphasis of stern discipline and what appears to them as a cold impersonal attitude on the part of the coach. What often develops is that the faculty members view the cause of coach-faculty strain as being the direct result of the unusually stern authoritarian leadership behavior of the coach.[3]

In contrast, coaches take the view that authoritarianism does not cause strain and that the strain is caused by the overreaction of the uninformed, antiathletic faculty. Sage described leadership behavior in American sport and identified a major point that is often overlooked by people outside the field of coaching. He maintained that people often erroneously assume that authoritarian leadership is always bad, overlooking the fact that the motives of coaches are often for the good of the team members, as well as for the good of the team and the school.[4]

The problem of authoritarianism in coaching is deeply embedded in the occupational milieu of the expected coaching role. According to Beisser, a coach must also fulfill many of the functions of the traditional father. He must be strong, virile and tough. Although firm discipline is disappearing from the home, it is still expected in athletics by parents, fans, alumni and other interested pro-athletic groups. The father role is seldom initiated by, or expected of, other members of the faculty. The father role is expected of the coach. However, he seldom receives extra credit for merely fulfilling this role. He must win to receive extra credit. If the coach feels that the faculty is attempting to strip him of his father-like authority, and he views this authority as a prerequisite for molding a winning team, coach-faculty strain is greatly increased.[5]

3. J. Scott, *The Athletic Revolution* (New York, Free Press, 1970).

4. G. H. Sage, "The Coach as Management: Organizational Leadership in American Sport," *Quest*, Vol. 19 (1973), pp. 35-40.

5. A. Beisser, *The Madness in Sport* (New York, Appleton-Century-Crofts, 1966).

Faculty members often view the authoritarian control of the student by the coach as an infringement on the students rights and freedoms, and an unnecessary restraint on the total educational development of the student. The coach seldom questions this infringement, for he considers himself the faculty expert in coaching and the authority with the ultimate responsibility for the total performance of the team. He demands dedication, obedience and loyalty, for he is held responsible for losing, not the team members. Success is expected of him, through his leadership behavior and his decision making power. In this sense he is an executive, a decision maker with legitimate authority and he dislikes interference from faculty members who are unqualified to work in his area of expertise. Other faculty members seldom have an appreciation for the complexity of his occupational role as executive.

Although the coach may be hired as a bonafide faculty member, his responsibilities and occupational role differ markedly from other faculty members. He seldom is fired for his academic reputation. Winning will often substitute for academic inadequacies, if inadequacies exist. However, academic excellence and teaching expertise will seldom substitute for losing. Other faculty members do not work under this dilemma and seldom understand the problem. This dilemma adds to the problem of coach-faculty strain, often creates polarization and results in the formation of a very homogeneous group of coaches, both locally and nationally.

It appears that specific responsibilities of the coaching role cause coach-faculty strain and then the strain is intensified by the decision making powers of the coach. An important aspect of coaching decisions is the method and manner in which these decisions are made. Coaching decisions are characteristically practical, rational, expedient and often made in the shortest possible time. This manner of decision making comes easy to the coach, since it is the type he is forced to use in day-to-day and game-to-game situations. Success with this type of decision making may be the main reason that coaches constantly criticize the decision making processes of the faculty and the administration.

As a group, coaches often criticize faculty and administration decision making, and most of the criticism revolves around delay tactics and the use of theory instead of basic down-to-earth reality. Coaches often view indecision as no decision at all and usually maintain that even a bad decision is better than indecision. Many coaches also view indecision as weakness and weakness is seldom acceptable to coaches, since it is a trait that is not allowed in their occupation.

What coaches view as weakness or even incompetence in decision making on the part of the faculty and administration is clearly evident in some of the responses of prominent coaches interviewed by Underwood.[6] Typical remarks of the coaches were: college administrators started the athletic rebellion by backing down, they were scared to make decisions, they knew nothing about what we were trying to do, they were incapable of judging coaches, they do not understand the coach-player relationship, faculties cannot understand coaching responsibilities, administrators were weak under pressure and administrators displayed gutlessness in one form or another. It is clear that current administrative policies and procedures used in modern education can definitely cause coach-faculty strain, if the coach adheres to his traditional occupational role.

Because of coach-faculty strain, coaches have attempted to use athletic governing bodies and professional organizations to bolster what they view as a diminishing authority structure within their occupation. While this movement increases coach autonomy, it also increases coach-faculty strain, especially when public policy statements are issued that attempt to reinforce the authority of the coach.

The coach continually attempts to gain complete control over his position, although he realizes that complete control is impossible. However, the more control he gains, the better he views his position, since he is continually reminded that he is ultimately responsible for team performance. The coach willingly accepts total responsibility, but with this responsibility he insists on no interference from anyone. He asks for, and completely accepts,

6. J. Underwood, "The Desperate Coach," *Sports Illustrated*, Vol. 31(11) (1969), pp. 68-70.

responsibility for a position filled with uncertainty, in order to eliminate as much uncertainty as possible.

According to Edwards, authoritarianism and inflexibility in coaching is caused by the institutional demand that coaches be given total liability for outcomes in a situation filled with uncertainty.[7] When coaches are held liable for the total performance of a team, they demand the complete authority to make any decision they deem necessary for team success, regardless of whether the other faculty members view the decision as necessary or not. This decision making technique can often cause coach-faculty strain and in recent years has fostered overt action by some faculty members.

Along with the causes and considerations previously presented, there are several smaller issues that cause a continual irritation to coach-faculty strain. Items such as: coaches with higher salaries than other faculty, peer group evaluation for faculty expertise but not coaching expertise, conflicting views of standards of academic achievement, the social prominence of the coach in the community and athletes receiving special consideration in the school and the community.

CONCLUDING STATEMENT

Although it is impossible at this time to accurately determine the exact causes of coach-faculty strain, for they vary from school to school, the uniqueness of the coaching role is surely a large contributing factor. The consideration of the coaching role is important, since role change is inevitable in the schools of the future. Currently men are being forced out of coaching due to role strain and the number of men being forced out will probably increase according to Edwards.[8]

The competence of the coach will probably continue to be determined by winning and losing, although the coaching role may change. However, the occupational milieu of the coach will probably continue to affect faculty relations as much as any oth-

---

7. Edwards, *op. cit.*
8. *Ibid.*

er factor. Regardless of the type of strain caused by the occupation, the coach will have to adjust to the occupation, or he simply will not make it as a coach. Coaches will probably continue to contribute to coach-faculty strain as long as they view factors that cause the strain as being the same factors that are necessary for winning performance.

CHAPTER 17

RELATIONSHIPS BETWEEN ATHLETIC OFFICIALS AND COACHES

RICHARD J. DONNELLY*

A PROPER CONCEPT OF ATHLETICS and their role in the education of youth is basic to the development of an understanding of the relationship that should exist between coaches and officials. It is also important to recognize the unique roles that coaches and officials play in this specialized process of education. Once a recognition of these roles is visualized, then it is possible to discuss in an enlightened manner the procedures that coaches and officials can utilize to better carry out their roles. In this framework it is also necessary to consider the athletic director and the techniques that he may employ to make it easier for coaches and officials to do their respective jobs effectively. The ultimate result would lead to better coaching and better officiating as well as to better relationships between coaches and officials. These in turn would further enhance and strengthen the educational values of school athletics.

SCHOOL ATHLETICS AND EDUCATION

Just what is the fundamental relationship of school athletics to education? Are school athletics education or entertainment? The answer is obvious. Everybody wants school athletics to be educational, but many also demand that they be sponsored for the entertainment of the spectators. However, it should be remembered that whenever an athletic event neglects or loses its educational significance there is no reason for it to be included in the school program.

---

* Richard J. Donnelly, "Relationships Between Athletic Officials and Coaches," *Athletic Journal*, Vol. 37 (May 1957), pp. 30-32 and 53-57.

Do school athletics need to be amateur in order to be educational? Of course, they must be. However, everybody wants schools to promote amateur athletics, but many also desire a professional performance.

Is the win-at-all-costs ideal an enemy of school athletics? It most certainly is. In fact, this ideal is at odds with the very framework of social morality which guides people in the democratic way of life. It is also a fact that the public is always interested in the final score, but is seldom concerned with how the boys played the game or how the crowd behaved. If this false philosophical principle of the ends justifying the means is allowed to run unchecked, it will become like a Frankenstein monster ready to turn and vent its most violent fury upon its creators and most avid supporters.

In our society today, we are committed to the philosophy that athletics are an integral phase of education. In such a philosophy the following points are important:

1. The purpose of athletics must always keep in step with the purposes of education.

2. School athletics are sponsored primarily for the participants, not the fans, the coaches, the officials or the school.

3. Winning is not all-important, since a team that wins its fair share of games over the years will only break even. On the other hand, instilling the spirit and the will to win is all-important. The overriding principle is that this desire to win should always be kept subservient to the fundamental code of the sport and to the ethical code of sportsmanship. The founder of the Modern Olympic Games, Baron Pierre de Coubertin, has most aptly phrased this ideal in words that have been immortalized and which will continue to endure as long as the Olympic flame burns: *The important thing in the Olympic Games is not winning but taking part. The essential thing in life is not conquering but fighting well.*

4. Athletics are only one of many vehicles for educating boys and girls. As such they are liked by some and disliked by others.

5. There are many athletic sports and no one sport should be purposely built up to overshadow and exclude others. Every school should promote as many sports and as many teams as it

possibly can. This is in accordance with the psychological principle of individual differences, one of the most important characteristics that has distinguished American psychological thought from European.

6. To make reasonably sure that the educational objectives are most effectively attained, it is essential that professionally trained leaders be given charge of the athletic program. Lay leadership may function in an advisory capacity, but school administrators must never yield to pressure for complete lay control of the school athletic program.

Unless school athletics are rigidly controlled and carefully supervised, there is present at all times an inherent danger that the educational value of athletics will be diminished and athletics will eventually lose any semblance of education. It seems ironic that the first argument used to advocate athletics in schools is now being used in turnabout fashion to curtail them. The early supporters of school athletics maintained that they were a safety valve for the release of pent-up animal spirits in growing boys. Athletics were supposed to curb juvenile delinquency. In recent months, athletics have provided an opportune setting for the promotion of delinquency in a few of our large cities. The situation has become so serious that some schools have discontinued night football, in some cases even night basketball, and have reverted back to afternoon contests.

ROLE OF THE COACH

First of all, the coach is a professionally trained teacher. Secondly, he is a professional specialist whose duty it is to teach his boys not only how to play, but also how to win with humility and how to lose without rancor. It is his duty to teach his boys to have courage and to do their best at all times, to control their emotions and to be gentlemen in all situations no matter how trying. It is a coach's duty to instill in his boys a desire to win in accordance with the letter and spirit of the rules of the game and not at all costs.

The coach occupies a position of strategic influence. He is the leader who should set the example for his boys, his school and his community.

ROLE OF THE OFFICIAL

The athletic sports official is an honest, impartial judge whose duty it is to see that the game is played according to the rules and to see that no team or player secures an advantage by violating or circumventing any of the rules. His role is secondary to the game. It must be assumed that he is honest and also that he may make mistakes. Everybody makes mistakes—doctors, lawyers, engineers, teachers, businessmen, coaches, players, even officials. There are probably very few officials who can say that they have not made mistakes on rules and rules interpretations at some time in their officiating careers. But they are honest mistakes. We believe that today officials are making fewer such mistakes than ever before. Credit should be given to officials' associations and officiating clinics and to the state high school athletic associations for their unceasing efforts to improve the caliber of officiating. As for judgment decisions, who can definitely say an official is wrong? So much depends upon the angle from which the play is viewed. Officiating procedures and techniques are designed so that the best all-around coverage can be given to all types of plays. Judgment decisions usually have to be made instantly and there is no opportunity to rerun the play.

THE ATHLETIC DIRECTOR

It is probably safe to assume that the athletic directors who have the best records in relationships with officials are the directors who have proved to be competent in handling their jobs. The competent director does everything within his power to see that he secures the best possible officiating. Some of the procedures which he employs are as follows:

1. Provides more information about an open date other than the date only. An official should also be advised of the time of the contest, the opposing schools, fellow officials who are being contacted (if possible), the officiating assignment and the customary fee. These additional facts may prevent an unhappy event that might otherwise have occurred. For example, an official may be able to work a night game but not an afternoon contest. For personal reasons he may prefer not to officiate games in

which certain schools participate. He may have relatives in that school system or as members of the team. Or, he may not get along with the coach of that school. Furthermore, he may not work very well with the other officials and prefer to pass up the assignment and work with somebody else.

2. Use written contracts for the hiring of officials. The contracts include all of the information given to the official in the initial communication as well as the location of the contest plus the names, addresses and telephone numbers of fellow officials and the home team athletic director.

3. Sends to each official a written reminder of his contract to officiate so that it will be received about three to five days ahead of the event. The location of the contest should be made clear and if it is a difficult place to reach, directions or a diagram of how to get there should be included. Information should also advise about parking and dressing facilities. Another idea is to include a post card that can be returned by the official who indicates that he has received the reminder notice and confirms his intention to fulfill his contract. A double post card serves this purpose very satisfactorily.

4. Sees that the field or court and surrounding area are properly marked and roped or fenced off in accordance with directions in the rules books. In football the most frequently overlooked item is the failure to mark off the football field by five yard lines. Other common mistakes are poorly marked in-bounds lines, no restraining fence or rope around the field, and the coaches' and players' boxes inadequately designated. In basketball the customary practice is to neglect to provide enough clearance on the ends and sides (national standards recommend a ten-foot minimum). Also ignored are protruding objects that are not well padded. In baseball the proper marking of the three-foot line, coaches' boxes, and the on-deck batter's circle as well as markings that would facilitate enforcement of ground rules are most often forgotten.

5. Provides trained and competent assistant officials such as scorers and timers in basketball and the *chain gang* in football. The director also sees that they are on hand in advance of the contest so that they can receive instructions from the game offi-

cials. The officials should not have to hold up the start of the game or hustle around at the last instant trying to get a *chain gang crew*. Neither should they be expected to spend an undue amount of time explaining the duties to the assistant officials. These are routine duties that the competent director never fails to carry out.

6. Treats the official as his guest and proffers certain social courtesies and amenities upon the official's arrival at the site of the contest. These courtesies include convenient parking, dressing facilities separate from coaches and players, and being available or having somebody else available to greet the official upon his arrival. He also sees that each official is provided with soap and a towel for a shower.

7. Handles pregame arrangements in an efficient yet courteous manner. These may be summarized as follows: a. Introduces officials to the coaches. b. Introduces officials to the assistant officials. c. Provides the officials with advance information on pregame and half-time band performances or other festivities. d. Has the necessary game equipment such as the ball, watches, whistles, and the like easily available before the start of the game. It is also prudent to have spares on hand.

8. Makes prompt payment of the fee to each official. Occasionally, it may be necessary to mail the official his check, but in such cases the official should be advised of the situation as soon as possible.

9. Gives a courteous farewell to each official as an invited guest of the host school. In extreme circumstances it may be necessary to provide an escort for the officials.

10. Rates the official's work in an unbiased and objective manner and turns this rating into the state association, if such ratings are requested.

THE COACH

The competent coach is also interested in doing everything in his power to improve the caliber of officiating. A coach can materially assist in this endeavor by consenting to employ younger and newer officials in reserve and junior high school games, so that a supply of trained and experienced officials can be developed. However, it goes without saying that the coach makes his greatest contribution in this area by adhering to high standards of ethical conduct. Some of the practices that a coach must employ if he is to uphold this high idealism of athletics are as follows:

1. Avoid talking to officials during the game and between halves. Before the game he should merely extend a greeting to the officials and tell them the names and numbers of his captains. It is also good practice for the coach to introduce his captain or captains to the officials. He may, if he thinks it necessary, explain any unusual maneuvers that his team may attempt to execute. This explanation gives the officials advance warning so that they are not caught off guard by the unusual tactics. This technique is acceptable to the vast majority of officials, although there are a few officials who resent that type of *inside dope*. On the other hand, there is nothing more irritating to an official than to have a coach advise him before a game to watch a particular player of the other team, or caution an official that the other team *has gotten away with murder* in previous games and that they *play dirty*.

2. Learn the rules and teach the players the rules. The coach instills in his players a respect for the spirit as well as the letter of the rules.

3. Does not allow the players to bait the officials. The good coach removes players from the game whenever they are baiting or arguing with officials or with opponents or teammates.

4. Instruct the players to address the officials in a courteous manner.

5. Accept judgment decisions of the officials without outward signs of emotion and demand the same of the players.

6. Permit only the captain to discuss an interpretation of a rule with the official. The captain should be instructed to do this in a polite manner.

7. Shake hands after the game with the opposing coach and with the officials in full view of the spectators. A handshake in the locker room, while commendable, is not as effective as one within sight of the crowd. Most assuredly, a handshake in the locker room is not a fair exchange for a histrionic effort by the

coach when he was protesting an official's decision in front of the emotionally charged spectators.

8. Talk courteously to officials at all times. Never criticize an official on or off the record to players, the public, officials, coaches or sports writers.

The competent coach is aware that a judgment decision once made cannot be changed. He also realizes that an official who is affected by a coach's theatrical extravaganza is usually more apt to be looking for an opportunity to call a foul on the coach, thus penalizing the team even more severely. The good coach knows that constant baiting and bickering with officials upsets the players who start fighting the officials instead of concentrating on the opponents and sometimes even turn against the coach himself. He has learned that this type of situation creates a boisterous group of fans and lessens considerably the educational benefits of athletics. Past experience has taught the competent coach that he has the responsibility of setting the example for others by his own conduct on the bench. In the final analysis, the competent coach has found that only the incompetent coach uses the official as a crutch or an alibi for losing games or as an excuse for his team's mistakes or poor caliber of play.

THE OFFICIAL

The problems of officiating are twofold and the officials must bear their fair share of responsibility in meeting them. There are various degrees in the quality of officials just as there are different types of coaches and athletic directors. The competent official known that his officiating ability depends, and is also judged, by certain overt acts of behavior that he follows as a matter of habit. Some of the more important of these are:

1. Promptness in answering business correspondence about open dates and contracts for games.

2. Sending a reminder to the home team athletic director two or three days ahead of the game signifying intention of coming.

3. Early arrival at the site of the contest—at least 30 minutes ahead of time.

4. Thorough knowledge of the rules and the ability to interpret and apply them to the game. The good official regularly attends the rules meetings sponsored by the state high school athletic association. He also joins a local officials' association and attends its meetings where rules, play situations and officiating mechanics are discussed.

5. Hustle and being in good position on all plays. This means that the official must keep himself in good physical condition. He should adopt a preseason training regimen to get into condition before the season starts.

6. Consistency in making decisions—throughout the game and all over the court or field. The good official calls plays the same way in the last quarter as he did in the first quarter. He calls plays inside the 10-yard line in the same way as he calls plays at midfield.

7. Control of emotions, especially temper and tongue. The official must always use proper language and never employ profanity.

8. Courteous treatment of players. The official's attitude toward the players should be a friendly one; firm, but not dictatorial; fair and impartial, not biased. A controlled sense of humor is a valuable asset for any official. He should know when to be serious, when to joke, when to say nothing, when to praise and when to chastise.

9. Avoiding explanation of decisions. If the captain courteously requests an explanation of a play ruling, the official should respond in a courteous manner. He should explain the ruling to the captain as quickly as possible, if he feels that the situation justifies it. In some cases, it may be necessary to consult with fellow officials. However, a consultation should be avoided as much as possible, unless it is absolutely necessary.

10. Act as an official only and not as a scout for a friend or as a coach on the field. In this same vein, officials should avoid a lengthy lecture on rules of the game just prior to the start of the game. It is essential to cover the ground rules, but it is not necessary to give the captains a five-minute lecture on how the game is going to be officiated.

11. Unobtrusiveness in carrying out the duties as a game official. An official is not hired to be a show man or to make a spectacle of himself.

12. Calling decisions loudly and decisively so that everybody concerned (officials, players and coaches) knows what has been called. There are official signals that each official should master and use at all times. These signs enable the coaches and the spectators to know what the decisions of the officials are.

13. Wearing of the same uniforms by all officials in any one game.

14. Use of similar game officiating procedures and mechanics by all officials in all games. This means teamwork on the part of the officiating team. The officials should be able to depend upon each other. An official also has a right to expect the support and assistance of his fellow officials in his judgment decisions.

15. Fulfilling a contract even though it may mean losing out on a higher paying game. An official should not send a substitute unless he has obtained the permission of the athletic director or coach who hired him.

16. Never talking about other officials or coaches on or off the record. Most of all an official never berates a fellow official or a coach.

These points are by no means a complete coverage of the acts and actions that are consistently used by competent officials. However, they are the most important ones. The competent official also has the ability to get along with the players. He always keeps them and the game under control. He possesses the courage to call plays as he sees them, even though he may be right in front of a team's bench. Neither does he let the remarks of the spectators upset him. Never should he make the mistake of explaining a play or decision to a spectator during a time-out in the course of the game. The competent official realizes that mistakes are possible. He also knows that some mistakes are made which should never be made. The reasons for this are lack of hustle and anticipating decisions. These are sins that no official has any excuse for committing. To guard against falling into these errors an official cannot ease up for a single play. He must bear down, hustle and work hard on every play for the entire game.

By following the principles and procedures outlined, considerable improvement will result in the relationships between coaches and officials. The aforementioned procedures and guides to action are merely the end result. Obviously, some planned program must be instituted to assure that these desirable practices are consciously and deliberately sought after. For such a program we propose the following ideas:

1. A change in the method of hiring and assigning officials to games.

2. A tightening up of the requirements that are necessary for officials to be licensed and to retain their licenses.

3. A change in the method of training new officials and giving in-service education to experienced officials.

4. The raising of professional and certification standards that are required for coaching.

5. The instituting of a better sports education program in our schools and communities.

Each of the above suggestions will be discussed in turn.

NEW METHODS OF ASSIGNING OFFICIALS

It is our suggestion that the appointment or hiring of officials for high school games be taken out of the hands of the coaches, athletic directors and officials' associations. Instead, this function should be entrusted to a state or regional commissioner of high school athletic officials. As long as the local school hires the officials the following beliefs will continue to persist. First, a few officials will either consciously or unconsciously favor the home team on more than their fair share of close decisions. Secondly, some people as a result of possibly one or two episodes will brand all officials as *homers* and come to the conclusion that a visiting team never gets an officiating break. With an impartial board or commissioner, who is not affiliated with either of the contesting schools, assigning the officials to a game, these false beliefs will not have the slightest shred of evidence left to support them.

Local schools would have a hand in setting up the administrative machinery for this program. Perhaps they would wish to make it one of their rules that a local school could have veto power over an official for a game. If such were the case, it might *also* be wise to limit the number of officials any one school could veto for a season.

Even if this recommendation were not adopted, there are certain principles that local schools can follow in order to avoid untoward episodes and unhappy incidents in the management of their athletic contests as far as officials are concerned. These may be summarized as follows:

1. Use the same care in selecting officials that is used in selecting faculty members.

2. Use written contracts.

3. Hire out-of-town officials. If possible, avoid hiring local officials or close friends for officials.

4. Hire an official for no more than two home games during a season.

5. Avoid the evil of trading games on the part of coaches. This practice operates somewhat like this. The football coach of School A will give the basketball coach of School B two football games, if the latter will give the former two basketball games to officiate.

6. Hire officials early; do not wait until the last minute.

TIGHTER REQUIREMENTS FOR OFFICIALS

When it comes to raising the standards for high school athletics, the official appears to be the forgotten man. To those who know athletics best, the official is an important cog in the educational program of athletics and must be considered in any program which is designed to augment the educational importance of athletics. It would be in order for state high school athletic associations to tighten up on the requirements that are necessary in order for the officials to be licensed and also to retain their licenses. Some of the requirements that might prove effective are as follows:

1. Rules examination and a practical officiating examination for all new officials.

2. An annual physical examination for all officials.

3. An annual rules examination and a practical officiating examination for all experienced officials.

4. Compulsory attendance for all officials at rules meetings sponsored by the state high school athletic association.

5. Compulsory membership for all officials in a local officials' association.

6. Compulsory attendance of all officials at a specified minimum number of meetings of the local officials' association.

NEW METHODS OF TRAINING OFFICIALS

As matters now stand, there is practically no method for training officials except through the old-fashioned way of actual game experience in officiating. In the early days of athletics this was undoubtedly an answer. It is now as outdated as the ancient method of a father educating his son in all aspects of life as was done in primitive societies. The school has been established to help the father in this process, because it is a duty now too complicated for a father to perform alone. Thus, we must find some way to assist in the process of training new officials. There are several things that might be done to help.

State high school athletic associations and our institutions of higher education that are training men for teaching and the other professions could cooperate in a program designed to provide practical experience in officiating for future officials. We have the pattern to follow in the student teaching idea. A student teacher does not need a teaching certificate to practice teaching, but he does his practice teaching in a real classroom under expert supervision. A student or an apprentice official could do his practice officiating without a license in actual games under experienced supervisors. Certain prerequisite standards could be drawn up before a student could enroll in practice officiating just as is done for the student teacher. Such a training program should not be limited to physical education majors or minors, or even to any teaching major; but it should be broad enough to include students in other professional or preprofessional fields.

HIGHER STANDARDS FOR COACHES

We have traveled a long way since the days of the transient part-time coach who in most cases had no affiliation with the school except during the few short months his special sport was in season. Today a few states require a major in physical education as a minimum standard for certification to coach, some require a minor in physical education; and most demand that the coach be a regular member of the school faculty or else be registered with the state high school athletic association as certified to coach. The trend is in the right direction.

If in-service education is necessary for officials, it is just as essential for coaches. Many of the disagreements between coaches and officials would never arise, if both parties had a mutual knowledge and understanding of the rules and rules interpretations. Rules can be learned by self-study, but in the case of interpretations there is no substitute for group study and discussion. Many interpretations of the National Federation and of the state high school athletic associations never reach the coaches until it is too late. If the coaches had to attend the state rules meetings, they would receive these rulings in time to avoid *rhubarbs*. Compulsory attendance of coaches at state rules meetings is a must if relationships between the lazy coach and officials are to improve.

A BETTER SPORTS EDUCATION PROGRAM

We have little reason to be proud of our efforts and success in educating the American public on the place of sports in American life, on the educational values of athletics and on the public's role as a spectator and participant. This is a program that should be started in the early elementary grades and carried on through the colleges and universities. The schools should offer regularly scheduled classes in the appreciation of sports. The parents, students and the whole community should be involved in the planning and execution of the sports education program.

CONCLUSION

Many practical suggestions have been made on how to improve the relationships between coaches and officials. Many have not been mentioned. For example, schools should employ capable announcers who not only know the technical job of announcing, but who also have a high code of sportsmanship that always guides them in performing their job of announcing. Trained students, teachers and parents can be used to help supervise the spectators at all athletic events. Cheerleaders can be taught ways of helping to keep the crowd under control. Law officers, plainclothes as well as uniformed ones, can lend weight to the rules and regulations set up for crowd and traffic control at athletic contests.

In brief, whenever a school is sponsoring an athletic event, the school authorities, including the superintendent, principal, athletic director, coaches and officials must always be alert and on the job. They cannot afford to relax for a single moment. If things should get out of hand, or if a rivalry with an opposing school has become too hot, a temporary break in scheduling them would probably be beneficial to everybody concerned.

CHAPTER 18

ROLE OF COACH, PHYSICIAN IN PROGRAM

HENRY F. DONN*

A CLOSE RELATIONSHIP always has existed between teachers of physical education and members of the medical profession. It is primarily because of the interest shown and the help given by many physicians that physical education enjoys its present status.

Physicians more than anyone else, perhaps, have impressed upon them the fact that a child's mind is not separate from his (or her) physical self—that body and mind are one entity, greatly in need of training to meet the problems of life. Even today, however, there are some educational authorities who accept the principle of *mens sana in corpore sano* in theory only.

SPECIAL TRAINING FOR TEACHER-COACHES

With the change in emphasis from a medical background to advanced study in the field of education, physical education lost the strong support of its medical friends. There has been some cooperation on a national scale between the American Medical Association and the National Education Association, but only sporadic efforts at cooperative work on a local scale.

Athletics is but one branch of physical education. It simply is an educational experience, provided by the school, in order that all students who are physically gifted may have an opportunity to display their talents in competition with their peers. It is not

* Henry F. Donn, "Role of Coach, Physician in Program," *The American School Board Journal*, Vol. 153 (August 1966), pp. 44, 45, and 48.

an entertainment program for the community. Its importance should not be overemphasized or exploited. It has grown from the traditional four-sport seasonal program of football, basketball, baseball and track to include soccer, wrestling, fencing, swimming, hockey, gymnastics, tennis, golf and bowling, in addition to the girls' intramural program. This growth has placed an unprecedented demand for facilities and has created a shortage of trained leadership that has become a growing problem.

With few exceptions, the athletic coach is a teaching member of the faculty. As a teacher, he has met the training and experience requirements for state certification. Our medically trained leaders knew the importance of and insisted on the inclusion of special courses in the training of physical educators. Anatomy, physiology, kinesiology, biology, chemistry, hygiene, first aid, and accident prevention, adolescent psychology and mental hygiene are included in his training.

Quite often, the coaching coverage cannot be met with the physical education staff alone. Of necessity, the administrator must supplement his coaching staff with classroom teachers who have had only playing experience. Unless the classroom teacher has had some physical education training, he should not be employed as a coach in contact sports, particularly football. Administrators, physical educators and physicians should suggest minimum standards for coaching certification.

PROFICIENT TRAINERS ARE GOOD AIDES

A close relationship between medical men and the coaching staff is mandatory. The coaches need medical assistance and supervision to determine the physical condition of athletes and the medical examination provides this information. In some schools the athlete is examined once each year. Experience indicates that a medical examination should be given for each sport. In contact sports, examinations are desirable not only at the beginning of the season but during and at the end of the season as well. The medical profession should take a stand on the frequency of examinations for athletes and, even more important, determine how thorough the examination should be.

The coaching staff then must make effective use of the information obtained from the medical exam. Experiences have indicated that the physician should help weed out from among the athletic candidates those who are a risk in athletic activity.

In many schools funds are not sufficient for the services of a physician on a daily basis. This situation forces the coach to act as a trainer and to care for minor injuries. Most coaches do not like this situation and compensate for it by appointing a firstaid-trained adult or student as a trainer. Many of these individuals have become quite proficient in their work and have received accolades from members of the medical profession. In this situation, only those injuries come to the attention of the doctor that are serious or have failed to respond to recommended treatment.

The American Red Cross First Aid Textbook defines first aid as follows: "First Aid is the immediate and temporary care given the victim of an accident or sudden illness until the services of a physician can be obtained."

To render care is one thing, but to give treatment which includes preventive measures becomes a questionable practice when it is done without the direct supervision or instruction of the physician.

UNDERSTANDING, RESPECT NECESSARY

In these days of high insurance claims, increased numbers of liability cases and the awareness by parents of acceptable standard procedures, it becomes essential for the coach and the trainer, if there is one, to work under close supervision and instruction of the doctor in any matter that concerns the players' health. The most minute details of a doctor's instruction must be carried out. There must be mutual respect for their professional training and experience between the coaching staff and the doctor. Adolescents are alert to take advantage of a situation where there is a lack of professional harmony.

In working as a team, the physician and the coaching staff should, before the season starts, set up a check list of items to be discussed in order that a common starting point be established for efficient and professional performance of their respective duties. The following suggestions for such a list are basic.

1. *Specific responsibilities for the injury prevention program should be clearly defined.* Under no circumstances should trainers or coaches be considered a substitute for the physician. In football and other contact sports, the physician should be the one who examines an injured player to determine the advisability of his continuance. No football game should be permitted to start unless there is a physician in attendance. This is the usual practice during varsity games, but not during junior varsity play. The junior varsity squads in most cases, consists of ninth and tenth grade boys. These boys lack the physical maturity found in boys on the varsity teams.

2. *A good accident and record-keeping system should be established and adhered to.* A system very easily can be developed in a local situation. The collection, analysis and use of such data is invaluable for the improvement of coaching and can be the base from which a program of injury prevention can be guided. All first aid cases can be recorded on an individual player's card and on a daily log sheet. Student athletes should be instructed on the necessity of having every injury, no matter how minor, examined and recorded. No injured player should be permitted to dress for practice or for a game until he has been examined by the coach. The exam should be repeated at the end of the game.

3. *Sound practices should be established for the immediate care of injured players.* Medical men report that sprains, strains, contusions, dislocations and fractures are the common types of injuries found in sports. Failure to apply immediate first aid and early treatment frequently results in prolonged convalescence or permanent injury. A fully-equipped first aid kit, stretcher, blankets, ice packs, water and other necessary equipment should be easily accessible during practices and games.

4. *The coaching staff should have accessible information as to where parents, physician, emergency equipment and the police can be reached in an emergency.* A member of the coaching staff should accompany an injured or sick player to his home or to the

hospital and remain with him until a parent or guardian arrives. A written record of the facts should be made.

5. *An adequately-stocked and properly organized first aid room should be planned.* The uses of therapeutic devices, such as whirlpool baths and infrared lamps, should be used under the direct supervision of the physician. The practice of permitting unauthorized personnel to use specialized equipment is fraught with danger. The first aid room should not be a hangout for players or coaches.

6. *Sanitary hygienic practices should be discussed and deviations from accepted procedures should not be tolerated.* The use of a common drinking cup or of a common towel, the borrowing of clothing and protective equipment, are evidences of a lack of professional supervision.

7. *A line of communication should be established between the home, the coach and physician.* Parents need to understand before injuries occur, just what insurance coverage the school policy (if there is one) provides. The family physician should inform the team doctor about any of his findings. Training rules, dismissal times and general procedures must be understood early in the season, if cooperation is expected.

8. *Coaching personnel and players should be schooled to recognize the hazards they are going to be exposed to, the need to remove those hazards that can be removed and to compensate for those that cannot be removed.* The prevalent causes of injuries, the necessity for individuals to wear protective equipment at all times, the importance of an adequate warmup, the avoidance of horseplay, the checking of playing facilities before use, the need to recognize the whistle as a safety device and to immediately stop activity when it is heard, all are items which need to be discussed.

9. *The selection, care and fitting of protective equipment should be carefully reviewed.* The results of research on helmet fitting and protection, shoulder and hip pad fitting, changes in shoe design to prevent injuries are important. Prepractice and pregame taping instruction can be given. Ankle wraps should be mandatory. In football, players should wear all protective

equipment, including headgear, face protector and mouthpiece, during practice as well as games. All protective equipment should be carefully inspected to insure an adequate fit.

10. *The preseason and early-season conditioning should be carefully planned.* In football, it is almost an impossibility to get a boy in good physical condition for body contact if he starts his conditioning on September 1. There should be a minimum of two weeks of graduated physical conditioning before there is any inter-squad scrimmage. Definite practice plans to a preset time limit for each phase of the day's work will aid in obtaining alertness and will minimize injuries that occur through carelessness and inattention.

11. *Coaches should follow suggestions by sports safety experts.* No practice session or game and no facility should be used unless there is adult supervision. Other suggestions include the following: In contact sports, younger boys should not be used in scrimmage against the varsity. Abnormal size and age differentiations put a needless risk on the smaller and younger boy. Players should not be used as tackling dummies unless they have protective padding. Players who present constant behavior difficulties, who are adverse to teaching and following instruction, who insist on horseplay, who become involved in too many personality difficulties, should be dismissed from the squad.

12. *All players must be taught the rules of the game and the procedures to follow during "time-out" periods.* Exemplary conduct should be demanded at all times. Belligerent players should be removed from the game. Players must be taught that the decision of the official is final and must be abided by.

GAME OFFICIALS HAVE RESPONSIBILITY

The code of any game permits competition to be conducted in an interesting and equitable manner and, at the same time, specifically prohibits unnecessary roughness, unfair tactics and unsportsmanlike behavior. The action of the players must be in conformity with the rules and game officials accept the responsibility for enforcing the rules. The judgment and skill of the official determines to a great extent the manner in which the rules are enforced.

Only competent, trained and qualified officials should be hired to handle games. These men generally are teachers, lawyers, merchants and even physicians. The vigilant administration of the rules starts before the game gets under way. Each official has a specific responsibility to inspect game facilities, the wearing apparel of players, any bandaging if worn and to instruct assisting personnel in safety procedures. A good rapport is established between coaching personnel, players and officials. It is at this time that the officials consult with the doctor and agree on signals to summon him when needed.

During the game officials constantly must watch for equipment that may become dangerous through play. A lost cleat, a torn lace, a ripped pair of pants, a loose chin strap, a discarded mouthpiece are common occurrences. Officials develop a "second sense" in recognizing trouble before it starts. The goading of opponents, the exchange of verbal threats, a belligerent attitude, a constant complainer, all are signs of impending trouble. A mere shift of an official's position or a cautious word may be all that is necessary to forestall trouble.

Coaches, officials and physicians have the same objectives in the prevention of athletic injuries. Mutual understanding of their respective duties and responsibilities will assure satisfactory results in the prevention program.

CHAPTER 19

"UNACCUSTOMED AS I AM . . ."

Douglas Fessenden and Seth Fessenden *

PUBLIC SPEAKING HAS BECOME an essential part of the coach's job. In fact, some coaches, particularly football men, must do almost as much speaking as coaching—their talks ranging from full-dress speeches before civic or professional gatherings to informal chats with special interest groups.

Almost any program chairman who can announce "a talk by Coach Doake" is pretty sure to have a good turn-out.

Until he has actually tried it, the coach may have no idea of how effective a speaker he is. He may find that he is very good in front of an audience or that, despite his lucidity on the gridiron or basketball court, he stutters and stammers upon a speaker's platform.

Since good public relations is an integral part of modern coaching, it is of the utmost importance to be well-received. The wise coach will develop an effective speaking style very early in coaching life.

Actually, public speaking is not as difficult as it sometimes appears. A critical self-analysis is half the battle and diligent practice will do the rest. Here are three fundamental tenets to consider first:

1. Platform speaking is a group activity.
2. The effective talk organizes the thinking of the listeners.
3. Physical appearance and vocal style are vital factors in the transmission of ideas.

The speaker's task involves considerably more than mere verbal output. He must somehow "get over" to the audience and in a manner that will generate warmth and interest.

* Douglas Fessenden and Seth Fessenden, "Unaccustomed as I am . . ." *Scholastic Coach,* Vol. 23 (March 1954), pp. 30-34.

The soundest of speeches may die in midair, where the speaker dissociates himself from the audience. The speaker should consider himself as part of the whole, not apart from the whole. A speech is really nothing more or less than a sincere conversation with another person, excepting that the "person" is a crowd.

Good speeches are carefully prepared. Lincoln is said to have written the Gettysburg Address on the back of an envelope while en route. But such masters of the art as Stevenson and Churchill sweat bullets in preparing a talk. Certain principles will help the beginner:

1. *Try to identify yourself with the audience.* Consider the people who will be there, their interests, ages and knowledge. What do you want to accomplish with them? Remember, the more you seem to understand your listeners the more they will consider you one of them and the more influence you can exert.

2. *Try to make your comments relevant to the common interests of the audience.* Almost every gathering of people is an evidence of mutual goals. In their own fashion, civic clubs, pep rallies and Downtown Quarterback clubs are groups with reasonably common purposes. Decide what these are and talk in terms of them if you want to be well-received.

3. *If you want to change attitudes, do not do it with a head-on clash.* A good approach will warm up an audience and lower their resistance to your arguments. Where you try to harangue them into a change of attitude on some issue, you might very well increase their resistance and build up additional tension. Approach your goal by first removing any objections to the changes you have in mind. In other words, set up your play before you run it.

4. *People do not always hear the same thing.* It is a great fallacy to assume that an audience always understands what you have said. Some people with poor attentive ability keep tuning the speaker in and out, so that they digest only portions of the speech. Also, certain words may have varied meanings to them. What, for example, does a "winning team" mean? What do you mean by "character?" What constitutes a "good crowd?" How do you give the boys "real backing?" Be careful to explain your terminology and even then expect a varied interpretation of your comments.

The organization and development of a talk is probably the most important single element in its success. The speaker should make the audience feel they have a real part in the presentation.

A good guide never reaches the top of the mountain first; he seeks to inspire confidence in his knowledge and to set an appropriate pace. A good speaker employs the same techniques. He never beats his audience to the climax; he makes sure that he and his audience know where they are going and that they respect his knowledge of the area. Meanwhile, he watches their reactions to be sure his pace does not exceed theirs.

As a rule, your planning should include careful outlining. But do NOT write the speech out completely and then either read or memorize it. Concentrate on getting the main points and the pattern of organization well in mind. For, while your talk will need to have shape and body, it must at the same time remain flexible.

In organizing your talk:

1. *Write a single declarative sentence containing the specific idea you want to present.*

Be sure it is explicit and does not cover more ground than your time limit will permit. This sentence should set forth your subject and your attitude toward it. It should not be a mere statement of fact. For example, consider such a topic as "basketball." A thesis sentence on such a topic might be, "Basketball can play an important role in education," or "Basketball is the most widely used intramural game," or "Watching basketball is more fun when you know the rules." The number of these approaches is almost limitless, but note that each is made in a complete, definite statement.

2. *The next thing to do is plan a method of explaining and clarifying the basic statement.*

After you are satisfied with the statement of the idea, ask yourself, "How?" or "In what way?" or "To what extent?" or "Way?" or any similar question which might arise in the mind of a listener. Answer this question with as many statements beginning with "by" or "because" as seem desirable. You may then need to gather further information to support these answers. Your listeners will expect you to be specific. Be prepared to offer illustrations and examples.

3. *Next, determine the manner in which these ideas are to be grouped.*

Some of the more common methods are time-order, space-order, topical-order, logical-order, problem-solution order. The principal ideas, arguments or answers and examples devised in the above step need to be given some form, and one of these suggested will usually suit the purpose.

4. *No one definite plan can be used for all situations,* but the speech almost always will have an introduction, body or discussion and a conclusion.

The introduction should accomplish three things, each of which develops according to the situation. It should help establish a desirable rapport between you and your audience; it should arouse interest in the subject by showing how it applies to the needs and interests of your audience; and it should set forth and clarify the basic idea which is to be developed.

The discussion should also do three things. It should deal with the phases of the subject that the introduction indicated it would; it should develop each of these phases with details that are specific, moving, and within the experiences of the listeners; and it should use transitional means to show the relationships and the sequences of ideas.

The conclusion should round out the entire presentation through a summary or application and it should leave the audience with a feeling of satisfaction. Never apologize or thank your audience for listening. You have provided them with ideas. Clinch the talk with a specific stand.

The delivery of the talk is important not only because it transmits your ideas to the listeners but also because they react to mannerisms just about as readily as they do to ideas.

One of the vital elements in speech is the attitude of the speaker. If he is bored, his listeners will tend to be bored; if he is animated, his listeners will tend to reflect his spirit. The speaker should be interested in his topic and his audience; his desire should be to help his audience understand and appreciate his point of view.

TALK TO AUDIENCE

He should not look over their heads or merely in their direction. He should see them as people, talk with them as people, and note their reactions. Upon finishing, he should be able to point out those in the audience who listened most closely, who seemed to understand his comments most readily, who seemed bored or uninterested. He should also know which of his ideas were most readily accepted, which caused doubt or concern, those which puzzled.

The speaker should analyze his audience before he speaks and evaluate his analysis during his speech. The speech is not a presentation or a performance. It is part of a communication situation and it is the speaker's responsibility to judge his success in communicating his ideas and attitudes.

In addition to the directness of eye-contact, *the speaker should attempt to improve his poise, posture, gesture, dress and other physical characteristics.* Very often we are influenced as much by what we SEE in the speech situation. Many people seem to be predominantly visual-minded.

Flexibility is desirable. The speaker should seek a variety of ways to express ideas and attitudes through bodily action, facial expression and gestures. Alertness and interest are often best indicated by the way you stand and talk.

Following are some important dos and don'ts guaranteed to aid all public speakers:

1. *Have something to talk about.* Outline it, but do not try to memorize. Some of your best stuff will develop after you start talking. However, do not go in cold.

2. *Talk to your audience's interests.* The more you know of your group beforehand, the better you can plan your talk.

3. *Do not talk down* and do not use a lot of technical terminology. Say things in such a way that your audience will understand and appreciate it.

4. *Tell them the truth.* You do not have to claim the makings of a state champion, but at the same time do not ridiculously misrepresent the facts and thus stamp yourself as a man whose public statements are not to be taken seriously. The coach with the courage to put it "on the line" will always be believed when he really needs to be believed.

5. *Be natural.* Most nonprofessional speakers who attempt to

imitate senators merely succeed in becoming ridiculous. The best speaking is most conversational in style.

6. *Do not be a coin juggler or a tiptoe rocker.* It often annoys the listener and at best distracts his attention. Keep the hands out of your pockets and your heels on the floor.

7. *Praise your opponent.* If you cannot find something worthwhile to say about him, leave him out of your talk. Hate-doctrines have no place in interscholastic athletics.

8. *Do not alibi.* It is no go anyway. If you really need an alibi, let someone else make it for you.

9. *Do not tell hand-me-down jokes,* and under no circumstances smutty stories. Unless you are a Herman Hickman or a Fritz Crisler, the chances are that the laugh you get will not add much to your lustre as a speaker; and, besides, most of the crowd have heard it anyway. Use actual stories about your boys to keep the interest going.

10. *Give your boys a build-up.* If you have an incident to relate, be sure it reflects credit on the player. The parents and most of the fans will never quite forgive you for humiliating a boy in public—to say nothing of how the boy feels about it.

CHAPTER 20

LEND HIM YOUR SON

EVELYN MITSCH[*]

W HEN YOUR FIFTEEN-YEAR-OLD SON comes running home excited and out of breath, yelling, "I'm going out for sports! I need a doctor's okay on a physical. Practice starts next week,"— what does a mother say?

Does she yell, "No! No son of mine is going to participate in such a rough game. I didn't protect you all these years just to have you break an arm or leg now." Or does she say, "Oh how nice!"

Can she lend him to the coach for a little while, let him go out for sports and not worry about him?

Some mothers have to make this decision only once. As the mother of four sons, I had to make it several times—each time with more and more doubt, skepticism, qualms, indecision and a full knowledge of the possible damage that sports could do to my sons.

I wondered if the benefits derived from participation and training could off-set the fear of accident, injury and permanent disfiguration?

I also asked myself this question: Is all the time spent in athletics worth the hours lost from study, music, church functions and other extra-curricular activities which seemed more important to me?

Does it make any difference whether it is football, basketball, soccer, hockey, wrestling or track? Aren't they all just as dangerous? Or is one safer than the other? Which one? These were the questions that bothered me.

---

[*] Evelyn Mitsch, "Lend Him Your Son," *Scholastic Coach*, Vol. 39 (October 1969), pp. 62-69.

In a household of five males, the activities and interests of the one female member become rather insignificant. Her opinions on sports, the focus of masculine interest in her home, are definitely in the minority and usually ignored.

With the sport page for breakfast, the night finals when she goes to bed and play-by-play accounts of sport highlights in between, she just naturally retreats into a secluded land of femininity. She learns to close one ear to the constant din, but one ear only.

She cannot escape entirely because their lives are her life; their health, their activities and their schedules constantly affect her day, too.

She remains the silent partner until the glaring headlines disclose the irregularities in the sports world: suspicions of fixed fights controlled by gangsters, pro football players betting on their own games, college basketball players guilty of point shaving, hockey becoming gang warfare on ice and the farce of professional wrestling on television.

"No more sports!" she will argue and complain, but in vain.

She will receive no support from her husband or his friends. He will see his son's name in the headlines and envision the boy doing what he himself only dreamed of.

So I ask: "What are you going to say? Are you going to say yes, too?"

You may as well, for sooner or later you will give in. Your son will hound you day after day until he catches you in a weak moment and against your better judgment you will finally agree to sign the permit and arrange for his physical examination.

And then your life will change. The coach will move in with you; not actually of course, but in spirit. His quotes will dominate the conversation at the dinnertable . . . he will tell you what to cook, how to cook and when to serve it. You will always be making a quick meal before dinner or keeping one warm long after everyone else has finished. You will be so conscious of him that you will almost feel it necessary to set a place at the table for him too.

Your son's habits also will change. This remote-controlled

robot who looks like your son will now go to bed by the clock, look cleaner, dress better and walk a little straighter with an important air about him. On that day of the first game away from home, when he comes down to breakfast in his new suit, white shirt and tie, you will almost choke on your coffee. You will stifle a gasp.

Shortly thereafter all your fears will become realities; the little accidents will begin happening. I remember so well the many trips to the doctor's office and the hospital, the dislocated collar bone, and elbow, the water on the knee, the sprains and chip fractures of the ankles, the broken finger and nose, the broken arm that needed surgery, the puffed ear and the four front teeth (which had been straightened out for a mere eight hundred dollars) knocked out by one quick flash of a hockey puck.

Your natural instincts will make you cry out: "Oh, no! Is this what I protected you for? To gorge yourself to gain weight for football, only to starve yourself for the next three months to reduce for wrestling; to lift weights and do push-ups until you look like a boiled lobster; and to watch you as you eat your heart out waiting for those magical words from the coach, 'Suit up!'?"

I remember my sons' cotton-mouth from dehydration and the shinsplints from too many running trips around the athletic field or up and down the bleachers. Their hobbling home like old arthritic men, wincing with every step, plopping in front of the television with pop and popcorn while I delivered each one's paper route and then drove each in turn to school the next day.

There also was the long siege of complications after mononucleosis from too much activity during and too soon after the attack.

You will wonder: How can all this be worth it? You will attend all the meets because you cannot possibly stay away. You will watch with your heart beating fast, your hands clenched, balancing yourself on the edge of the bench, anticipating the worst yet hoping for his sake that his match, his play, his contribution to the game will bring him the recognition that all this training has been for.

You will look guiltily around at the other spectators and slide back in your seat, trying to join in the excitement and the fun without letting your anxiety show.

You will see the principal looking up at you and smiling because he claims that he can pick out the parents of the athletes by their tense, anxious looks and actions during a game.

But when the crowd yells your son's name, you'll stand tallest in the stands, waving and screaming, gladly sacrificing your voice for the pride and joy, the admiration, the relief and thanks for that dynamic wonder down there who is your son.

After the game on Parents Day or at the Athletic Banquet, wearing the corsage your son gave you, you will meet the coach. This stranger who is not a stranger . . . this man who has spent more time with your son than any other one person, this man who knows your son as you will never know him. His influence, his ideals and morals, his outlook on life have left their mark on your son, as on all the boys who have trained and developed under him.

He shares intensely the joys and heartaches of each of the boys, sometimes to the extent of impairing his own health. He instills in all the desire to win, but stresses even more the importance of losing like a gentleman.

He teaches them teamwork and sportsmanship, health, personal hygiene, family relationship, gentlemanly manners in speech and dress and respect for authority.

His hand is like the tool of the sculptor who, surely but firmly, presses the soft clay into place or adds a little, bit by bit, until the definite shape of the man he is creating begins to take form.

When the coach meets your son for the first time, he says hello to a boy, but when it comes time to part, when the period of growing up, learning and training is over, he says goodbye to a man . . . a man who is much better qualified to meet life's challenges as a result of this close association with a high school coach.

A boy needs someone by his side as he takes that big step from boyhood into manhood—not someone to hold his hand and lead him as a mother would, not to tell him how as a father would, but another man, one whom he can admire, respect and ask for advice.

So I have learned the difficult truth that physical fitness programs and athletic training do benefit boys in later life. I told a high school coach that my son had written a paper in college entitled "The Man I Admire Most Is My High School Coach." This remark convinced him that he had chosen the right profession, and I knew that I, too, had made the right decision.

So, say "Yes!" when your son wants to go out for sports. Lend him to a high school coach for this little while . . . gladly.

THE COACH AND
THE COACHING STAFF

CHAPTER 21

HEAD COACH AND ASSISTANT RAPPORT

Don Veller*

A HEAD COACH IS NO STRONGER than his assistants and behind every successful coach will be found competent assistants.

Coach Woody Hayes said: "Good morale starts with the relationship between the head coach and the other coaches on his staff. If there is friction among these men, the players on the squad will sense it, and the most important factor on the squad, morale, will be in jeopardy."

Unfortunately, some head coaches, mostly in the high school ranks, have too little influence in the selection or dismissal of their assistants. Of course, in most cases, the assistant will have other teaching duties for which he must be qualified; therefore, it is understandable that the principal and/or some other administrator will have to have a hand in the selection. However, in our modern competitive, high pressure athletic picture, it is most helpful to the head coach for the assistant to realize that his future depends to a great degree upon the effectiveness of his work for the head man. As an example, at one time we were in a college head coaching position where even recommendations for salary raises were entirely out of our hands. Naturally, this did not enhance the prestige of the head coach nor the importance of his sport in the eyes of the assistants. It made the job tougher.

When the head coach has a part in the selection, as he should, he must look first for character in the assistant—a man with high ideals and good work habits. This is more important than such things as what school he graduated from, or to what system

---

* Don Veller, "Head Coach and Assistant Rapport," *Athletic Journal,* Vol. 48 (April 1968), pp. 66-69 and 77.

of play he is accustomed. An assistant can be taught new systems
and techniques; but character, an interest in the welfare of
youth, a penchant for hard work, a strong desire for excellence
—these he had best already possess.

Two of the most damaging character deviations for coaches
are those which involve *boozers* and *women chasers.* Since men
with these traits, especially the latter, are seldom cured, the
moral is to make certain they are not hired in the first place.

Another important question which can easily be answered in
a simple interview is, "Will the candidate be satisfied with the
job? Is he eager for it?" If the answer is negative, and he is subsequently employed, then there is trouble ahead.

In selecting assistants, the head coach should, where possible,
search for those who possess qualifications which will counter-
balance his, the head coach's known shortcomings. An ex-line-
man, for instance, would want at least one assistant who had
played a backfield position. The coach should research thoroughly the qualifications, personalities, special interests and capabilities of his assistants. Only upon the basis of this knowledge,
and, of course, the needs of his squad, can he delegate assignments and responsibilities intelligently.

A rather common but fatal mistake among leaders in athletics,
as well as business and industry, is to give subordinates responsibility without corresponding authority. Players easily recognize
a situation in which an assistant is given assignments with little
or no backing from the head coach. Some coaches, only the
stupid ones, correct assistants in front of their players. When
the assistant is teaching something wrong, the head coach should
take him aside unobtrusively for advice and correction.

A subordinate should neither be reprimanded nor corrected
in the presence of his subordinates. When this is done, an assistant loses face and the respect and confidence of the players. He
becomes a *nothing* in the eyes of the players and his effectiveness is seriously and almost irreparably damaged. This is anal-
ogous to a commander giving a soldier a gun but no bullets.

An assistant should be considered somewhat like a military
staff officer. After having been given an assignment, he works out

the plans and submits them to the head coach for approval. If approved, then they are carried out.

Some head coaches, again, not the successful ones, fail to define properly the specific duties of their assistants. Not knowing what his job really is, is most frustrating to the helper, and certainly makes him of less value. Surely most head coaches who make this mistake are unaware they are doing so. Would not a written job description for each coach help solve this problem?

Another positive outcome resulting from the assignment of exact duties with a corresponding degree of authority, is that it tends to make the assistant feel he is an important part of the organization.

Loyalty is a two-way street. The head coach expects and must receive loyalty from every member of his staff and conversely each coach on his staff has a right to expect loyalty from him. When either side of this union breaks down, then it is time for the assistant to move to another job.

A cardinal sin among assistants is to speak disparagingly of the head coach either to players or outsiders, including news media. To do damage they do not necessarily have to say anything. They can undermine the head coach by such nonverbal communications as facial expressions, shoulder shrugging or remaining silent when he is attacked by critics in their presence.

Neither should the head coach criticize assistants, except in private face-to-face situations; never, as pointed out previously, in front of players and with rare exceptions never in the presence of other assistants. If the head coach is not satisfied with something the assistant has done he should tell him so in a constructive way. Remaining quiet, or telling others is not the solution.

In order that he may adapt himself to the ideas and philosophy of the head coach, an assistant must remain flexible in his thinking. No two people can possibly agree on everything. Disagreements must be thrashed out in private; and, of course, when differences cannot be resolved, then the head coach has the prerogative to make the final decision. As long as the assistant is on the staff, it is his duty to carry out such an edict in good faith. This does not mean that the prudent head coach will always remain adamant in a controversy. He might subsequently decide the assistant was right.

In staff meetings each coach must be encouraged to speak up and state his views. Surrounding himself with a bunch of *yes men* will result in incontrovertible harm to the head coach. If assistants are unable or unwilling to contribute their brain power, then the coach has access only to his own knowledge and judgment. Often that is not enough. Why have a staff, if they do not share their brain power?

On the other hand, ill-tempered and dogmatic coaches have been known to intimidate their assistants to the point where they were actually afraid to make suggestions. But that is another story—not a success story.

Where the coach encourages assistants to give their views freely, staff meetings can become rather noisy and controversial at times. This is to be expected. On occasions it may even be prudent to take a vote on issues which seem difficult to solve otherwise.

The head coach should make certain that decisions are not made for personal reasons, but on the basis of what is good for the team. Therefore, when the staff walks out on the field or floor, final judgments must be accepted in good faith by each member. Unless otherwise indicated, matters discussed in staff meetings are confidential.

Staff meetings must be planned in advance, with an agenda, not just nondescript affairs with no objectives. The meetings should be held in a comfortable room, uninterrupted by telephone calls, salesmen, well wishers, and the like. Everyone should be on time, including the head coach. Do not drag the meetings out. Adjourn at a prearranged time.

An attempt should be made to schedule meetings when convenient to most of the staff. We witnessed one coach who arbitrarily and without warning, scheduled meetings at odd times, early in the morning, or in the evenings, without consulting his assistants. Sudden changes in family plans did not endear him to the assistants and especially to their wives.

Frankly, the most effective time for staff meetings is immediately after practice when everything is fresh in mind. In addition, there is a better chance that all will be present. Sometimes it is difficult to get everyone together during the day, especially in a high school situation where coaches normally have other teaching duties.

There was a college coach, who, when out of town in the off-season, had the dubious habit of calling his secretary early in the morning and/or near the end of the normal working day, checking whether or not his assistants were on the job. Making clock punchers out of assistants is definitely not recommended by human relations specialists nor assistants.

One successful head coach likes to think of his coaches as partners, as personal friends, certainly not rivals. He gives every man a job and lets him do it with the mutual feeling that they are each helping the other. This head coach, as all coaches should, insists on top-notch performances by his assistants—and they know it. For example, if an assistant is placed in charge of the defense, then he really is in charge of that phase. If the defense does well, that is his job; if the defense is ineffective, then he bears the brunt.

Titles are powerful ego inflators. Titles such as head backfield coach, pitching coach, head defensive coach, coach of field events, will lend a feeling of importance to the assistant. There seems to be a trend to name an assistant head coach. This is commendable when and if the recipient really qualifies for the title.

Another popular arrangement is embodied in the system wherein no person is called assistant coach. Each is just called coach. Deemphasizing the term assistant tends to elevate the status feeling.

The relationship of the assistants with each other must be harmonious. Each must recognize his position within the staff framework and not attempt to *feather his own nest* by embarrassing or criticizing colleagues to the head coach, other assistants, players or the public. Such actions will indubitably create dissension, an intolerable condition among staff members. They must work cooperatively at all times, realizing that a successful team is their mutual bread and butter, and only through united effort is this possible. In order to implement this *togetherness* among assistants, Coach Hayes established an unwritten rule that any coach may feel absolutely free to ask any other member of his staff, including the head coach, for help. His coaches make it a policy never to say, "I did not have time to finish it." They might on occasion say, "We did not have time to finish it."

Constant effort must be made to assure each assistant that he is an important cog in the success or failure of the team. In addition to creating an atmosphere in which they feel free to present their opinions, he should offer them a voice in such things as assigning personnel to positions, planning the attack, making up the schedule, etc.

One college football assistant learned by observation prior to the official opening of a Wednesday practice session that the team's only passer could throw a running pass much more accurately than the drop-back variety currently being used. Since this passer and his team had experienced only mediocre success in the first three games, the assistant promptly told the head coach of his discovery. He answered with a perfunctory remark. However, the head coach did put in two running passes that session. On the following Saturday this previously impotent passer broke a conference one-game passing record.

The head coach did not mention the incident to the squad, press or to the other assistants; nor did he even give the responsible assistant a private *Thank you*. Even a simple pat on the back, or a nod of encouragement will work wonders in increasing or maintaining the efficiency and morale of a subordinate.

Assistants should not forget, either, that the head coach may also need a little encouragement, now and then.

We learned a great deal about how *not* to treat assistants from a head college coach we used to know. Rarely did he even hint to his coaches what the practice schedule was going to be. They found out bit by bit from him as practice progressed on the field. Frequently he would add or change plays on the field and sometimes the coaches would learn of these changes from the players themselves. When changes such as additions to the schedule, new assistants, personnel switches and the like were made, the assistants often heard of them first by reading the newspapers. This is a story of now *not to win friends and influence assistants.* The only way that type of head coach can ever win is by having personnel much superior to that of his opponents.

If, unfortunately, there is an argument, or altercation between an assistant and one of the players, the head coach must overtly support the assistant. Otherwise, the line of authority is broken and the assistant is placed in an untenable position. This type of problem can best be resolved behind closed doors and with the least fuss possible.

Assistants must have confidence and believe implicitly in the head coach. All successful head coaches have this going for them. Coach "Bear" Bryant, it is reported, personally makes the plans for his practice sessions. The assistant coaches can suggest changes but rarely do. This may not appear to be democratic, but it is a time saver, and since they have complete faith in his judgment, they can spend their time working on other important things.

One hard-nosed head coach said facetiously: "The head man should keep his staff sullen but not mutinous." Perhaps that is a slightly extreme view, but it is the duty of the head coach to offer constructive criticism when and if there is a need for it, and the assistant must always try hard to put himself in the place of the head coach to see his point of view. The head man should offer criticisms in the proper manner and spirit. To resurrect the old chestnut, *It is not what you say, it is how you say it that counts.*

As inferred previously, the head coach must not be afraid to make decisions which involve criticisms. Criticisms are not easy to give, and certainly nobody wants to either give or take them as a hobby. It is tempting for the coach to postpone unpopular or controversial decisions too long in the hope that things will work themselves out.

Efficiency should not be sacrificed for popularity and the head coach must assert himself at times. If given in a firm but friendly manner, the affected assistant should respond to criticism in the same spirit in which it is given. A chip-on-the-shoulder attitude is most objectionable and unprofessional.

Frankly, there is no way for an assistant to know what a head coach contends with, or how he really feels, until some day he becomes a head coach himself.

When things are not going so well, the head coach should take the blame. He will get it anyway. When things go well, he may give credit freely to his assistants.

An erudite coach is aware of the specific talents of his individual assistants. It is possible, even probable that they are better informed than he in certain phases of the activity. Therefore, he will take full advantage of their skills and knowledge in making assignments and in asking their advice.

A coach need not be reluctant to train assistants to take over his job if and when the occasion arises. They should be made to realize by the discerning head coach that he will help them secure head jobs or promotions any time openings occur in which they are interested. Coaches have been known to hold on to an assistant when just a word or two, a telephone call or a letter to the right person, would have secured a well-deserved promotion for him. On the other hand, an assistant who is incessantly looking for another job is of dubious value.

Bear in mind, please, that the prerequisites for being a head coach are not the same as for an assistant's job. There are many ambitious assistants who aspire fervently to be a head coach, but who do not possess the natural talent or necessary leadership qualifications. They will, therefore, never become successful head coaches. It is indeed a difficult task to transmit such information to an ambitious helper, since it is often obvious to others but not to him.

Assistants should be extremely careful when talking to representatives of the press. Quite often statements are made, either through ignorance, or otherwise, which when quoted have a deleterious effect upon the team's success. Many successful coaches discourage assistants from talking to reporters, explaining that releases and quotes are often misunderstood when they emanate from more than one source. Some even suggest that all statements, or news be disseminated either through the head coach or with his personal approval. This system has merit even though it might appear on the surface to be harsh and selfish on the part of the head coach. When using this technique, or any other kind, it is wise to make a special effort to credit assistants whenever and wherever the opportunity arises.

An unhappy, discontented wife can definitely lower the efficiency of a coach. Therefore, the astute head man will be alert to seek ways to effect a happy situation. The assistants' wives may be brought into the picture by occasional invitations to the home of the coach. Other suggestions include giving the wives special seats at games; taking them on out-of-town trips; introducing them at games, and banquets, etc. These are just a few ideas. There are more. The friendly treatment and/or relationship of the head coach's wife to the assistants' wives is vitally important. We know of one situation where the assistants' wives were never invited to the head coach's home in seven years. The rapport was not very good.

Off the field and off-duty with his assistants the head coach may be *one of the boys.* But on the field they must be respectful, and all their words and actions should point up to the players that he owns the show—he is the head man.

CHAPTER 22

SEVEN GUIDELINES FOR
THE ASSISTANT COACH

ROBERT B. KENIG*

A NYONE WHO WANTS to become a successful assistant coach and eventually a successful head coach must possess certain qualities and observe certain principles.

1. Loyalty is the most important quality. If you are loyal, all the other qualities will fall into place.

Loyalty does not mean being a "yes" man. Express your own ideas and opinions and disagree with the head coach whenever you feel you are right. But do this at staff meetings, not out in the public.

Once the head coach decides on a course of action, abide by his decision and never openly disagree with it. It is easy to be loyal when your team is ten and zero, the test of loyalty comes during a few zero and ten seasons.

2. Have a burning desire to improve yourself and to become a successful head coach. The only way to achieve such goals is through hard work, not only during the season but throughout the year. Make yourself a twelve-month coach, not a four-month one.

Once the season is over, go right into your normal post-season activities, such as attending clinics, caring for equipment, setting up a conditioning program for the squad and preparing for the next season.

Also do a great deal of work on your own. Set aside a period of time every day to work on your sport. Communicate with

* Robert B. Kenig, "Seven Guidelines for the Assistant Coach," *Scholastic Coach,* Vol. 43 (December 1973), pp. 69 and 72.

coaches who have more experience and knowledge—who can help you acquire different ideas.

3. Sacrifice is as essential for the coach as for the player. Without a great deal of sacrifice, a potentially outstanding player may remain ordinary and a potentially outstanding coach may wind up jobless.

If you are primarily concerned with monetary rewards, you are in the wrong profession. You must be willing to trade wealth for the satisfaction of coaching and of working with young people.

You must realize that during the season you are not your own man; you practically belong to the head coach and the team. Even during the off-season you must spend a great deal of your time on trying to improve both the team and yourself.

This is time that could be spent doing many other things. You must be willing to give it whenever the team needs it.

4. Your family must be very understanding, as they are called upon to make even greater sacrifices than you. They live four months with a part-time husband/father, and they must always share you with forty boys whose names they hardly know.

Let your family know that they are the most important people in your life, that without them success would be impossible and meaningless. Make arrangements for them to attend all of your games. Make them a part of your coaching life.

5. Be an active teacher as well as an active coach. If you do not do a good job in the classroom, you will not do a good job on the field. The qualities necessary to become a good assistant coach are quite similar to those necessary to become a good teacher. Your class work must not suffer because of your coaching.

When most school districts hire a coach, they look for a teacher first and then a coach. An assistant coach with a poor classroom record will find it extremely difficult to find a head coach position.

6. Always set a good example. You actually are closer to the players than the head coach and they will look to you for guidance and leadership.

Never allow yourself to be anything but a gentleman in both

action and appearance. Learn to control your emotions; never let them control you.

You cannot expect the players to avoid smoking if you are constantly seen with a cigarette in your hand.

Attend an many school functions as possible. Let everyone know that you are an active member of the school community, not just a sport buff.

Never miss a team function. Whenever you stay away from one, the importance of the activity will diminish in the players' eyes. Not only must you be present, you should arrive early. This will encourage the squad to be on time.

Never even slightly disagree with the head coach in the presence of the team. The boys may wind up losing confidence in one of you.

Talk about the sport whenever you run into a team member during the off-season. It will let the boys know that you are a year-round coach and will encourage them to think about the sport all-year round.

Develop a sense of humor (if you do not have one) and be willing to exhibit it on and off the field. Practice can become drudgery and an occasional joke or two can make it more pleasant.

Dispatch all of your duties with enthusiasm. If you work with enthusiasm, your players will do the same.

7. Love your job and do it with pride. If you do not love it, you will not give it the time it needs and you will not be a success. If your job is work rather than enjoyment, better start looking around for another field of endeavor.

Encourage others to feel the same way about the sport as you do. Do not be afraid to let others know how dedicated you are. You must believe that your profession is the greatest in the world. Every day you walk on the practice field, your love and enthusiasm for your job should be apparent to every player and coach on the team.

Show the boys that you care deeply for them and have great respect for their feelings. They will usually reciprocate your feelings and play far above their capabilities in order to please you.

Show your affection for them in overt ways, so that it cannot be missed. But be ready with a severe reprimand when they break the rules. Without discipline a team will never develop the character necessary to become a winner.

Strive for perfection. Never present an idea to the head coach, the team or the public without having thought it completely through and being completely convinced that it is correct and the best you can do.

Neatness, accuracy and efficiency should be the guidelines for all your written reports to the head coach and the staff.

Be proud of your team and your school. Wear shirts and jackets bearing their names. When the students and the athletes see that you are proud of them, they will become proud of themselves.

CHAPTER 23

THE HEAD COACH AND HIS ASSISTANTS

HARRY EDWARDS*

B ECAUSE OF THE CHARACTER of the coaching role, there is an in- herent potential for strain between head coaches and their assistants. We have already observed that the head coach histor- ically has had a paternalistic, "father surrogate" role in relation to the athlete. But this role extends beyond the direct coach-ath- lete relations. The sports organization as a whole is generally conceived of by coaches as being akin to a "family" with the head coach—the ubiquitous "old man"—as patriarch. The en- deavors of the athletic "family" are usually portrayed in the sports creed as a "team effort." This "team effort" refers not just to the efforts of the athletes participating at any given time, but to the input of every person affiliated or identifying with the athletic organization. Thus, fans often state *"we lost"* when their favorite team loses. For, according to the sports creed, they are members of the family and a loss by "their sports family" affects them deeply and personally.

The hard, autocratic stance of coaches toward their athletes may be softened somewhat by the conception of the sports unit as a family. Family members can be disappointed in one another without hating. A father can punish his son because he wants him to be better rather than because he arbitrarily wishes to hurt him. Similarly, two brothers of the same family can compete against one another with a ferocity which often times exceeds that brought to bear against strangers, but in the face of a com- mon external threat, *"all other things being equal,"* they forget their differences and cooperate toward the accomplishment of

---

* Reprinted with permission from Harry Edwards, *Sociology of Sport* (Home- wood, Ill., The Dorsey Press, 1973 c.), pp. 156-158.

a common end. So it is with athletes who are part of the same sports aggregation. They compete for starting assignments, star status and so forth but when they compete against an opposing sports unit, differences in individual personal goals are at least suppressed. The characterization of sports units as families probably serves an integrative function within sports aggregations—in the coach-athlete and athlete-athlete relations—and also in reducing tension between head coaches and their assistants.

Because the head coach bears complete liability for his unit's outcomes, he has traditionally demanded and received total autonomy with regard to "running his shop." Accordingly, the authority structure in any given sports unit has always been rigid and monarchical. But, whereas the head coach has always been able to openly "discipline" his athletes for failure to follow his directives, this has never been possible with assistant coaches—short of firing them. For it has been thought that the visible disciplining of an assistant coach would essentially place him in the same status relationship with the head coach as exists between the head coach and his athletes. This would tend to undermine the perceived status and authority differences between athletes and assistant coaches. Without such perceived differentials, it is believed, athletes' respect for assistant coaches would diminish. And without the respect of his athletes, the difficulty of any coach's task becomes greatly magnified.

Assistant coaches typically harbor the same aspirations which head coaches had before obtaining their head coach positions—to wit, they aspire to become head coaches. Similarly, they have their own notions about which strategies are best, what coach-athlete relations should be like and so forth. Because these views do not always correspond to the head coaches' ideas, it is inevitable that some tension should emerge between the two.

Out of the assistant's continuing ambition to advance professionally there emerges an ongoing incongruity of interests. On the one hand, it is in the assistant coach's personal professional interests to prove his capabilities by actively devising strategies, giving advice and otherwise demonstrating his competence. On the other hand, he must follow the directives of the head

coach who wields ultimate authority over the team. If the assistant coach argues too fervently for his own suggestions, he is likely to be seen as overly ambitious, uncooperative or even as a
threat to "family" unity and morale. But if he fails to show
sufficient creativity, and passively follows the head coach's directives, he may be accused of not shouldering his share of the
coaching burden and thus harm his chances of being appointed
eventually to a position as a head coach. Most assistant coaches
relate to head coaches well within the polar boundaries of being
overly aggressive or submissively passive. But, in relation to any
given incident or issue, the assistant always runs the risk of
erring in one direction or the other.

If participants actually do regard the athletic unit as a "team"
or a family, the potential tension in this situation may be less-
ened or controlled. As family members, assistant coaches and
head coaches can disagree without being disagreeable. Inherent
deep-seated role conflicts and conflicts of interest can be "explained away" by the ideology. *Loyalty* of the assistant coach to
the athletic unit becomes the norm and supposedly precludes
conscious or deliberate encroachment upon the prerogatives of
the head coach. The head coach is the "quarterback" calling the
signals and for the good of the whole "team" the assistant coach
should not contest his decisions.

THE COACH AND
COACHING METHODS

COMPENDIUM OF COMMONSENSE PRINCIPLES IN MODERN COACHING

DON VELLER*

A T MOST ANY COACHING SCHOOL or clinic, the mere mention of a play diagram or a team defensive maneuver will be the signal for all to grab their pencils and notebooks and begin copying like mad. Everyone seems to be looking for a panacea to win those ball games. But we doubt whether there are any.

After years of coaching and lately teaching and observing sports, we believe more than ever that there are decidedly more important facets to successful coaching than that of inculcating the latest offensive diagrams and defensive strategies. Call these facets psychology if you like, but "horse sense" is perhaps a more pertinent term.

Among the more important coaching "musts," of course, is that of establishing the proper rapport with the players. One component of proper rapport is confidence in the coach. Have you ever seen a coach demonstrate a skill he could not do well? The players, especially in high school, frequently (as they should) believe that the coach should be perfect. And watching a coach demonstrating punting with weak twenty-five-yard squibs will not engender much confidence.

One might ask then, who is going to do it? Space here does not permit a full discussion, but couldn't it be done by an assistant or by one of the players who already does it rather well?

For similar reasons, the coach should not compete against his players unless he is pretty certain he can win, or at least look

---

* Don Veller, "Compendium of Commonsense Principles in Modern Coaching," *Scholastic Coach*, Vol. 28 (October 1958), pp. 68-74.

good losing. How about the basketball coach who, while scrimmaging against his players, repeatedly has his dribbles stolen or misses crip shots? What effect might it have on his players?

Prior to a football practice session in a certain midwestern college, a 235-pound ex-All-American lineman was engaged in a little "horse play" with one of the squad members. This big coach got a little boastful and the squad member (the 155-pound Big Ten wrestling champ) picked him up and flopped him resoundingly on his back. He remained there a few minutes, stunned and breathless. The resultant loss of prestige in the eyes of the fifty or so on-looking squad members was obvious.

SELL YOUR PLAYERS

Speaking of instilling confidence, you must "sell" your players on what you are trying to teach them. It goes without saying, of course, that one must first believe in a thing before he can "sell" it.

Elementary psychology tells us that we like best and have more confidence in the things we do well. For example, if a coach wishes to successfully introduce a new play in football, especially one that takes finesse, he should be wary.

To hastily give the play to his first team and have them immediately scrimmage it against a good second team is liable to be disastrous. Since the first team are apt to get their heads bashed in (what with poor timing, etc.), they may lose all confidence in what otherwise might have been a good play.

In such instances, it would be best to thoroughly practice the play with opposition against whom it will work even at first! Many more such incidents could be cited. Just keep in mind the principle that one nearly always enjoys and has more confidence in the things he does well.

Another tip in selling your system to the players is to *keep it simple*. This goes for all sports, but it applies particularly to team activities. Too many coaches, especially young ones, have been guilty of over-estimating the mental capacities of their charges. Would anyone refute the sagacity of the trite old statement that it is better to be able to "do a few things well rather than a lot of things poorly"?

It is a real temptation to put in "just one more play" or "one more defense." Some coaches are like drug addicts when it comes to this. They must have just one more. But it is doubtful if any coach ever got fired for making his system too simple!

Over-coaching is also frequently done on individual skills. Again, do not try to teach the boys *all* you know. The writer has known at least three high school punters whose college mentors "coached" them down from sixty-yard high school booters to thirty-yard college "sensations." How easy it is to coach a 6-4 high jumper down to a consistent 5-10'er by merely making him change the take-off foot.

All this does not mean that a good boy cannot be improved upon. But, remember, do not be greedy!

Many coaches are rather adept at teaching "how" to do things, but fall short in emphasizing "why" certain things are done. A player is apt to react more favorably and remember better if he knows "why" he is asked to perform a certain task.

For example, a lineman in a certain play may be instructed to put a partial block on a certain defensive lineman, and then go down for the secondary. If he is informed that the play is designed to trap the defensive lineman, he will be more apt to put on a realistic block. He is more likely to realize that if he does the job well, it will influence the defensive man into a position vulnerable to the trap.

Each player should know the philosophy of each play or defense. He should know where and how the play is going and not merely his own individual, unconnected job.

It is also of tremendous importance in coaching not to just tell them, but to show them! Tell them *and* show them!

Another cliche which a coach should frequently recite to himself is: "Many a contest has been lost on the practice field (or court) the week before." A young man's hunger and eagerness for competition, especially in contact sports, cannot be honed by scrimmaging nearly every afternoon in practice. A lazy coach will often scrimmage too much because it takes very little planning. The best advice available is: "When in doubt whether or not to scrimmage, then don't scrimmage!"

Be truthful and sincere in what you tell your boys. Insincerity is not only unethical, but dangerous. The boys will catch on to phony stories sooner or later. Nothing is worse for the coach's prestige than to have his players realize that he is insincere.

Some coaches, in order to "key up" their players, have been known to say derogatory things about their opponents, whether or not they were true; or to consciously exaggerage the strength of a very weak opponent and then crush the helpless opponent by a lopsided score. Do not cry "wolf" unless you mean it. The boys may not believe you later when you need help.

The writer is completely sold on the "no swearing" rule he has enforced during fourteen years of high school and college coaching. The rule worked out beautifully, even though the only penalty for swearing (in football) was a trip around the goal post for each offense.

Try it and you will be surprised how swearing will decrease from week to week and year to year. The kids get a kick out of it and even the most habitual offenders will take pride in abstinence. Naturally, the parents love it. It may even help the coach a little, since he also must abstain from a "pool room" vocabulary.

DIRTY PLAY IS MAJOR SIN

Encouragement, or even toleration, of unfair or dirty play is a major sin. Besides being unethical, it has a tendency to encourage the player into taking the "easy way out" instead of concentrating on clean, hard play.

For the sake of morale, it often pays to have a "clown" on your squad. This is especially true if the clown knows when, how and where to be funny.

A coach, too, must develop a sense of humor, not only for its favorable effect upon the players, but for his own mental hygiene as well. Along with its many assets, the coaching profession is replete with disappointments. Taking them too seriously may impair the efficiency of a coach.

Apropos of this, however, is the temptation to be too entertaining and/or too "familiar" with the boys. Being popular without commanding respect will not help create the rapport necessary to get the job done.

With few exceptions, much more can be accomplished by criticizing your players privately than by yelling at them in the presence of other squad members. The temptation is to shout at them. But, with rare exceptions, taking the boy aside is much more effective. This is especially true of certain sensitive types who are sincerely doing their best *all* the time.

Unfortunately, in all athletics, especially in the contact sports, injuries will occur. When a player is hurt, the coach must, of course, see that he receives prompt and adequate treatment. However, for obvious reasons, it is poor psychology to stop practice completely and allow the squad to congregate around a player who, say, has an ugly-appearing wound or who may be moaning in pain.

Without delay, place the injured player in charge of the trainer, an assistant or a doctor, if available, and move your squad promptly to another part of the practice area. This maneuver may smack of brutality, but it is definitely best.

A wise coach, though, will be thoughtful of injured squad members and the least he can do is visit hospitalized players. One coach we know would completely ignore injured players, even to the point of not speaking to them until they were able to play again. This coach's tenure ended rather abruptly.

TRAINING RULES ENFORCEMENT

One facet of coaching which can be perplexing is that of training rules and their enforcement. There is no positive solution, but here is a suggestion or two. Permit the members to set their own rules and let them as a group enforce them. It is really surprising and gratifying to observe how mature they will be in their judgment.

Several successful cases have "sold" us on this method. A typical example occurred in a certain high school. A sophomore who was reared on the wrong side of the tracks was caught smoking and was turned over to the players for a decision. The captain led the hearing and the squad, after some deliberation, ruled that the offender should be given another chance.

This "tough" boy came to the head coach with tears in his eyes and thanked him for giving him this opportunity to continue in the one activity in which he had a chance for status—"to *be* somebody."

Do not fret about your boys being too easy on offenders. One of my squads once dismissed (for drinking) a first-string tackle. History has shown that the players' decision on such matters will usually be more severe than that of the coach.

Also, do not forget that dismissing a boy from the squad frequently creates a controversial situation. The coach is presented with plenty of other pressure decisions, and this is one he will not have to make if the boys take over. If you *do* decide to make your own training rules, then be certain they are enforced. The morale of the squad certainly is threatened when exceptions are made.

To help unify your squad, encourage them to mingle off the court or field. One method for implementing this unified spirit is to attend a movie together prior to a contest. The movie manager in most communities can be prevailed upon to provide free admission for the playing squad. Among others, such affairs as weiner roasts and hamburger fries at the coach's house are also effective.

There is a considerable difference of opinion as to whether captains should be elected or appointed. Most coaches, however, favor electing a captain. In the latter case, careful orientation by the coach prior to voting is compulsory.

It must be carefully and forcibly explained that the election is not a popularity contest, but that a captain must, above all, possess the qualities of leadership. Explain these qualities to them. If the vote is close between two top men, make the higher (class) one captain and the next man alternate captain. If the vote is a runaway for one boy, then perhaps it is best to have just one captain.

Another successful method is to elect a captain for the season and in addition let the seniors appoint an alternate captain for each game. Among other advantages, this latter method will help compensate for a mistake if a bad season choice has been made.

It has been our experience that the coach can, through word of mouth, subtly influence squad members to eliminate poor choices. Through a good leader who has been chosen by the players, a coach can have a "finger" on the "pulse" of his players.

Do not hesitate to call upon the parents for aid. Parents can help tremendously with such vital things as proper diet, observance of training rules, school attendance, proper facilities and general morale. Meet with them as often as necessary.

Many communities subsidize the coach's salary by private contributions. While this extra money will buy "goodies" for the wife, remember, if you accept such contributions, they "own" you.

DON'T PLAY TOO FEW BOYS

One of the blunders the unwise coach frequently makes is to play too few boys. Let your subs play at every opportunity. You will thus make a lot of kids and parents happy, give experience to future regulars and endear yourself to the opposing coach. In addition, the game will be more interesting to the fans.

On trips take *only* squad members who have a chance to play, excluding injured regulars who are unable to participate. This may seem harsh, but if you select one injured boy you must take them all. Encourage rides for the wounded, but do not let them displace an active player.

In general, beware of all deadwood on trips. This includes big shots, politicians and the like. The person who knows he is not going to be called upon to play is apt to be light-hearted and gay and thus distract the players from the mission at hand.

Another application of this deadwood rule applies to the dressing room and the bench. One coach coming into a new town found so many former players on the bench that he could not find seats for the active players. He was forced to make a ruling that nobody could sit on the bench except players, managers, coaches and a doctor.

This ruling also had to be enforced in the dressing room. The previous coach had let the situation mushroom until it clearly had gotten out of control.

The new coach must be extremely cautious, however, about

suddenly eliminating a school's long standing athletic traditions, even though he does not believe they are sound or helpful.

DON'T CRITICIZE PREDECESSOR

If you really want to make a giant "booboo" when starting a new job, criticize your predecessor. If you cannot think of anything nice to say about him, then do not say anything at all. He may (and usually does) have lots of friends around.

Never belittle your opponents, especially to the press. At one time in the writer's career as a coach, he was using the straight single wing. The head coach of one of our opponents, in speaking to a service club audience about our upcoming game, made this statement: "I have never been beaten by the old-fashioned single wing, and I never will be."

That remark got into the press, and, of course, our boys read it. It steamed them up to a fighting pitch and that is all it took to change a pregame toss-up into a rout.

The best advice to the young coach in his relationship with the press, radio and TV people is "be honest with them." For various reasons, coaches sometimes make the mistake of telling untruths relative to injured players, starting line-ups, etc. When in doubt, give the press the truth.

Never publicly criticize game officials. Opponents (and sometimes hometown fans) will classify you as a "cry baby" even when the officials are incompetent. If you are the kind who *must* violate this principle, then be sure you have won the game. Otherwise, you cannot be right.

Most experienced coaches will agree that it is wise to insist on your boys dressing neatly on trips. How frequently have you seen a squad traveling in jeans, T shirts, old sweat socks, unshaven and in general looking like a bunch of derelicts? Surely the reaction was unfavorable to you and all others who saw them. Many wise coaches insist that coats and ties be worn.

But more important than proper dress is good behavior. One offense for which there is no excuse is whistling and yelling at girls. Gambling among the players is also a frequent occurrence on trips and this can lead to no good. The coach's insistence on proper dress and gentlemanly conduct will definitely lead to greater pride and better team morale.

At home contests, treat your opponents as guests. Make arrangements to meet them or have them met by a representative of your school. Provide them with the services of one of your managers, who should show them around, lock and unlock their dressing rooms, furnish towels, etc.

Make certain that your visiting dressing room is clean and comfortable. How often have you been called upon to dress in a place which resembled a pig pen? Many times there is an absence of lockers and frequently there is not even a hook available for hanging clothes. Also provide such necessities as a blackboard, chalk, hot water, soap and heat.

Furnishing a dirty, inadequate dressing room for the visitors can be as effective against you as a well-planned pep talk. Do not make them angry. It is tough to beat anybody in that frame of mind.

Treat your officials as guests, also. Provide them with adequate, desirable parking places and a private dressing room with showers away from the players. Frequently, officials are herded in with the players, or near public toilets with a resultant "Grand Central Station" atmosphere.

At one gym, the basketball officials were placed in the furnace room nearly in the middle of a coal pile. They were not anxious to return. Officials should be addressed by your captain as "Sir," and be sure the captain is the only one who talks to the officials.

DRESSING ROOMS

Much of the *esprit de corps* of a squad can be "caught" in the dressing and training rooms. Keep these rooms clean, neat, well-painted, light, dry and cheery in every way. Also see that clean equipment is issued often. Some coaches also favor the use of a radio or phonograph in the dressing room as an aid in maintaining morale.

If you have a trainer, be sure he is firm with the squad members. Otherwise you are apt to have a bunch of malingerers and training room "babies" on your hands. Players should be in the training room for business only. If encouraged, there will be loafers on every squad and their headquarters will be the training room.

Watch for shoddy excuses to miss practice. Make it a rule to get permission to miss practice prior to the practice rather than the following day. Then if the excuse is invalid, the boy can be so informed before it is too late. One football coach of our acquaintance makes each injured player who is ambulatory to dress in full pads even though he may not be able to participate in any rough stuff.

Be firm with your boys in the care of equipment, because the slipshod handling of gear had a tendency to carry over to other activities. The old term, "Give them an inch and they'll take a mile," certainly applies to the equipment situation. They will lose stuff and "steal you blind," if firm policies are not established. A good, honest manager is imperative.

Though it may sound like defeatism, it is wise to make players lock up all valuables at each session. One "rotten apple" on a squad can wreck the morale by stealing and thus creating a suspicious climate.

Be extremely watchful for the "locker room lawyer"—the player who undermines the coaches and/or other players. This type of guy can wreck a ball club by spreading discontent among the players. Your captain can aid in detecting such a "termite." Rehabilitation is possible, but dismissal from the squad is more often the ultimate solution.

COACH-AIDES RELATIONSHIP

A favorable relationship between the head coach and his helpers is indispensable to success. An assistant who is to do a good job must be made to feel he is appreciated and important to the success of the team. Assistants should have, among other things, a voice in planning the attack, making up the schedule and placing of personnel in positions.

The head coach must create an atmosphere in which the assistants are not afraid to make suggestions and he should ask them frequently for their opinions. Furthermore, he should give them certain specific responsibilities with authority to carry them out.

Assistants should, when the occasion arises, be given credit for their contributions. These credits may be given before the squad, and/or to the public through the press.

The writer learned a lot about how *not* to organize for coaching and how *not* to treat assistants from a head college coach we used to know. Rarely did he even hint to his coaches what the practice schedule was going to be. They found out bit by bit from him on the spot as practice progressed on the field. Frequently he would add or change plays on the field and sometimes the coaches would first learn of these changes from the players themselves. The only way a head coach like this ever wins is by having much better material than his opponents.

Also, when such changes were made as additions to the schedule, new assistants, personnel switches, and the like, the assistants often learned about it through the newspapers or the radio. That is not the way to win friends and influence assistants!

If by chance there is an argument or difference of opinion between an assistant and one of the players, the line of authority must not be broken. With rare exceptions, the head coach must publicly back up the assistant. Otherwise the assistant will lose face. This type of problem can best be ironed out behind closed doors, with the least possible fuss.

Likewise, do not embarrass, criticize or point out an assistant's mistakes before the players. Remember, an occasional kind word or a pat on the back will be most welcome and will work wonders in maintaining the efficiency and morale of a helper.

In developing this democratic relationship, one word of caution is pertinent. With all this effort to upgrade the role of assistants, it remains inportant that they, as well as the players, realize who the real boss is—the head coach. As they say in the military, unity of command is absolutely essential.

The unethical assistant coach can undermine the confidence and wreck the morale of a squad by belittling the head coach and/or usurping his duties. On matters of disagreement with the head coach, an assistant may talk it over privately with the head man. If he feels he must criticize the head coach to the players and/or the public, then he should get another job, but quickly!

It is rather generally accepted that a large percentage of games are won or lost on the practice field or court. If that is accepted as true, then it follows that it is extremely important for the coach to know the elements of successful practice sessions. There is no excuse for just "busy" work. It also must be made known to the players "why" they are performing certain skills and exercises. Psychologists and commonsense tells us that one is more apt to learn a skill if he knows why he is practicing it.

Many coaches undo a lot of otherwise excellent coaching by dragging out their practice sessions. Usually these practices are accompanied by a lot of standing around by a large number of players. As much as is feasible, keep everyone busy (except when fatigued) all the time. Short, snappy, purposeful, well-planned sessions will pay off.

MAKE PRACTICE INTERESTING

As pointed out previously, practices should be made as interesting as possible, because we do things better when we enjoy them. For example, in conditioning, a short, competitive shuttle relay race is more fun and subtly accomplishes more than a series of dull wind sprints or several slow laps around the field or floor. Bobby Dodd is one of the foremost examples of a successful coach who believes in combining hard work with fun in practice.

Insist on your players reporting to the practice area on time. This also means, of course, that the coach and his assistants be on time. As a matter of fact, it is advisable for the coaches to report considerably earlier than the appointed time.

Also, start the business part of practice on time. Do not stall around after the players are ready to go to work. One coach we used to know stalled around so much that his players started purposely reporting a half hour later, knowing that they would miss nothing important.

In outdoor activities at least, have your players run from the dressing quarters to the field at the beginning and end of practice. When a player is beckoned during practice, insist that he run, not walk. This snappiness soaks in. Also, when substituting during games, players should, unless injured, run, not walk, on and off the field.

For disciplinary reasons, many coaches will not permit their players to sit or lie down during practice sessions. While listening or observing, they must either stand or rest on one knee.

Some coaches also ask their players to dress in full gear for all practice sessions regardless of the day or the activity in which they are engaged. For example, in football they are asked to wear all pads and their helmets even the night before a contest. The coaches argue that this is not only disciplinary, but that it is more realistic since a player *must* wear them in games.

PRACTICE PLANS IN WRITING

Another helpful reminder is to put your daily practice plans in writing and file them for reference during the following years. Practice planning is difficult and last year's plans are handy to have around. Helpful too is a complete checklist to remind you of things you must cover during the season. This can be placed on your office wall for ready reference.

One of the shortcomings of many coaches is that they spend too little time evaluating and placing personnel. Leaders in business and industry consider it of paramount importance to get "the right man in the right job."

In football, for example, it seems foolish to spend hours trying to develop an effective quarterback out of a boy with no natural ability when perhaps switching, say, an end to that position might solve the problem quickly and effectively. In our experience, such switches from one position to the other has frequently made the difference between a losing and a winning season.

A word of caution is necessary here. You, as well as other leaders, will have "favorites." That is only human. But remember, just "good" boys cannot win for you—they must be players, too.

Have you ever heard of a coach getting fired for being too *firm* on his boys? Probably not. But you *have* heard of a coach getting fired for being too *easy* on his players. Lack of firmness in such things as excuses from practices, thorough conditioning, stealing of equipment and breaking training rules are prime examples. Do not be a "softie." It will get you in real trouble.

Unwise behavior on the bench can also be a coach's undoing. A parent is seldom overjoyed when a coach jerks his boy and gives him a tongue lashing before the whole crowd. Corrective instruction can and should be made, but the coach must be subtle. Loud swearing and rough treatment of his boys on the bench recently cost one nearby high school coach his job—and after an undefeated season, too!

An unpardonable sin for the coach on the bench is to snap back at a heckler in the stands. Early in our coaching career we got peeved at a derogatory remark about one of our players. We proceeded to challenge the anonymous heckler. That was a mistake. It seemed that everyone in the stands joined the heckler in making life miserable for us the remainder of the game. Older and smarter coaches do not do this sort of thing.

How often have you heard fans say this about a coach: "If they could just keep him at home during the contests, we could win more games." The most frequent target of such criticism is the coach who gets all excited during the contests. He loses his head at intervals, making bad substitutions and in general thinking poorly, while the critical action is taking place. This is a rather common and serious coaching weakness and frequently spreads to the players.

Care must be taken in preplanning bench maneuvers during a contest, i.e. sequence of substitutions, game strategy, orderly seating of players by positions on the bench, specific duties of assistants, etc. The chaotic bench scene usually belongs to the losing team.

GOOD CITIZEN

The coach should exemplify the good citizen both by his civic interests and his private life. Although most coaches are busy creatures, they should make every effort to mix and lead in such community interests as church, Sunday School, civic clubs and Boy Scouts.

While the coach might not be asked to follow the path of a clergyman, he should not divert far from the straight and narrow. His unethical behavior certainly would not develop confidence in him among his players, let alone the parents, school board and the community in general. All will agree that the coach is a trifle out-of-bounds.

While under the influence of alcohol a few years ago, one of our colleagues in an adjoining town ran into a porch and demolished it. It was a Baptist minister's porch and the time was Sunday 3 A.M. That opened up a coaching job in that area!

The following is another case of a mistake in the personal life of a coach. The fellow, an assistant in a certain town, moved to a smaller town as head coach. The following year the head coaching job opened up in the town where he formerly assisted. Even though he had the reputation as an excellent assistant, he did not get the job.

Reason? When moving away from the town to accept the head job, he had left the house he was renting in a very dirty condition. So his former landlord, a prominent man in the community, influenced the school board into not hiring him. His argument was that a coach who mistreated other people's property was not the kind of man they wanted to influence the youth of the community. Who could refute that argument?

Many a coach has started off on the wrong foot by not making friends with some important people, namely, the principal, the teachers and the janitor. The principal in most cases is the boss, so it is obvious that one must get on well with him.

Pages could be written on how and why the coach must make friends with the teachers. Suffice it to say that a teacher will be flattered by your interest in his or her subject area. A coach must also work hard to be friendly and to speak and write correct English. Many teachers still picture a coach as "just another dumb athlete." Surprise them!

A word of praise or a game ticket now and then will go far toward winning over the janitor. Cold showers, dirty dressing rooms, unmarked fields are three of the many results of an uncooperative maintenance man.

While this article cannot elaborate on safety, two or three words of advice can be given. If a doctor cannot be made available during practice sessions, have a telephone immediately available. Near the phone, in large blown-up figures, list the numbers of three or four doctors and an ambulance facility.

How often have you heard the P.A. announcer at a football game blast out with, "Will a doctor please report to the bench?" It not only scares all the mothers, but it indicates poor planning. Arrange in advance to have a doctor on each bench.

To summarize, then, the successful coach will need to develop, among other things, a cooperative relationship with the people of the community, the parents, and the principal and other school colleagues. In addition, he must inculcate sound principles of psychology in his teaching, be able to control himself under duress and set a good example by his own personal behavior.

However, if there is any one single item that is *most* important to the coach, it is surely the establishment of a favorable rapport with his players. If they both like and respect him, they will play hard for him.

In conclusion may we say again that there are many more important facets to successful coaching than fancy plays and tricky defenses. Success will come your way only when and if you place the proper emphasis upon developing these less-heralded facets.

CHAPTER 25

ANALYSIS OF ATHLETIC COACHING FAILURES

Robert L. Dodd*

THE FOLLOWING IS AN EFFORT to list the more common causes of athletic coaching failures. Many of these failures are due to carelessness or thoughtlessness on the part of the inexperienced or untrained coach, and merely by calling the failures to his attention he may avoid making the same errors again. To this extent, he will make a greater contribution to his school and community, and his tenure of office in athletic coaching should be longer. For the purpose of this discussion, seven separate areas of failure are listed, although it will be seen immediately that these areas are often closely related and react upon each other.

THE ATHLETIC COACH IS SOMETIMES ACCUSED OF LACK OF EFFORT AND INTEREST

Success in athletic coaching goes hand in hand with hard work. Over a period of years it cannot be considered a matter of luck. Too frequently the inexperienced coach does not comprehend all the duties and responsibilities of his work and, due to this fact, he creates the unfortunate impression in the community and among his players that he is lazy and indolent. The duties and responsibilities of an athletic coach include:

A. *Reading and study of books on coaching, athletic conditioning, first aid, physiology of exercise, psychology, education and the like.*

B. *Detailed and business-like organization of that part of the*

---

* Robert L. Dodd, *Bobby Dodd on Football* (Englewood Cliffs, N. J., Prentice-Hall, Inc., 1954), Chapter 3.

program assigned to him for administration. This may include any or all of the following: organization and administration of the budget; purchase, repair and care of equipment; supervision of ticket sale; general publicity and special game publicity; seating and comfort of spectators; automobile traffic and parking; arrangements for officials, etc. Space prohibits detailed discussion of the elements of organization. Needless to say the alert and conscientious coach will spend the time and energy necessary to carry out efficiently any administrative duties he undertakes.

C. *Study and analysis of strength and weaknesses of his coaching system and of other systems in order to plan intelligently for the season of coaching.* It is not the coaching system that determines success but the thoroughness and efficiency with which the system is taught. Young coaches should hesitate to change from the system they know best and, instead, should concentrate on thorough teaching of the better known system.

D. *Study and analysis of the playing strengths and weaknesses of the members of the team.* Individual instruction should be given to overcome weaknesses and to take maximum advantage of playing strengths.

E. *Outline of a daily plan of practice before the practice session begins.* Lesson planning or practice planning is essential to success in the coaching profession. Also, the coach will find that an occasional unprejudiced introspection of his own efforts will be helpful.

BELOW AVERAGE AND INEXPERIENCED PLAYERS CONSTITUTE AS COMMON COACHING PROBLEM

Although it is generally agreed that there are factors of good and bad fortune connected with the playing strength of every athletic squad, the energetic coach will have several legitimate methods at his command by which he can improve both the quality and size of his squads:

A. The coach should make friends with promising elementary and junior high school athletes and should encourage them to remain in school.

B. The poor students of the squad should be helped with

their studies and encouraged to set up some plan for their adult life that includes graduation from high school and university.

C. A preseason canvass of all boys in the school should be made and they should be invited personally by the coach to try out for the team. In this connection it is frequently necessary to see the parents to get parental consent.

D. The athletic coach should promote modified intramural athletics in elementary and junior high schools and should cooperate with the school authorities and Parent-Teacher Associations in providing sports supplies and equipment for use by these younger players.

E. Junior varsity teams should be organized for younger and smaller players. Unpaid coaches can usually be secured from among recent graduates and a schedule of intramural play can be arranged either to precede varsity games, or to be played during intermissions. In another year many of these young players will be of varsity size and physique and the previous playing experience will be of real value to the next year's varsity squad.

POOR PHYSICAL CONDITION ON THE PART OF THE PLAYERS IS A FREQUENT CAUSE OF FAILURE

As a general rule, the athletic coach is held responsible for injuries and poor physical condition of his squad members. He has the following procedures to help and protect his players:

A. A medical examination *must* precede active participation in strenuous competitive athletics. An examination of the heart and lungs, a test for hernia and a check of recent illness and operation are the important items here. This service can be obtained either free or at a nominal charge by a physician who is interested either in the school, or sports, or both.

B. In the absence of a qualified trainer, the coach should secure the needed technical knowledge to apply first aid and he should treat minor injuries promptly. Minor injuries that are ignored frequently become infected, the result being that the injured player is prohibited from playing for from one to several weeks. Of course, the danger to health is even more important.

C. The athletic instructor should work to condition his squad so that they will be physically fit to play an entire game at top speed. Conditioning results from exercise taken daily over a period of several months. There is no short cut to physical conditioning and endurance. Successful coaches attempt to measure the amount of physical work included in each practice session to the point where the participants definitely feel the tiring effects of the work, but practice should be stopped each day before harmful fatigue or exhaustion sets in. Adequate focus on conditioning is a frequent omission of coaching duties and must not be overlooked.

D. Except with the approval of a physician, the coach should not run the risk of playing a boy in a game when he is injured and when he might receive a permanent physical defect as a result.

INEFFICIENT TEACHING METHODS RESULT IN MISTAKES BY PLAYERS

The athletic instructor should plan all practice periods and teaching procedures intelligently. There are many accepted principles and psychological laws of learning that have practical application in the field of athletic coaching.

A. In general, we may think of athletic coaching as the teaching of motor habits. These complex motor coordinations are learned slowly. Drill, practice and more drill are necessary parts of this learning procedure. Explanation and demonstration by the coach are important elements, but there is no short cut to learning. Nothing will take the place of participation by the learner. These drills should be made as interesting as possible to the participants—but regardless, the practice must be carried on.

B. A few fundamentals (blocking, ball-handling, footwork, etc.) well taught are more conducive to success than having all skills explained but none habituated. The coach should work for perfection of execution and focus on attention to detail.

C. It is not what the athletic instructor knows that determines his success—it is what he teaches. The correlation is not always a positive one. This psychological principle of teaching should give confidence to the coach who was not a regular on his college team and should serve as a warning to the former college star.

D. Performance is more important than form. The coach should hesitate to require detailed mechanical movements of a player if his present performance is highly effective. Remember there are many football punters ruined by coaching for every punter helped by it. Also, it is absurd to see ten different university basketball squads using ten different mechanical techniques in foul shooting with every boy on each squad carrying out the detailed mechanical method prescribed by his particular coach. It would seem that at least nine of these ten coaches must be teaching inaccurately. However, the coach should make an accurate measurement of performance before he permits unorthodox execution.

E. The well-known, widely accepted and little used psychological laws of cause and effect have most important applications in athletic coaching. The wise coach will keep them uppermost in his teaching focus. These laws tell us that a habit to be made lasting should be followed by satisfactory results and a habit not to be lasting should be followed by unsatisfactory results. As a general rule, praise of effort is more effective than criticism.

F. Constructive criticism is necessary; destructive criticism is harmful and demoralizing. Do not tell a player he is poor—tell him how to correct his inaccuracies.

G. Teaching effort and energy should be directed to the end that the coach may expect his team to win from those opponents who are potentially just as good or a little better than his own team.

H. There are individual differences in learning capacity. Be patient with the slow learner. A team is no stronger than its weakest player.

POOR TEAM MORALE SPELLS FAILURE IN COACHING EFFORTS

This is a phase of coaching that can be analyzed and developed intelligently. It is possible to provide an intelligent analysis of the causes of poor morale in any athletic squad. Here are suggestions for improvement of morale:

A. When the team is losing, it needs encouragement and not destructive criticism and sarcasm. The coach should take the blame for any game that is lost and should point out to his squad an encouraging analysis of the defeat as soon after the game as possible. When the team is winning, it may be best to assume an unsatisfied and critical attitude—but give the players the credit for the victories.

B. Require group loyalty. Prohibit criticism, wrangling and jealousy within the squad at any cost. There must be a feeling of all for one and one for all. The first indication of criticism, wrangling or jealousy among teammates must be dealt with promptly, fairly and in a friendly but business-like manner.

C. The athletic coach must be loyal to his team at all times. This is necessary if he expects the players to be loyal to him. He should criticize the player to his face and not when the player is absent. He must defend the player against criticism when the player is not present. (If the drug store "cowboys" are capable of respecting anyone, this action will cause them to respect the athletic instructor. Also, the player defended will hear of the defense by the coach and will feel friendly toward the coach.)

D. The athletic coach should try to treat all players fairly. He must be tolerant to the extent that he will not permit a known feeling of hatred toward him on the part of one of the players to interfere with a just selection of his team on a strict basis of playing ability. The coach must remember that this feeling of hatred may, and frequently does, change to one of respect and friendliness within twenty-four hours. Also, the coach should re-member that the antagonistic feeling on the part of a player is most frequently due to some treatment by the coach that the player interprets as unfriendly or unfair. In such cases, a friend-ly conference will erase the misunderstanding and establish a feeling of friendliness between the two individuals. In this, the coach must take the initiative.

E. The athletic coach must feel friendly and kindly toward every boy on his squad. When he has this feeling it will be found that the boys generally have a similar feeling toward him and a feeling of harmony will soon develop throughout the en-tire squad. Again, the coach must take the initiative. A thoughtful coach will soon realize that this group feeling comes from the heart, not from the mouth, of the athletic instructor.

F. The athletic coach should be friendly with all of his players, but not too familiar. He should not be friendly toward some and sarcastic, critical and domineering toward others. This latter attitude will soon lead to friction and poor team morale.

G. The coach may prevent inferiority complexes on the part of young second-string players by talking with them, pointing out to them their playing strengths and weaknesses, and encouraging them in their efforts to improve. To ignore or unduly criticize a substitute player will generally break his confidence and ruin him as a player. Criticism should be made in keeping with the potential abilities of the individual criticized. If this policy is made known to the players, they will welcome criticism. To attempt to show off by directing harsh criticism at an awkward, unskilled player is an act unworthy of any athletic coach.

H. In dealing with each disciplinary situation, the following procedure is suggested: do not speak until there is absolute quiet; then, talk with a low tone of voice; do not say too much; be sure a penalty can be enforced before it is announced; and do not hold any malice afterward—treat the incident as closed.

ATHLETICS COACHES ARE FREQUENTLY ACCUSED OF FAILING TO COOPERATE WITH THE ACADEMIC FACULTY AND OTHER EXTRACURRICULAR AGENCIES OF THE SCHOOL

In the majority of cases, these accusations are either unwarranted, or are caused by carelessness, thoughtlessness, or shyness on the part of the coach. Men in the athletic coaching profession should show an interest in all other phases of school work and should go out of their way to cooperate with people in these fields. To eliminate these accusations, the following additional points are suggested:

A. A friendly cooperation regarding the use of school and community facilities, supplies and equipment reacts favorably upon the athletic program.

B. In like manner, a fair, unselfish, cooperative attitude toward the use of school appropriations and athletic funds for other school projects indicates a desirable character trait of the athletic coach.

C. The avoidance of criticism of co-workers, employers and townspeople indicates cooperation. It is important to remember that even a door knocker is always on the outside of the door. Boosters are usually accepted in a social group; knockers or critics are usually regarded as small, social outcasts.

D. The ability to accept adverse decisions and criticisms gracefully is important. In order to develop professionally, it is wise, but difficult, to take the attitude that they are given in a spirit of helpfulness. Then, the coach should analyze the criticisms factually and revise conduct or policies in keeping with the factual analysis.

LACK OF COMMUNITY RESPECT CAN REDUCE TENURE IN ATHLETIC COACHING WORK

In this connection, the athletic instructor should dress appropriately; guard his reputation zealously; be mannerly, not boisterous and rowdy; choose his friends carefully—avoid the "tinhorn" element and make friends with the better element of the community by showing an interest in them, in their work and in their recreations. He should take an interest and active part in community affairs; refrain from criticizing people or projects— instead, be an optimist and a booster; prohibit swearing, gambling, drinking, questionable stories and other unsocial actions on the part of the players, and the coach must avoid these same acts himself.

CHAPTER 26

FACTORS INFLUENCING A COACH'S ABILITY TO ANALYZE

ANDREW GRIEVE*

S UPPOSE A BASKETBALL TEAM is facing a defense which is constantly thwarting their offense and the regular offensive patterns are proving to be completely ineffective. The ground game
of a football team is gaining very little yardage, even though in
previous games certain plays worked successfully. A soccer team
finds itself completely inept at penetrating an opponent's defense using their normal strategic attacks. In these situations the
coaches must analyze the situations and make the correct adjustments, or at least those which they think are correct. This is what
we infer in reference to a coach's ability to analyze.

As the situation now exists in most team and some individual
sports, the coach has assumed this responsibility. There are many
who feel these solutions should be left strictly to the players, but
in actual practice this is not the case, at least not at present. The
team members often do make decisions but the overall plan and
the necessary adjustments are most often made by the coach.

Our purpose is to determine what factors influence a coach's
ability to make adjustments. Some are quite obvious, while others may not be. In some instances, it would be possible to correct
negative influences, while in others it is doubtful if such
changes can be made. For some individuals this could be a problem without an answer, but a realization of the factors which influence such decisions might assist coaches in improving this ability.

From our personal experience these situations have arisen on

---

* Andrew Grieve, "Factors Influencing a Coach's Ability to Analyze," *Athletic
Journal*, Vol. 51 (June 1971), pp. 42-45 and 53-54.

numerous occasions. They have involved our coaching staff, coaches with whom we have worked and opposing coaches. The latter proved to be the most satisfactory situation. From such observations it would seem this ability varies among coaches. There are coaches who can recognize changes immediately and make the proper adjustments. On the other hand, there are numerous coaches who cannot make on the spot adjustments and this could be due to any number of factors. The recognition of such factors is the purpose of this article.

The time element has a great deal to do with an understanding of this problem. There are four periods of time when the coach must utilize his ability to analyze the opponent. The first is in his preliminary planning, where he utilizes information available on the opponents, usually gained from scouting reports, to prepare his overall plan for the particular contest. Some coaches have the ability to make the most of such information, while others do not recognize certain important aspects.

The second phase would be in formulating the practice plan which would be an outgrowth of preliminary planning. A comprehensive plan would depend upon the coach's ability to include in his practices factors related to the overall plan. Once again, there is a variation in ability among coaches in this area.

The third time period, and probably the most critical, would be the ability to analyze during the game itself. A coach who is able to analyze during all the other time periods may not be able to do so during the actual contest. This ability is the one with which we should be most concerned and where most of the problems exist.

The fourth time period where ability to analyze is necessary is following the contest. Many coaches make post-game notes immediately following the contest while the information is still uppermost in their minds. While this procedure has no effect upon the outcome of the recently completed contest, the coach will be able to note where the team was successful or unsuccessful and why. He should be able to use a great deal of this information in future contests. This is one of the many values of filming athletic contests. However, the coach must remember that hindsight is always more correct than foresight. Many coaches will say, *If we had done this we would have been more successful.* The question is, why did they not do so during the game rather than stating the correct adjustment following the contest?

There are numerous factors which influence the coach's ability to make the proper decisions. We feel the major influence is the emotional involvement, which would be considered as an intrinsic factor. Emotional involvement will be discussed later, but we would like to begin with the effects of what we refer to as outside influences. Although we may refer to them as outside influences some could have a definite effect upon the intrinsic or emotional involvement. In certain areas it would be quite obvious to the coach that there is no possibility of his changing such factors and he will accept them with little emotional response. On the other hand, there are other areas which will develop an emotional reaction even though there is little the coach can do about them at that particular time.

The nature of a sport will have a great deal to do with a coach's ability to analyze, or at least the rapidity with which he can do so. In activities such as wrestling, tennis, fencing, etc., a coach may be able to analyze the strategy of the opponent rather easily due to concentration. With only two competitors as the focal point, a capable coach can readily point out proper adjustments to the athlete. On the other hand, team sports may be somewhat more difficult to analyze. Football, because of the close action and the number of players involved, demands tremendous concentration and a rather effective ability to analyze. Basketball, because of the rapidity of movement and constant action, also develops a difficult situation.

There is always the question of player influence. Being closer to the action, often they are able to analyze more effectively and are better able to judge the situation. Is it more appropriate for the coach to indicate adjustments since he has a better overall view of the action? In this situation there have been numerous occasions when players have influenced the decision of the coach. In many instances these influences have had negative effects. During their careers many coaches undoubtedly have had some second thoughts on following the suggestions of their players as the ultimate results proved such suggestions to be incorrect.

The time of the season will have a great deal to do with the coach's ability to analyze. This is particularly true in preliminary planning. Early in the season a coach may not have sufficient information on an opponent due to a lack of scouting reports and it will be difficult to determine the overall strategy. Previous experience with these opponents in other seasons might be of value but often opposing coaches will make radical changes which make previous information of little value.

The location of a contest might very well affect the analyzing procedure. In certain sports the home court is a definite advantage due to the home team's familiarity with the facilities. However, crowd reaction is more important. A coach, as well as the players, can be tremendously influenced by crowd reaction. There would be, without a doubt, some emotional reaction on the part of the coach and the players in an obviously hostile atmosphere and this could influence the coach's ability to analyze the situation properly. It would be valuable if a coach were slightly deaf at away contests so he might not hear the crowd reaction. During the past several years there has been an increase in afternoon games. In this situation the spectators are almost always a home crowd and this develops an unusual condition as all positive reaction is limited to the performance of the home team.

Weather conditions at outdoor contests will often demand a change in strategy on the spot. The coach can do little about the situation but he must be ready for such eventualities. Thus many coaches schedule practice sessions during inclement weather in order to familiarize the players with making adjustments which the weather conditions may demand.

The coach has little control of the factors related to the trip if the contest happens to be away from home. A short trip in comfortable circumstances will have little effect on a coach's ability to concentrate. On the other hand, a rather lengthy, uncomfortable trip may develop an atmosphere which acts as a deterrent. Arriving at the site of the game rather late will not only affect the players but also the coach. Arriving too early results in a long waiting period and can also have negative effects.

The matter of concentration and its effects upon the coach's ability to analyze is also influenced by his individual personal problems. If certain problems are pressing such as family difficulties, finances, and health, these could very well detract from his ability to concentrate and thus influence his capacity for analyzing.

Officials have a considerable effect upon a coach's ability to concentrate and avoid emotional reactions which detract from his ability. The coach often feels that officials tend to favor the home team. This is another area which could well be the basis of a psychological study. Are there factors which definitely influence officials, without their knowledge, to favor the home team? Disregarding the factor of the possibility of *homers,* a coach is influenced by his judgment as to the competence of game officials. Officials who, in the coach's opinion, are not performing in a competent manner will cause emotional reactions which will hinder him in the task of analyzing the necessary facets of the contest. In many instances this question arises due to rule interpretations by officials in various parts of the country. There is no doubt such interpretations on judgment calls do vary and if a coach has become accustomed to one type of interpretation he will experience difficulty when exposed to another variation.

One of the major dangers of excessive concern over officials and their calls is that a coach may spend a major part of his time being critical of officials. His energies and concentration are directed almost completely to this criticism and he is usually not capable of analyzing the game situation. When a coach is busy criticizing officials, he is not coaching.

There are several other factors which might well influence the coach and his ability to analyze. Assistant coaches can do a great deal to enhance this ability. However, this depends upon their individual ability, and the method they use to inform the head coach of their observations. A team's season record might also influence the degree to which the coach feels extensive analysis is necessary. Injuries will also have a similar effect because a coach may be limited by the capabilities of the athletes in the contest.

We believe it is possible to develop this particular ability, at least to some degree. The first method would be through training or educational background. During his period of education there are courses which should help a future coach develop this ability. Such information should be one of the major units of any coaching course but, unfortunately, we have rarely observed this problem discussed extensively, even though it has tremendous ramifications in the area of coaching.

Experience is probably the greatest teacher but this does not mean that all coaches have analytical ability as a result of their experience. The beginning coach is often limited in this characteristic. A simple lack of experience in recognizing the need for adjustment is typical of younger coaches. Some who do recognize the need for such adjustments may not have the background necessary to provide the players with the needed changes.

Another notable characteristic of young coaches, and of some experienced coaches, is an attempt to introduce a new strategy or technique in the midst of a game. Obviously, a team which has not practiced such a variation will definitely experience difficulties. A knowledgeable coach will usually have provided his team with a variety of adjustments for particular situations during practice sessions. If one strategy is not effective his team is prepared to attempt another, but not without some experience in its intricacies.

If it would be possible to eliminate or regulate the negative influences, and provide the ideal conditions for every athletic contest, the factor of emotional involvement would still be the determining factor in the coach's ability to analyze and provide the necessary information for the team. The major problem for many coaches is not being capable of providing possible solutions due to the emotional involvement. Extremely strong emotions, which the coach is unable to control, will interrupt or deter logical thinking. Although it may be somewhat difficult to describe the problem, one might say the coach is looking at the wrong things. He becomes strictly concerned with the performance of his athletes at a focal point. This focal point would be the point of attention, or that point where the typical spectator directs his attention. In football it is usually at the ball-carrier, in basketball it is the man who has the ball, and in baseball it would be the pitcher and the batter. Although there are twenty-two players on a football field, 99 percent of those in attendance are watching the man with the ball. Naturally this is the focal point of the game, but the coach who is concerned with analyzing the game must direct his attention to numerous other areas. Is the blocking in the line effective? Is the quarterback carrying out his fake when he does not have the ball? Is a decoying receiver holding the defensive secondary?

Basketball also provides numerous observation points. Did the screener do an effective job in freeing the man with the ball? If the team is using a pattern are the players away from the ball following the proper movement, or are they standing around watching the ball? In playing against a zone defense, rather than watching the ball, is the coach watching the defensive shift to determine where there might be a weak spot?

There are numerous other examples but these should suffice. Actually, the coach who recognizes that there is more than just one focal point will be concerned with an overall view of the situation. It is this overall view which will provide him with the information necessary to analyze and provide the needed information to the team. Telling the team they are not gaining yardage, or are not putting the ball into the basket is not news to them. They recognize these factors; they want to know how to overcome these shortcomings. By recognizing the overall situation on the field or on the court, the coach should be capable of indicating to them what adjustments should be made and will probably result in more success.

Another danger of a lack of emotional control is exemplified by the coach who uses the time-outs or the half-time period to berate the players. As in the situation of constantly badgering officials, a coach who is guilty of this action is not coaching. There are reasons why players may be performing poorly and one reason may be that the opponents are superior. Coaches must learn to accept this in certain situations. However, in many cases the athletes' performance, or lack of the same, is due to poor strategy by the coach. Even slight adjustments will often provide the players with opportunities that were not previously available to them.

There are factors which influence the emotional impact of the contest. The more important the game, the greater is the emotional effect. A game for the state championship will most certainly develop a greater emotional reaction on the part of the coach than possibly the opening game of the season. A contest with an arch rival is another example of a situation which will arouse strong emotions. There are degrees of emotional response.

The closer the outcome of a game, the greater is the emotional involvement. Many coaches will indicate they would rather win by twenty or lose by twenty points than have to go through the stresses of a tight contest. Some coaches virtually freeze when it comes down to the last few seconds of a close game and they must decide what has to be done. Many make the wrong decisions because their emotions interfere with their logical thinking processes.

The pressures of having winning seasons will depend upon circumstances. Many coaches are under constant pressure to have winners, either by the spectators, the athletic department, the students or the alumni. This is the type of coach who must be under extreme emotional strain because his future in the profession is at stake. Most coaches, however, develop such pressure on themselves, and even though the outside pressure may be at a minimum, they are still under an emotional strain which is often self-developed.

Finally, in this area of emotional involvement, a great deal depends upon the emotional characteristics of the coach. This is a part of his personality, and according to many psychologists, is determined at a very early period in his life. The emotional reaction of the coach may not only be characterized during his coaching responsibilities, but the same would be reflected as he faces other situations which develop tension. The individual who is emotionally mature in his day-to-day experiences will normally reflect a similar maturity when he is coaching.

What is the solution or solutions in controlling the emotions as a coach so one might better develop the ability to analyze? As mentioned previously, experience can do much to improve this ability. Self-discipline is probably the term most appropriate as one attempts to improve. If the individual takes a self-inventory, he must recognize instances in his coaching responsibilities where he did not analyze properly due to his lack of emotional control. The coach who can recognize such instances will be well on his way to improving this ability.

The coach must consciously work to develop this ability. He might observe other teams in competition and concern himself with a strict analysis of the strategies used by these teams. He should consciously recognize the numerous variations and practice such recognition. Oddly enough most coaches do this in the scouting process because it is imperative for them to provide all the pertinent information on an upcoming opponent. However, too many coaches lose this ability when their own teams are involved due to the emotional concern. We think practice and the observation of other teams in action constitute a good starting point.

When the team is playing, the coach must be as objective as possible. If the players are not capable of performing as the situation demands then they should be replaced. If the replacements are not capable then the coach may be in for a long, lean season.

This reminds us of the coach whose team was playing up to their potential but were behind forty-eight to zero at half-time to the best team in the state. What was he to say? Being a rather emotionally mature individual he did not berate his players, but rather corrected some of their minor errors and the team went back out for a sixty-four to sixty defeat.

A coach cannot be involved without emotions, but these must be kept in check in order not to interfere with his objective approach in observing an overview of the situation. He must analyze the situation as calmly as possible, making notes on a pad if he considers this necessary, but when the team surrounds the coach during a time out or at halftime, he should have something constructive to tell them. A team that has confidence in the coach knows he will provide them with information which should improve performance.

CHAPTER 27

NINE WAYS TO IMPROVE YOUR COACHING

VERNE CANFIELD*

CURIOSITY, A LITTLE HUMILITY and an open mind can carry a coach a long way. The wise coach recognizes that there is always something to be learned and there is always room for improvement.

He accepts the fact that others may have equally good or better ways of doing things. He is constantly aware of learning situations and constantly searching for ways to improve his techniques and adjust his philosophy. Methods and philosophy are always undergoing change and the wise coach will change with the times.

By keeping an open mind about new ideas, the coach can constantly reinforce his thinking. One of the most helpful and reassuring things about attending a clinic is learning that some other coach (usually a successful one) is thinking or doing something the way you are.

It is vital for a coach to study, analyze, compare and experiment with every aspect of his sport. This does not imply changing for changing's sake, but rather a willingness to learn and then change if it can improve your coaching and the team performance.

Following are suggestions for improving your coaching. Though they cover familiar areas, you might find an idea or a reminder that can help you.

---

* Verne Canfield, "Nine Ways to Improve Your Coaching," *Scholastic Coach*, Vol. 39 (December 1969), pp. 48-49 and 54.

Reading

This obviously includes books on skills and techniques as well as articles from several fine coaching magazines. Included also could be a biography or a text on psychology.

The newspapers and general magazines often carry articles on an outstanding coach or team that can give you an insight into the coach's personality or mention something about his way of doing things.

In your reading, be sure to mark the sections that apply to your particular situation. This will enable you to check back from time to time without having to go through everything.

The summer months offer a good time to catch up on your reading. Membership in coaches' book clubs and subscriptions to coaching publications can keep you amply supplied with reading material. Any coach who sincerely desires to improve should take advantage of any and all reading opportunities. He should develop his own library and endeavor to keep it as current as possible.

Clinic Attendance

Every coach should make an all-out effort to attend at least one clinic a year. This is the time to look, listen, compare, ask questions and seek other opinions; a time to pick up one or two fresh ideas. It does not have to be a fancy new offense or complicated defense. Just one new idea or confirmation of an old one can make the attendance worthwhile.

Clinics also provide the inspiration to "get to work," motivation to bone up on an area in which you are weak, and a reminder that there is so much to be learned.

To glean the most value from a clinic, you must take appropriate notes and reminders which you can refer to when you get back home and then file away for future reference.

Closely related to clinic attendance is serving as a counselor or instructor at one of the many summer sport camps. Much of your free time there can be spent in comparing notes with other instructors.

Offensive and Defensive File

Information on fundamentals, coaching methods and techniques, and other related information taken from your reading, clinic attendance and talking to other coaches should be filed for quick reference in the future. Your file system can be divided into offensive and defensive sections and then broken down into specifics through the use of manila folders and neatly typed index tabs.

Notebooks and Manuals

Notebooks and manuals can be used to file tidbits of knowledge picked up along the way from other coaches and reading sources. By placing them in a notebook or a manual, you build up a complete future reference source. I have found that separate notebooks for offense, defense and general ideas prove very helpful in maintaining an organized catalog of information.

Offseason Projects

Since most of us have little time during the season for any extra reading or studying, the offseason offers an ideal time to catch up. Take a particular phase of your sport that you feel you need to learn more about or perhaps need to review and then read everything you can on it. You can also confer with other coaches to get their ideas on the subject.

From your reading and conferring, you can firm up your thinking and perhaps develop a sounder approach to this particular phase of the sport. While doing such research and study, it is a sound idea to make notes and place them in your designated notebook or file.

Use of Assistants

Use your assistant as a sounding board for new ideas, practice procedures, teaching techniques or some phase of game strategy. Be willing to listen to his suggestions. It is important to make the assistant coach feel free to disagree with you and to present cogent reasons for doing so. He might come up with some small point that you possibly may have overlooked. An assistant coach should always be encouraged to contribute his ideas and feelings.

Observations

Watch as many games as you can, observing other coaches' strategy, substitution and technique. Think of what you would be doing in the same game situations. If you see a good idea, do not be afraid to use it. You can always learn by imitation and from the mistakes of others.

Write for Publication

One of the most important things about writing for a coaching magazine or possibly even writing a book, is that it forces you to reorganize or review your thinking on a particular subject. It also forces you to review other sources of information such as your files, notebooks or the opinions of other coaches. This type of review can be most helpful in your growth as a coach.

Such writings are also extremely prestigious and can bring you into contact with coaches from all over the country. You should be willing to share new thoughts and ideas with other members of your profession.

Self-Evaluation

Evaluating your own coaching methods, techniques and philosophy is an essential step in climbing the ladder of success. This self-evaluation should include an honest look at every phase of your coaching career, including your goals.

Specifically, you must evaluate your offensive and defensive philosophy and your methods of handling practices, game situations and player discipline. You must ask yourself questions about strategy and substitutions. In other words, you should be able to second guess yourself, be able to take an honest look at your mistakes and learn from them.

I have found that a short evaluation after each practice comes in handy at the end of the season in looking back and summarizing the entire season. You should take a long look at everything you have done and write down the weak areas as well as the strong ones. What must you change or adjust for next year?

It might be helpful to keep a sort of personal log of mistakes, decisions made (both good and bad) and the way you handled things. Player questionnaires at the end of the season, a record of daily practices or conferences and comparative observations can also be helpful in your self-evaluation. Make an attempt to rethink many of your decisions.

Although I have mentioned various ways to grow and improve in your techniques and philosophy, I am not suggesting that you should constantly change your style. It is most important to be yourself and not a carbon copy of some name coach.

But neither should you be the same old coach year in and year out. Your coaching methods and philosophy need your constant evaluation and adjustment.

CHAPTER 28

IMPROVE PERFORMANCE BY UTILIZING FUNDAMENTAL PRINCIPLES OF MOVEMENT

Dale O. Nelson[*]

ONE OF THE MAIN DIFFERENCES between championship performance and mediocrity, between good coaching and just coaching, and between proper training and another workout, is the adherence to fundamental principles of movement. Certain of these fundamentals apply to many different sports and skills. Once they are learned, these fundamentals should be transferred and utilized in any activity requiring their application.

It may be noticed that children are able to learn sports at a very early age, since some have learned to swim before they could walk and many are championship performers of one kind or another while still in their teens. Most of the learning which takes place in the early life of the child is the trial and error, nonanalytical type. He imitates older performers, tries first one way and then another until some degree of skill is attained. One important question which relates to this thinking and is now confronting us is: Would it not be easier and simpler to know and practice more of these basic movements that apply to many skills? It seems that the trial and error period for both the coach and the athlete could be reduced in obtaining satisfying results if the fundamental principles of movement were applied in the initial stages of learning.

Physical educators and coaches now have at their finger tips more scientific information about various sports than at any

[*] Dale O. Nelson, "Improve Performance by Utilizing Fundamental Principles of Movement," *Athletic Journal*, Vol. 39 (November 1958), pp. 26-28 and 48-51.

time in history, yet many are not able to apply and utilize the available methods and techniques because they seem too complex or too encompassing with all of the details involved. It may come as a surprise to some coaches when they realize that many types of movement are transferable from one activity to another, and that most of these fundamental principles are scientifically established. Very often the coach and athlete learn the intricate details of each skill separately, never realizing that there are fundamental types of movement which apply to many different skills and activities. The best results often come to the teacher and athlete when relationships are readily recognized.

The purpose of this article is to discuss some of the fundamental principles of movement and cite examples of skills in which they are applied. As a result, we hope to improve performance.

PRINCIPLE DEFINED

It seems appropriate to preface the discussion with a definition of the term *principle*. A principle is a guide to forming judgment and determining a course of action. It is a fundamental belief based on both fact and theory. Some of the chief characteristics of a principle are that it should (1) imply action or direct action rather than cite techniques for effecting it, (2) be a belief or conclusion based on the best facts or near facts, or on the best judgments presently available and to which men of good reason should agree, (3) be applicable, attainable and interpreted similarly by men of good reason.

The principles under discussion in this article are not the only principles applicable to various sports skills, nor are they necessarily the most important. They seem to be representative of the types of things that, when applied, will make teaching and learning more meaningful, as well as easier.

PRINCIPLE I

In many different sports and skills, the body, parts of the body or the implement being used should be in a moving position.

Newton's first law of motion states that every body at rest tends to remain at rest and every body in motion tends to continue in motion in a straight line unless compelled by external force to change that state of rest or motion. This law is the tendency to stay put or keep going, sometimes referred to as inertia. Force is an element required in most types of activity in one degree or another and is defined as an action exerted by one body on another, tending to cause the body acted upon to change its state of motion. Momentum is a product of force, and as every coach and athlete knows, is essential to good performance in many skills. Consequently, it is easier to derive force and momentum, as well as increase speed and decrease reaction time with a moving body or object. In this case force and momentum are also related to coordination which, when properly applied, improves performance in many sports.

Skill Examples: 1. Gymnastic skills on the parallel bars, rings, high bars and other equipment require that the body be kept moving.

2. Good tennis players are usually found in a moving position of readiness when preparing to receive the ball.

3. Bowling utilizes this principle before the ball is released.

4. Baseball batters start moving with a short stride forward as the pitcher delivers the ball.

In addition to moving readiness, it is also important to keep the body balanced. This means that the body should be spread over the base of support or kept moving over a spread base to maintain a balanced position.

PRINCIPLE II

Since many activities require starting from an inert or stationary position, the first principle leads naturally into the second.

In order to develop force, momentum, and speed, the body should be kept low in the initial stages of the skill.

It is important to have a low center of gravity so that the muscles can supply force through the ground or contact surface to start the body moving. Joints are placed in a flexed position so that extension will overcome inertia and create the forceful movements necessary to gain momentum.

Skill Examples: 1. Sprint starting and the emphasis on keeping low in the first part of the dash are excellent illustrations of this principle.

2. Slow motion movies of Parry O'Brien, U.S.C.'s Olympic champion in the shot put, and Sim Iness, another U.S.C. Olympic champion in the discus, bring out the importance of starting low and staying low as they cross the ring. The momentum necessary to throw the shot approximately sixty-three feet and the discus approximately 196 feet is initiated by adhering to this principle. It should also be noted that these men keep to a straight line across the circle and to ground-skimming steps so that all momentum is exerted in the most effective direction.

3. Baseball has many examples of speed which mean staying low in the start, base stealing, the sprint to first after hitting the ball, fielding, etc.

4. The pulling linemen running interference in football. Some coaches teach their players to turn and reach for some grass so that they will stay low in starting the run. The principle also applies to the speed backs and ends when bursts of speed are required.

5. Basketball players often need speed and should be taught to stay low in the first stages of moving.

Any activity requiring force and momentum (speed included) should be performed with the body kept low in the initial stages of the skill performance.

PRINCIPLE III

The third principle is also a natural sequence and is related to the first two. *Force and momentum are increased by greater range of motion.*

There is another law of physics that applies to the development of force and momentum. The more time or the greater distance a force is applied to a body or object, the greater will be the momentum. Range of motion becomes extremely important for this reason. Force can be applied longer over a greater distance and greater momentum results. Many skills need tremendous momentum for top performance.

Skill Examples: 1. Track has many events in which range of motion is important. The revolutionary technique of putting the shot introduced by Parry O'Brien employs this principle. Facing the rear of the shot circle permits him to increase his range of motion, which, when added to the employment of other fundamental principles, allows for greater distances and world records. Of course, we should not overlook the physical equipment of O'Brien, but he must utilize these fundamental principles to the greatest advantage. Sim Iness is another example of tremendous range of motion in throwing the discus. We have studied slow motion films of Iness and O'Brien (128 frames per second—double slow motion), and found the application of this principle to be extremely good. The javelin event also portrays the use of long range of motion in applying great force to gain distance.

2. Baseball pitchers throwing the fast ball must have good range of motion in order to get the necessary speed on the ball. Bob Feller, Carl Hubbell, Lefty Grove and others developed characteristic wind-ups which gave them great range of motion and helped build up the momentum so important to a blinding fast ball. All of these baseball players take a backward stretch and backward extension of the throwing arm, then a long step, all to increase the range of motion for the throw.

3. Golf utilizes greater range of motion whenever more distance is desired. The drive takes a full swing; whereas, the approach shot is only a part of the complete range of motion possible. Batting also has the utilization of this principle. Long-ball hitters hit farther when they can get a full swing, which means more range of motion.

This principle is not always the most important in a particular skill, but when momentum and force are requirements, its use becomes paramount. Many other skills and activities could be cited, but it seems sufficient to say that whenever striking power, force or momentum are involved in the performance of a skill, great range of motion becomes an important factor.

PRINCIPLE IV

Any movement of the head interferes with coordinated body movement, especially in the shoulders. Therefore, *it is essential*

to keep the eyes on the ball or object until contact is made so
that head movements will not cause a deviation in the correct
pattern of movement. Everyone has had the experience of missing a ball, both catching and hitting, as a result of disobeying
this principle. The following skills illustrate its use.

Skill Examples: 1. Football players often miss a pass because
they take their eyes off the ball before contact is made. They an-
ticipate being hit or want to look where they are to move before
actually getting the ball. Head movement interferes with the
catch. The place-kicker must keep his eye on the ball until it is
kicked. Many good kickers never see the ball go between the up-
rights.

2. The same can be said of baseball players, basketball players and any other activity which involves catching an object.

3. Whenever hitting an object is required, the same principle
is applied. The golfer keeps looking at the ball and even the
spot of the ball so that the principle is not disobeyed. Baseball
players, tennis players, badminton players, handball players and
other types of athletes involved in hitting objects follow the ball
almost to the point of contact so that head movements will not
interfere with the pattern of the swing.

PRINCIPLE V

All movements should have reasonably good follow-through.
At first glance, follow-through appears to be relatively unimportant, since at this time in the course of action the object has
left the implement or the important part of the movement has
been made and there is nothing the participant can do to change
the course of action. Alterations in follow-through should not
commence until after the central movement reduces its effectiveness. Therefore, the follow-through is an indication of what has
happened during the preceding central action and carries significance because of its effect on this prior action. Follow-through
also prevents tension in the muscles which otherwise would be
involved in an attempt to check movement at the end of the central action. Momentum from the follow-through may also be
utilized to accomplish subsequent movements such as getting the
ready position for another type of action.

Skill Examples: All of the striking examples listed under Principle IV require the application of the follow-through principle.

1. In addition, the charging football blocker and tackler must follow through after contact has been made with the opponent.

2. Jack Dempsey once said that he tried to hit his opponent in the back of the head. He meant the follow-through was essential so that the force of the blow was not stopped before contact was made with his opponent's body.

3. The baseball hitter and the golfer illustrate this principle after a powerful swing. The follow-through indicates that all possible force was exerted at the moment of contact with the ball.

PRINCIPLE VI

Generalize skills by practicing them under varying conditions and performing them at the normal desired speed. Performers who practice at reduced speeds usually develop techniques not successful at faster rates because the coordination and pattern of movement are not the same. At the same time, conditions vary in many sports so a person should practice under many different conditions. Distances vary, wind changes, terrain varies, the opposition is hardly ever the same, etc. Consequently, practice sessions must vary the conditions to meet these different situations.

Skill Examples: 1. In golf, the player pitches onto the green from various angles, in dry and wet weather, on a windy day or a still day. The swing is also at normal speed so that the performer gets the desired movement pattern.

2. Tennis players use different playing surfaces, backgrounds vary and game conditions differ. Consequently, all types of situations should be practiced under game conditions. When fundamentals alone are practiced, they should be at the normal speed.

3. Successful basketball teams play many games and scrimmage considerably in practice. Thus they receive practice under varied conditions and they are able to meet most game situations that arise.

PRINCIPLE VII

Strength type skills require the longest warm-up.

The best evidence available points to the importance of warm-up in proportion to strength being involved in the performance of the skill. This includes speed, because strength is important in determining speed.

Skill Examples: 1. Sprinters in track require more warm-up than distance men. Weight men require a good warm-up because of the tremendous strength involved.

2. Basketball players require considerable warm-up because of the speed involved in the game. The same can be said of football players, tennis players, baseball players, etc.

3. Throwing calls for a longer warm-up because speed and strength are necessary to initiate action.

More warm-up is necessary on cold days than on warm days, along with the application of strength in the activity. The coach and athlete should analyze the degree of strength involved and warm up accordingly.

PRINCIPLE VIII

Improvement in any skill is dependent upon proper increase of the resistance to the performance of the skill.

Resistance takes many different forms in its application to varied skills. One activity might involve weight as resistance, another speed and another endurance or combinations of these and other forms not mentioned. The important thing to remember is that resistance in any form should be continually increased.

Skill Examples: 1. The four-minute barrier in track has been surpassed mainly because of adherence to this principle in training. The technique of interval running (sprint, jog, walk, sprint) is the application of this principle. Over a period of time the runner builds up tremendous effort as a result of having increased the resistance to performance.

2. Weight-lifting in an effort to build strength applies this principle. Each day or week the weights are increased and the amount of work becomes greater.

3. Both sprint and distance swimmers also improve by training under conditions which increase effort, the same as track men.

All activities should increase the resistance to effort in one form or another.

Differences in good and poor performance, both in teaching and training, are based, at least inpart, on adherence to certain fundamental principles. Although this article has not attempted to list all principles of movement, nor give all possible examples, it has discussed some that are considered important to many different forms of activity. If these and other principles of movement are kept in mind, teaching and learning should help to improve performance, as well as make the activities easier and more enjoyable.

CHAPTER 29

GET THE RIGHT BOY IN THE RIGHT JOB

Don Veller[*]

IT IS AXIOMATIC with leaders in business and industry, a highly competitive group, that they must get the right man in the right job. This is so vital that annually they spend many thousands of dollars and countless man-hours to help assure success in this important area. Athletic coaching is similar to industry in many ways, but perhaps none more so than in this phase which pertains to placing people in their most effective positions.

Next to influencing players to perform to their maximum abilities, wanting to do the things the coach wants them to do, we feel strongly that solving this personnel problem successfully is the most important and certain road to successful coaching.

The typical coach does not give this vital area sufficient emphasis. He is too busy with other matters, technical details, "X's and O's," etc.

Astute evaluation of personnel is an inexorable prelude to getting the "right man in the right job." Hammer[1] says players can be measured by: (1) How well they do the required things; (2) How much they know; (3) How fast they are improving; (4) What kind of an attitude they have; and (5) Their dependability.

Some key factors involved in selecting personnel are said to be: (1) Background of the coach; (2) System or style being used; (3) Position openings; (4) Size of the squad; (5) Specific requirement of the particular sport, i.e. tall in basketball, love

---

[*] Don Veller, "Get the Right Boy in the Right Job," *Athletic Journal*, Vol. 46 (March 1966), pp. 46-54 and 85-87.

1. William Hammer, *Football Coach's Complete Handbook* (Englewood Cliffs, N. J., Prentice-Hall, Inc., 1963), p. 25.

of contact in football, etc.; and (6) Various other factors such as weight, build, speed, etc.

At best, evaluating personnel is a difficult job. The following story illustrates that although this knack comes more naturally to some than to others, even the gifted talent hunters occasionally make mistakes. It is generally accepted that the late Branch Rickey was a keen judge of talent, but could not transfer this ability to his scouts; so he gave them a rule-of-thumb to use on a prospect: "Can he run? Can he throw? Can he hit?"

His method produced nine pennants for the Cardinals in the next twenty-one years. Then he moved on to Brooklyn, where his farm system was already in operation under one of his many proteges, Larry MacPhail. Flatbush farmhands fashioned two more flags under Rickey in 1947 and 1949.

In *The Official Encyclopedia of Baseball*,[2] it is said of Rickey: "Rickey himself has a matchless gift for evaluating the baseball potential of even the most callow teen-ager . . . 'putting a dollar sign on a muscle,' his admirers termed it."

On the other hand, *The History of Baseball*[3] tells about Joe Garagiola and Yogi Berra working out at Sportsman's Park in St. Louis with the Cardinals. Both were sixteen years old.

"Rickey," says the book, "gave Garagiola many silvery words, a modest bonus of $500, and a contract with Springfield, Missouri of the Western Association."

And Berra?

"Yogi received only advice. 'You'll never be a ball player,' Rickey told the disheartened Berra. 'Take my advice son, and forget about baseball. Get into some other kind of business.'"

Tests which purport to predict success have been designed for almost every sport. We have received numerous questionnaires from graduate students who in research projects were hopefully seeking foolproof methods or devices for forecasting future levels of success for the young athlete. They were noble gestures, but most of them were returned with a discouraging note

2. Hy Turkim and S. C. Thompson, *The Encyclopedia of Baseball* (New York, A. S. Barnes and Co., 1963), p. 21.

3. Allison Denzig and Joe Riechler, *The History of Baseball* (Englewood Cliffs, N. J., Prentice-Hall, Inc., 1959), pp. 260-261.

simply because they did not include the necessary ingredients for measuring certain vital factors. To be useful a test would have to include a section which prognosticates ability to perform under competitive pressure—a prediction of the athlete's future performance as to spirit, determination, aggressiveness and other such intangibles. To this date no such test has been devised.

For many years industrial psychologists have advocated the principle that the best predictive test of ability is a sampling of the performance in the activity in which the prediction is desired. Nevertheless, the competitive coach must constantly attempt to prognosticate and/or measure the spirit of a candidate. He will save considerable time and trouble if he can answer this question early on each athlete, "Does the boy have that competitive urge so vitally necessary for excellence in athletic participation?" If evaluation indicates clearly that a candidate lacks that qualification, then the coach had best forget him.

Many things cannot be taught—improved on, yes, but not taught from scratch. For example, the accident of birth—having the right father and mother—is the most significant factor in making a boy a shifty ball-carrier, a fast runner or in possessing large bones, big hands, to name a few. A coach is somewhat like the horse trainer, who can almost always improve the speed of the animal, but, "he cannot make a Kentucky Derby winner out of a plow horse."

The qualities necessary for excellence in an athlete vary in importance depending upon the nature of the sport. For instance, football demands in addition to competitive spirit, agility, speed and size, in that order. Then there is the athlete's inherent inclination for cooperating with the coach and his peers, along with his motor ability and intelligence.

Dana Bible[4] in his book, *Championship Football*, aptly lists the important ingredients of a football player as the five S's—spirit, speed, skill, size, and savvy. All, or most of these qualities will apply in other sports to a greater degree as the level of competition rises.

---

4. Dana Bible, *Championship Football* (Englewood Cliffs, N. J., Prentice-Hall, Inc, 1948), p. 5.

In basketball, perhaps after competitive spirit would come such factors as muscle-eye coordination, shooting ability, agility and height.

The previously mentioned illustrations are only for two sports. These and other sports call for particular talents, but all demand the one great common denominator, competitive spirit, a burning desire to excel.

Selecting and evaluating personnel in the individual-type sports is more objective and therefore much simpler than in team sports such as football and basketball. At least that is so if we mean which athletes should currently be playing on the first team—and not necessarily predicting future performance. To find the first, second and third best 100-yard dash men, a coach should run them against each other, or compare their times. In golf, tennis, wrestling and swimming, it is almost as simple. There is still one question, however, which is still unanswered by practice performance, alone, even in the individual-type sports. "How will the boy perform in a game or meet?"

Consider the case of a high school boy who could broad jump well over twenty-two feet in practice, but who never reached twenty feet in meet competition; whereas, a teammate was a nineteen-footer in practice and a twenty-one footer in meets. Even though such stories are rather common in sports circles, coaches are still admonished to observe and weigh carefully the athlete's performance "when the bell rings."

Let us return to selecting players in team sports, a job that is difficult at best. It is admittedly frustrating in team sports to measure one player against another, especially since there are so many ramifications, combinations of play situations and skills. Evaluation is most often subjective and thus less accurate.

The use of films has been a tremendous help. A careful analysis is possible with movies and the grading is much more objective. But even with the use of films, and constant attention and comparison of notes, the coach is often in a dilemma as to whether he has the best players in the game. Often, after making what he thought was a wise choice, results proved he was wrong. Yet, movies can be a coach's best friend when it comes to evaluating performance. The universal use of high school films by college coaches for selecting grants-in-aid is patent evidence of the accuracy and value of that media for selecting talent. Another testimonial for the efficacy of movies is exemplified by so many coaches, who when asked by newsmen to point out their stars, answer, "I really cannot say until we have studied the films."

Consultation with other squad members is one of the most commonly overlooked aids in choosing personnel. With the proper approach, a great deal can be learned by asking a player in a subtle manner such questions as: "Which one of our players would you rather not have on the opposing team?" Specific positions or qualities also may be selected for questioning. Judicious use of such inquiry can be invaluable, especially in the case of the more doubtful positions. Do not worry about peers not being honest and frank with their judgments of each other. They will be.

Statistics in scrimmages, or in games after the season has started, are being utilized increasingly to help rate personnel. The number of tackles, bad passes, rebounds, hits, errors and effective blocks are common examples of these statistics. The inherent difficulty in analyzing and/or observing such things during the fast, tense action of a contest or scrimmage, dictates that the astute coach record and use such statistics. Successful football, and some basketball coaches, are spending many hours grading players through films with the results tabulated in written form. Although not fully developed thus far, electronic computers are being used increasingly for collecting and interpreting data on athletic performance. Watch for wide use of this device in the very near future.

Just as there is more than one right system of play, there are many different, effective ideas or gimmicks for selecting personnel. In football, for example, we have always believed that the best single device for discovering football aptitude is a simple head-on tackling drill. This drill will not expose certain special skills which are closely related to the game, such as the ability to pass or punt, but it will certainly measure a boy's taste for contact. Although there is no proof, we believe this same drill will measure or predict competitive ability for use in other sports, basketball for instance. No doubt, there are other predictive drills in the various other sports, but space precludes such a discussion in this article.

Aptitude analysis charts have been used successfully in various forms and levels of competition. One suggested chart on the high school level was used to acquaint coaches with aptitudes of new players coming in from junior high. Among other things the youngster was rated by his former coaches, principal and teachers on competitive spirit, attendance at practices, interest in sports, intelligence, etc. Such a written record of a prospect may save many hours of guessing and trial-and-error on the part of the high school coach.

A rating sheet[5] for practice performance has been successfully used to help select personnel in football. Using a specially constructed chart, coaches rated players on such items as blocking, tackling, willingness to learn, teamwork and attitude. Not only will such a chart help the coach in selecting personnel, but it will motivate and aid player morale by indicating in black and white the reasons why they are playing or not playing. Similar charts for sports other than football could also be devised.

Whether or not an actual written chart is used, it is essential that case histories be studied. It is important to know even such a simple thing as a youngster's age. Consider the case of the coach who becomes enthusiastic about a big boy who performs well in junior high school, only to learn much later to his chagrin that the lad was sixteen years old at the time. The chances for such a boy to improve appreciably are slight.

Coaches should know the parental background of each candidate. Boys from certain racial extractions will mature at a younger age than others. Those from southern European forefathers, for example, seem to blossom earlier, whereas those from such stock as German and Scandinavian mature later. Are athletes from lower socioeconomic groups better? No conclusive studies have been made, but in certain sports, at least, there would seem to be advantages to the boy who has come from a

---

5. John M. Austin, "Rating Scale for Practice Performance," *Athletic Journal* (September 1956), p. 54.

rugged, hard-toiling family. Perhaps these athletes have not been spoiled by soft home conditions. At least they often seem to be endowed with more ability and desire to endure and perform hard work.

Some sociologists and others use these factors to explain the rapid ascendance of the Negro and first generation American athletes to prominence in recent years. They point out, as we have, that the boy from the higher socioeconomic level is more likely to be self-satisfied, or at least not oriented to the arduous physical toil necessary to become a top athlete. The lower ethnic group, however, does not possess all the advantages. A recent study pointed out, for instance, that in a highly competitive salesmanship situation the higher socioeconomic group excelled over that of a less affluent group.

Perhaps such an argument will never be settled, but there is incontrovertible evidence to support the premise that the unspoiled lad has a tremendous advantage in athletic competition, but like the American Indian, his ilk is rapidly vanishing from the scene. It is true that a candidate from the lower socioeconomic group will probably have had less opportunity for experience in such activities as tennis and golf. Therefore, it can most likely be expected that a youngster from a more affluent family background will be a stronger contender in those sports.

Woody Hayes[6] in his book, *Football at Ohio State,* says that coaches soon recognize the boy who comes from a good home. He goes on to say, "To us a good home does not infer affluence whatsoever. We feel that a good home is one in which the youngster was shown in many ways that he was wanted. He was never shunted. That youngster who is wanted in a home is the one who almost invariably will react well under pressure for he does have a sense of security which is so extremely necessary in meeting pressure." Such things as domestic trouble, arguing between mother and father, can alter an athlete's personality and character. Without this case history the coach may be treating symptoms only and cannot intelligently improve a candidate's performance.

6. Woody Hayes, *Football at Ohio State* (Columbus, Ohio, The Ohio State University, 1957), p. 180.

The incidence of tardiness and absence from school can often be used as an attitude barometer and therefore should be carefully scrutinized and weighed when examining a boy's case history.

Knowing his physical defects, if any, is significant, too. For instance, in football a boy with defective vision might be better suited to the line than the backfield. This sort of defect may easily go unnoticed unless the coach is circumspect in such matters.

Obviously, a candidate with such a defect as a heart condition could be a poor present and future risk, not only for himself, but for the team and coach. Although all state high school associations and colleges now require medical examinations, many athletes are still being given approval to participate despite dangerous physical abnormalities. Busy doctors and careless coaches have unwittingly collaborated to make this possible.

When and if coaches carefully evaluate each candidate daily, the players will soon learn to evaluate themselves. This is good, for in any guidance program the ultimate of guidance is self-direction.

May we emphasize again that most coaches spend too little time on evaluation of personnel, and we have yet to learn of one who stresses this phase to excess. Yes, getting the right boy in the right job is a never-ending task.

In football, for instance, it seems foolish to spend weeks, days or even hours, trying to develop an effective quarterback out of a boy who may really lack natural ability for the position, when perhaps switching, say an end to that slot might solve the problem quickly and effectively. Such prudent switches from one position to another often make the difference between a losing and winning season. Merely switching positions around, of course, is not a panacea, but do not be afraid to make changes when they seem logical. Each day the coach should ask himself, and the other coaches, the question, "What position changes, if any, can be made today to make us a better team?"

How about the high school coach who plays his best pitcher only when he is pitching, even though he is also his best hitter? Perhaps by placing him in the outfield when not on the mound would have made the difference between a mediocre and a very good team.

Then there is the case of the meanest, toughest, strongest boy on the football team playing end on both offense and defense, where he has the opportunity to participate only in about half of the plays at the most. The team's effectiveness might be doubled by moving this player to fullback on offense and perhaps to middle linebacker on defense. Good players are scarce. Do not waste them.

A word of admonition here for the coach who has a compulsion for making wholesale changes when he loses. It is tempting to look for scapegoats and position shake-ups, when perhaps the winner just had better material, or even better coaching.

Daily and careful evaluation will assure that the five best basketball, the eleven best football or the nine best baseball players are on the first team. There may be a valid reason, but we doubt it, for having two strong players competing against each other at center when either of them could play forward more effectively than one of the starters in that position. Do not let a better player sit on the bench. Besides the scarcity of constant, daily, thoughtful evaluation, this situation is often merely the result of a reluctance to change, a human weakness in the case of many, it seems. A first team is often selected and that is it. Bear in mind, too, that youngsters fluctuate in performance. Not only do they progress, but they often regress as well. Watch for these changes. Such a policy will help assure that the best athletes will be playing, and in addition all squad members will be on their toes, realizing that successful performance means advancement and vice versa.

It is well to review occasionally the prerequisites for certain positions. Have coaches ever thought of actually writing a job description for each position? Industry does it, and they consider it a most important facet in the efficient utilization of personnel. A reminder here that qualifications for a position often change as the season or years go by, and job descriptions must be updated occasionally by the coaching staff.

Personnel evaluation is so important it even determines, or should determine, in most cases, what system a coach will em-

ploy, especially in the team sports. For instance, a smart basketball coach who has slow players would not select a fast break offense or a full-court press. The key factor, of course, is
whether or not the coach has evaluated his team's speed correctly.

Some coaches are pressured by fans and news media into using
a certain popular system of play when really the available personnel is not suited to it. Systems may be compared to girls'
dresses. Girls who have ugly knees would present a more attractive appearance in longer dresses, even though bare knees are in
style. There is really only one sound criterion. Does the system
operate most effectively with the current personnel?

It is a truism that we are going to like some people better
than others. Anyone who claims otherwise is definitely deluding
himself. Even parents have favorites among their children. The
problem then is for the coach to take stock of this human weakness and not simply choose the good boy over the better performer, merely because he likes him better. Usually this is an in-
voluntary act and coaches are unaware they are doing it. Just
good boys cannot win, they must be players too. So stay alert for
this human weakness.

Conversely, it is easy to get *down* on a boy to the point where
the coach just will not give him a fair chance. The coach may
conceive of himself as a friendly, helpful person to all his candidates, accepting and treating them equally. But how he actually feels may be a different thing. These feelings may show without his being aware of them. Like playing favorites, this preju-
dicial action will preclude a coach's playing his best performers. As suggested previously, it is more difficult to win when one
or more of the first team players is sitting on the bench.

In a sport which places a premium on size, a good big man is
obviously more effective than a good little one, and this
prompts a coach occasionally to ignore the smaller boy. Conversely, the coach is often prone to let the little boy's popularity
and/or scrap influence him to play him too much.

Coaches at some time or another in their careers are confronted with the possibility, or shall we say temptation to play the

sons of important people, i.e. school board members and politicians, over athletes who have greater talent.

We cite a true case which illustrates this point. One of our colleagues substituted a politician's son on a very good 880-yard relay foursome. Weakened by this substitution the relay team lost, came in second and did not qualify for the state finals in which they were favorites to win first place. This was obviously unfair to everybody, the school, the relay team, the remainder of the squad and especially to the substitute. Neither the coach nor the substitute ever lived it down.

Shouts or chants from the stands are often heard encouraging the coach to play favorite sons, neighbors, fraternity brothers and the like. Such suggestions come more frequently to replace boys who obviously are not doing so well, or when the team is losing. These spectators are usually unaware of extenuating circumstances which may preclude such moves, i.e. legal time-outs exhausted, replacement cannot play defense, does not know assignments, has been ill or injured, etc. When such advice comes from the stands, the best move is to ignore it. If it comes face-to-face, then a courteous reply is usually appropriate. He can always privately reserve the right to make his own decisions. All this is part of coaching.

We would like to cite an incident pertinent to this discussion which happened on the first day of our coaching career. Before football practice started officially, the high school candidates were out on the practice field, kicking and passing the ball around informally, and we were merely looking them over for the first time. A spectator came up from behind and said, "Coach, see that number 32 over there? He will never make a football player. He simply does not have it." Well, we do not remember that spectator's name, or even what he looked like, but we do remember "that 32." During his senior year, he made eighteen touchdowns, was unanimous choice for all-state and subsequently became a college star. The moral of this story is obvious.

Correct substitution is an art never mastered but employed to better advantage by some coaches than by others. If one basic rule is used as a guide, this strategic weapon can be employed more successfully. Substitutions should be made to strengthen the team's chances of victory. Yes, there is a genuine art to substituting, and many a contest has been lost by injudicious use of this opportunity.

Again, the winning coach knows his players, their qualifications, idiosyncrasies, weaknesses and potentialities. A specific case is exemplified by the coach who became aware that a certain boy was overly keyed up, and exceedingly nervous before each contest. He decided to start another player and then substitute the high-strung player after two or three minutes had elapsed. The results were most gratifying. Not only did the player like the idea, but his contribution to the team increased considerably.

Substitution procedures must be thoroughly planned and rehearsed prior to a contest. Various possibilities should be geared to the game plans with alternatives in mind as the game situation changes.

The seating arrangement on the bench should be so organized that key players are close to the coach or coaches who are doing the substituting. Substitutes should have specific places to sit, not be spread all over the bench in a nondescript manner. Insist, too, that all players sit on the bench and stand up only when they are beckoned to by a coach.

When assistant coaches participate in the substituting, careful correlation must be exercised in order that duplications and other such mix-ups are avoided.

Many defeats, especially in close contests, can be attributed to coaches who fail to remain calm and collected during tense moments. An overexcited condition precludes sound decisions by the coach, including substitutions.

Play all the boys possible short of losing a contest. In addition to providing game experience for future regulars, the coach will make many boys and parents happy, and endear himself to the opposing coach. In addition, the contest will be more interesting to the spectators. We believe that no coach has ever been able to justify the decision to run up the score on an opponent.

Take the case of the high school football coach who was not scored upon, and in order to keep his record unblemished, kept his first team of seniors in almost all the time, even when far ahead. In the next-to-last game three key men were injured, and unable to play in the last contest. The replacements had experienced very little game action and through this weakness the victory string was broken. There went his undefeated season. The next year was disastrous, too, largely because the returning players had very little playing experience.

Praise the substitutes at every opportunity and give attention to the most obscure members of the squad. The morale of many teams has been undermined by disgruntled substitutes or tailenders who felt they were not being given a fair chance. Prudent coaches provide scrimmage sessions on Monday for substitutes and all those who did not get a chance to play on the week-end. The coach should give them the feeling he is looking them over.

Sometimes a coach will let a boy sit on the bench because he was angry with him, a player who might have made the difference between winning and losing for his team. Not only is this stupid, but it is unfair to the other players.

We believe implicitly that seniors should not be substitutes for seniors. Perhaps there are isolated occasions where this might not be feasible, but when at all possible plan to have an underclassman competing against a senior. As a result, next year's regulars will have a better opportunity to get needed game experience. Imagine the plight of the basketball coach who had four senior guards, four senior forwards, and one senior at center? In rare cases it might just happen that way, but many coaches bring it on themselves by not planning for the years ahead. Playing seniors against seniors will often lead to a top-heavy senior situation —and that can be bad.

The correct size of a squad is dictated by the particular sport, the number of coaches available, facilities, schedule and enrollment of the school. When the squad becomes so large that all candidates cannot be kept busy, given proper attention and made to feel important, then it is too large. Do not allow the squad to become top-heavy with seniors.

Coaches who are familiar with physiological and psychological testing realize that there is a positive relationship between general intelligence and athletic prowess. Therefore, other things being equal, it would seem better to spend more time with the better-than-average student than with the borderline probationary athlete, even though his skills are advanced.[7] Also, the flimsy eligibility status of the poor student may make him a poor risk.

We do not mean to infer that only Phi Beta Kappa prospects should be used in athletics. History has disproved this premise. John Lawther[8] declares that democracy is not based on the idea of the world being ruled by an intellectual oligarchy. An attitude that favors to a great degree those academically apt individuals is a form of intellectual snobbery. Industry, devotion to duty, productiveness, morality and common sense are not special traits chiefly characteristic of the high I.Q. This does not mean that the coach should reward poor academic work. In contrast, he must constantly stress the importance of scholarship, especially now that it is so necessary for entrance into college.

In addition to natural ability, there are other factors to be recognized in selecting the event or position which a candidate should play. Industrial psychologists are aware of and have stressed that employees will perform better when they are working in jobs they like. The same is true in the case of athletes. Although not always possible, the coach should work toward such an end at all times. Try to give the young neophyte his preference and the chances are more than good that it will be the correct spot for him. It usually works out that way. If he and his chosen position or event are completely incompatible, then the coach can direct a change. Boys often choose a position of a longtime desire, or because their father or brother or another hero played that spot. Therefore, the coach must be circumspect if and when he changes him, and when doing so should make every effort to influence him to be satisfied with and understand the reason for the shift. This is particularly true if the new job is known to be less desirable or less glamorous, such as a shift of a back to the line in football. Never change a boy's

---

7. Glen Wilkes, *Basketball Coach's Complete Handbook* (Englewood Cliffs, N. J., Prentice-Hall, Inc., 1962), p. 298.

8. John Lawther, *The Psychology of Coaching* (Englewood Cliffs, N. J., Prentice-Hall, Inc., 1960), p. 185.

position without talking to him first. For more effective performance, we repeat, a boy should like the position in which he is competing.

The enterprising high school coach will be more concerned with where the boy is needed now, rather than worrying about whether he is playing in his future college position.

When selecting and evaluating a player, the coach is admonished to be truthful to him (and his parents) as to his capabilities. Naturally, the coach will want to develop each athlete to his greatest potential, but it is unfair to build up hopes that the boy will become a great athlete unless he really has the potential. For proper *esprit de corps* in the human being a happy balance must be established between aspirations and potential achievement. Therefore, building up the hopes of an individual or a team far above their potential achievement possibilities will most likely produce negative morale. Human beings judge the value of their experiences by relating accomplishments.

Prudent coaches are constantly alert to make certain that they have all the potential talent in school out for the team. One criticism frequently leveled at the losing coach is, "There are lots of boys around school who are good enough to make the team, but they just will not come out." Potential athletes can be found and recruited in various ways: by word of mouth, elementary and junior high athletic events, bulletin board notices, assembly programs or physical education classes, to name a few. Be sure that every potential athlete has been contacted, but if a boy indicates he does not really like the sport, forget him. That is the best reason of all for his not participating.

Frequently a good-looking young prospect who is not out will give the excuse that his parents will not give him permission to participate. We have never yet known a parent who would deny such a request if the boy honestly wants to come out and was persistent enough. In a case of this kind, or at any other time, however, a coach should not promise the parent that the boy will not be injured.

Our parting shot is this. Remember that the selection and evaluation of personnel potential will not win for a coach. It is performance that counts. Know the difference.

CHAPTER 30

RECIPE FOR ALL-AMERICANS

EUGENE SOBOLEWSKI*

THE TITLE "ALL-AMERICAN" is a symbol of excellence that many boys dream of but few achieve. Though fans may argue about certain selections, there is little doubt that any boy tapped for such an honor is an excellent athlete.

Many coaches and parents also dream of seeing their boy make All-American. But some of them, through ignorance or lack of dedication, hamper the boy's chances. Although every boy cannot make All-American, there have been many who could have made it but, for one reason or another, did not.

There is no magic formula or special program for developing the superstar. The number of contributing factors is enormous. What is more, the factors that help one boy may hinder another. Nevertheless, there are three elements which positively influence the development of All-Americans—athletic experience, parental guidance and coaching background.

To pinpoint the significance of these factors, the author sent questionnaires to the ninety-seven boys on the 1966 *Scholastic Coach* High School All-American Football Team. Of the ninety-seven questionnaires mailed, sixty-five were returned. The factors studied were:

Athletic Training in Grades One-Six

Many coaches question the value of athletics in the early elementary grades, and most physicians are violently opposed to such programs because of the possibility of injury to immature bones. However, fifty-six of the sixty-five respondents indicated

---

* Eugene Sobolewski, "Recipe for All-Americans," *Scholastic Coach,* Vol. 37 (October 1967), pp. 66-69.

that they had participated in organized competitive sports before entering junior high school, with the average boy beginning in the fourth grade.

Little League Baseball (50), Midget Basketball (32), and Midget Football (33) led the list of prejunior high activities. It is interesting to note that the highly organized Little League program drew many of the boys to baseball, and that *all of the responding quarterbacks* participated in the baseball program!

Junior High Athletic Background

In most areas, competitive athletics begin on the junior high school level. But junior high coaches often make the mistake of creating specialists—boys who participate in just one sport. They fail to realize that every sport has some carryover value to others and that variety prevents a boy from becoming stale or bored with one game.

Sixty-four of the sixty-five respondents participated in junior high athletics. The single exception, a youngster from Germany, began competition in high school immediately upon arriving in this country.

Our select group had well-rounded careers prior to high school, with baseball (51), basketball (56), and football (61) again the leading sports. Interestingly, five of the sixty-one junior high footballers were only substitutes in the ninth grade.

Varsity Athletic Background

At the varsity level, interest in baseball declined. Only twenty-nine boys continued their baseball careers, while forty-six played basketball. All sixty-five, of course, played football.

Two of the boys did not go out for varsity football until the tenth grade, but both did have prior experience in football as well as other sports. Fifteen were substitutes as sophs, and one was still a sub as a junior. Of the sixty-five respondents, fifty-nine played either baseball and/or basketball in high school, thus demonstrating that most of the boys did not specialize in football even in high school.

Parental Background

The parents' influence on a boy's athletic career may be just as important as their influence on his choice of vocation. At this age, a boy requires the encouragement and support that only his parents can provide. The parents of sixty-two of the respondents favored their boys' athletic participation in the elementary grades.

Fifty-nine boys said that their fathers were real sports fans and most of them found healthy attitudes toward athletics in their homes. This type of parental feeling clearly influences the boy's mental attitude in athletics.

The fathers of thirty-nine of the boys had participated in high school athletics, with twenty-nine having played football. Thirteen continued to play in college and eight played semi-pro or pro football.

Interestingly, the boys whose fathers played football beyond the high school level tended to rate their coaches poorer than the other boys. This was probably due to the counseling they received from their dads.

Coaching Background in the Elementary Grades

Another crucial factor in the development of a boy's athletic career is his early coaching. The elementary-level coach must be well-qualified or he might harm a boy more than help him. Of the fifty-six boys who participated in elementary-school sports, forty-six felt they had received good coaching.

The questionnaire asked the boys to evaluate all of their elementary-school coaches. The 285 coaches who directed the fifty-six boys in elementary-school baseball, basketball and football were rated as follows: Great coach (91), Wish he was my father (12), Taught me a lot (133), Knew a lot about the sport (130), Poor coach (44), Loud mouth (23), Did a lot of swearing (14), and Knowledge of the sport was limited (50).

Summary

Athletic experience, parental influence and elementary coaching are significant in the development not only of an All-American, but of any athlete.

A coach's success is also determined by the talent available to him. Few coaches can win consistently without good material. Athletic development, therefore, should begin as early as possible. A well-rounded program in the early grades not only increases a youngster's athletic potential, but also fills his need for supervised activity.

A community elementary athletic program should be supervised by the high school head coaches. The major goals of such a program should be the development of athletic skills and the establishment of proper mental attitudes.

A healthy athletic environment in the home is an important asset to a boy. The wise coach will meet with parents to explain his program and suggest ways they can help their child. The old adage, "Never underestimate the power of a woman," is quite applicable to coaches, especially if that woman happens to be a player's mother.

No program can be more successful than its leadership. Competent coaches will develop first-rate players, mediocre coaches will develop second-rate athletes.

CHAPTER 31

ARE WE REALLY COACHING FUNDAMENTALS?

PAUL E. MEADOWS*

The three stages in coaching fundamentals are: knowledge of correct and incorrect fundamentals, selection and presentation of fundamental drills, and recognition and adjustment of correctable faults. Each is essential to the learning process; the elimination or de-emphasis of any one results in ineffective fundamental coaching. Attention is given here to stage three, which has often been neglected by coaches; the challenge is to discover the best technique for adjusting the correctable fault. An awareness of the mechanics of movement in all phases of sport skills increases the coach's effectiveness and demonstrates itself in improved performances by the individual player and the team.

"COACH ANDERSON'S SUCCESS is due to his ability to teach fundamentals." "Coach Rawlings is an excellent fundamentalist." "Coach Sawyer's teams make few fundamental mistakes." We often hear such comments in teaching and coaching circles when the merits of a respected coach are being discussed. It is apparent that a coach who has a reputation for devoting considerable practice time to fundamental drills is favorably typed as a "sound fundamentalist"—a title which may enhance his coaching tenure even during the more difficult won-lost record seasons.

What are the important coaching principles necessary to qualify as a "sound fundamentalist"? Is the knowledge of the basic, intricate movements of the whole sport and the ability to impart this knowledge sufficient in attaining sound fundamental coaching? Do we have a tendency to be easily satisfied with our fundamental coaching as long as our drills are well organized, varied,

* Paul E. Meadows, "Are We Really Coaching Fundamentals?" *Journal of Health, Physical Education, and Recreation,* Vol. 34 (March 1963), pp. 34-35.

challenging and hold player interest during their rhythmical execution? Is it possible that we may be placing more emphasis on mass fundamental drill execution and actually becoming less sensitive and aware of the all-important "correctable faults" in our individual players?

It is vital that we recognize the difference between merely *exposing* our squads to fundamental drills and *coaching* fundamentals. In our haste to move through our practice plans, we may minimize our corrective approaches when confronted with an incorrect fundamental execution. This is particularly a temptation during the short weeks of practice prior to the opening game when a coach is confronted with practice plans that comprise not only offensive and defensive fundamentals but conditioning drills, strategy and chalk talk sessions, and break down drills leading up to the team's offensive and defensive maneuvers.

The important fundamental coaching task is incomplete unless we coach fundamentals in three stages. Each stage is interdependent and of equal importance in the learning process. The three stages are sequential and the elimination or de-emphasis of any one of them results in ineffective fundamental coaching. They are: stage one—*Knowledge of correct and incorrect fundamentals,* stage two—*Selection and presentation of fundamental drills,* and stage three—*Recognition and adjustment of correctable faults.*

How many times have we coaches become so absorbed in the first two stages that we have failed to place equal emphasis on stage three? For example, in basketball dribbling fundamental instruction we take time to explain finger-tip control, head up and flexed knee with an approximate mid-thigh height of bounce, and follow up with a demonstration of correct dribbling fundamentals. We then move into the organization of the dribbling fundamental drills and enthusiastically put our squad through the movements. The missing link, however, is our failure to take sufficient time prior to stage two to explain and differentiate between the proper and improper execution of the fundamental. We should also instill in our players an understanding of the common errors of execution. Only by doing this will the individual player be able to distinguish more capably between correct and incorrect execution and, therefore, increase the effectiveness of coaching stage three.

It is basic that knowledge of incorrect fundamental execution must be founded on correct fundamental knowledge. Only a coach who is well informed of the sound, fundamental parts of his sport can be an excellent diagnostician of fundamental errors. He is constantly looking for the correct in order to detect the incorrect.

The challenge in fundamental coaching occurs during the execution of the varied fundamental drills. As the players move through the drills, the coach observes the execution carefully and watches for deviations from the correct movement. The coachable moment appears when the experienced coach recognizes the phase of movement requiring correction. It is often necessary to allow the player to repeat his participation in the drill in order to further assist and confirm the coach's analysis.

The challenge of stage three is in deciding the technique to use to adjust the "correctable fault." The coach often resorts to shouting out corrective instructions to the player and then allowing him to continue on with the drill. Only if he felt the "correctable fault" was flagrant does he take individual action.

Selecting Corrective Techniques

Corrective action requires fundamental skill insight, time, patience and clarity of explanation of the deviation. The coach not only must be accurate in his analysis of the correctable fault as a part of the total fundamental movement, but he must determine whether his preliminary corrective technique will only stress the deviated part or the entire movement. For example, a jump shooter in basketball is shooting at a flat arc and the ball is striking the basket rim too hard with very little accuracy. The coach analyzes the deviation as being caused by allowing the ball to roll back in the hand as it is released. As a result, the ball is partially thrown out with corresponding poor arm elevation. He explains and describes the deviation to the player by stressing ball position in the hand as it is supported by the opposite arm and as the ball is released in the upward swing of the shooting arm. By stressing the deviated part with repetitive arm movements and simulated shooting, the coach establishes a part correctable fault concept to the player. A follow-up demonstration by the coach or another player of the proper execution of the complete jump shooting movement reinforces the coaching of the deviation. It allows the player to visualize the correctable fault in the total movement phase prior to his execution of the complete movement again.

Combining Fundamental Movements

Combining two or more complete fundamental movements into one fundamental drill is utilized by the coach in warm-up drills, advanced fundamental practice plans and in breakdown drills leading up to offensive patterns of play. It is in the combining of fundamentals into one specific drill that the correctable fault frequently appears at the point where the first complete fundamental movement ends and the second begins. This usually occurs when the player merges the two complete movements too rapidly. In basketball, the excessive merging of the stride stop with the pivotal turn in offensive footwork fundamentals is common. Football coaches also have this excessive merging problem in varied fundamental drills, such as in the fundamentals of cross blocking and trap blocking from the three or four point lineman stance.

The experienced coach is ever aware of the deviations which may arise in combining fundamentals into one drill. He strives to eliminate the excessiveness of the correctable fault by early emphasis on single complete fundamental drill execution. Once he has determined that he has attained proper execution of each complete phase, only then should he enlarge his drill presentation with the combining technique. The more effectively the coach has established correct execution, and adjusted correctable faults in each individual fundamental phase, the less difficult will be his corrective approaches after combining the phases into one drill.

Coaching clinics are becoming increasingly popular every year; they are excellent ways for a coach to secure new ideas and techniques for his offensive and defensive attacks. He is particularly interested in discovering new and challenging practice drills for his teams. Many coaches evaluate the coaching lectures not only on new team play information but on the quantity and quality of new practice drill ideas.

In addition to this drill information, however, we also need to realize that fundamental coaching goes beyond a mere selection and presentation of varied drills. What is really vital is an improved knowledge and ability to analyze the mechanics of the fundamental phases within the drill. What are the key extensive and flexive movements that apply the major force in the execution? Is there a strong possibility of over-extension in the early or late phases of the movement and how can it be corrected? These are typical questions that a coach must ask himself and be in position to answer as his squad participates in stage two. An analysis of this type differentiates the fundamentalist from the *sound* fundamentalist, who strives to improve his knowledge of the mechanics of fundamental movement.

Analyzing Mechanics of Movement

Sound coaching requires vision beyond exposing our teams to fundamental drills. The fundamentalist job only begins at this point as the coach uses drills as a foundation for improved knowledge of deviations from correct execution. By adopting a philosophy of increased awareness and sensitivity to mechanics of movement in both single and combined fundamental phases, the coach increases the quality of his fundamental instruction. He may be further challenged through a study of body mechanics, kinesiological principles and cinematographical analysis to strengthen his knowledge of the deviations of the fundamental movements in his sport. The individual player, as the beneficiary of sound fundamental coaching, leads to improved overall team performance dividends. An evaluation of the total performance of each individual player will reflect whether the coach is really *coaching* fundamentals.

CHAPTER 32

THE COACH'S HANDBOOK

ANDREW GRIEVE*

ALTHOUGH EVERY COACH has a good idea of the philosophy and operation of his athletic program, he frequently is confronted by questions in twilight areas. He can do one of two things in such situations: bring the question to the athletic director or extemporize an answer.

How helpful it would be to have some sort of reference source on policy and procedure. By laying out both the philosophy and duties of the coaches, the athletic director can establish a solid foundation for the program, assure a smooth relationship between staff and administration, and promote efficiency.

The accompanying format for a Coaches' Handbook stems from a project of the Southern Zone of the New York State Council of Administrators of Health, Physical Education and Recreation.

Much of the information was culled from handbooks already in existence. The basic objective was to compile, as concisely as possible, all the information considered essential to the proper functioning of an athletic program. The emphasis was placed on the practical—the daily responsibilities of the coach—while avoiding the danger of over-specificity. The objective was not a rigid code of rules and regulations but a flexible outline that an A.D. could adapt to his own circumstances.

The basic outline of the Coaches' Handbook was set up as follows:

Introduction

1. Purpose: The information will be used almost daily by the

---

* Andrew Grieve, "The Coach's Handbook," *Scholastic Coach*, Vol. 38 (March 1969), pp. 58-61.

coach and will provide the answers to questions directed to him from many sources, such as those pertaining to training regulations, award systems, eligibility regulations.

2. A Statement by the Chief School Administrator. This will indicate two important factors to every coach; first, that the administrator strongly supports the athletic program as an educational experience to the students, and secondly, that he strongly supports the information and directives included in the publication.

Table of Contents

This will enable the coach to pinpoint any particular area in which information is needed rather quickly.

Statement of the Director's Responsibilities

Coaches must understand the extent of the A.D.'s responsibilities. This statement should be rather broad in nature, but should indicate that the A.D. is responsible for all facets of the athletic program and that he, in turn, is responsible to the various administrators in the school system.

This section can include a chart of the chain of command so that the coaches can readily comprehend the relationship of the A.D. to the many school officers. This sort of chart will vary from school system to school system.

Code of Ethics for Coaches

The handbook should attempt to remain as objective and as realistic as possible on this score. It is also imperative to list the individuals and groups with whom the coaches will have to cooperate. Many young coaches do not realize that the success of an athletic program depends upon a large number of people.

Staff Relationships with Noncoaching Personnel:
1. Administration.
2. Principals of the individual schools.
3. General faculty.
4. Athletic director.
5. Nonteaching school personnel (custodians, bus drivers, etc.)

6. Newspaper, radio and TV personnel.

7. College recruiters.

Staff Relationships with Coaching Personnel:

1. Between head coaches.

2. Between head coaches and assistants.

3. Between assistant coaches.

Community Relationships: public relations.

Relationships with Athletes:

1. Influence of coach in students' selection of a sport.

2. Making predictions or promises to students on their possible success in a particular sport.

3. Academic guidance.

4. Personal guidance.

Relationships with Opponents:

1. As home team.

2. As visiting team.

Relationships with Game Officials.

Length of Practice Sessions: Some states have regulations in this area.

Time Between Seasons.

Sharing Facilities.

Scouting Ethics.

Responsibilities of Coaches

This informs the coach of his many major and minor responsibilities. Some are quite obvious; others are often unrealized. All must be attended to to assure a smooth-functioning program.

1. Safety.

2. Verification of the completion of medical examinations.

3. Team lists.

4. Procedure when injuries occur: first-aid procedure, injury reports, insurance reports, returning to activity following injury or illness.

5. Attendance at practice sessions: coaches, athletes.

6. Trip arrangements and trip lists: The A.D. usually is responsible for arranging transportation, but the coach must provide him with pertinent information.

7. Care of facilities: The coach may not be responsible for such care but he should see that no undesirable conditions exist in play or practice areas, locker rooms, shower rooms, etc.

8. Securing facilities at conclusion of activity: lights and locking facilities.

9. Issue of equipment: storage of equipment, maintaining records if so responsible.

10. Care of equipment: verifying that equipment is not being misused or misplaced.

11. Inventory of equipment: at conclusion of season to verify needs for following season.

12. Budget request: requisition procedures.

13. Attendance at meetings: staff, league, others.

14. Financial records, where necessary.

15. Knowledge of eligibility regulations: verifying eligibility of team members according to school, league and state regulations.

16. Knowledge of game regulations: usually listed in state athletic handbook (which will be mentioned later).

17. Procedures for making announcements: relaying important information to players.

18. Use of bulletin boards.

19. Award lists and procedures: maintaining records of participation.

ATHLETES' RESPONSIBILITIES

Responsibilities of the Athletes: Much of this information should be relayed by the coaches. They should be familiar with the various rules and regulations which affect the athletes, and it is advisable to indicate such information in a *Players' Handbook:*

1. Changing sports during a season.
2. Dropping from teams.
3. Attendance requirements.
4. Social attitudes.

Transportation Regulations: This will provide the coach with information on arranging transportation and the rules that must be observed on trips.

Assignment of Facilities: The coach must realize that the A.D. often will have difficulty obtaining facilities, particularly when they must be shared by various groups. This section should explain how assignments are made.

Team Training Regulations: These must be standard for all teams, as it would be unfair for one coach to be tougher or easier than another. This would immediately create internal problems.

School Eligibility Regulations: Most schools have eligibility regulations which supplement state or league eligibility regulations and are mostly concerned with academic achievement. These should apply to all athletes, with no exceptions made or requested.

Field or Court Preparation: Such requests are usually directed through the A.D. and the coach should know the proper procedure to follow. A coach should never go over the head of the A.D.

Game Result Procedures: Set procedures should be observed in reporting game results. This information may be provided by someone other than the coach, but he must make certain that it is reported to the various media. This should include the telephone numbers of all the news media.

It is advisable to have a standard form on which the coach can report the game results to the A.D. in order to maintain records.

The compilation of statistics will vary. But the coach should know what is required in this area and whether he or someone else is responsible for the collection of such data.

Award Regulations: Standards should be set for athletic awards. The requirements may vary from sport to sport, but they should be clearly spelled out for each sport.

Staff Regulations: Some school systems have certain regulations applying to coaches. These may involve released time, required coaching assignments, teaching load while coaching, etc. All such regulations must be included in the handbook to preclude misunderstandings by the staff.

Legal Aspects: It is wise to emphasize the factors of negligence and liability. Many coaches are not familiar with these factors and it would be beneficial to include a short statement on them.

VARYING STATUTES

The legal statutes vary from state to state and a short resume on such factors as the liability of the school, the individual coach and the immunity factor, as it exists, is extremely helpful. A list of legal definitions may also be advisable.

Inserts: It is possible to include the following pertinent items in a small pocket at the front or rear of the handbook:

1. State Athletic Association Handbook: This will include the eligibility regulations, game regulations, etc.

2. National Federation Handbook: Some individuals may feel that this is not important, but the Handbook includes information which can be extremely useful.

3. List of Coaches: names and sports coached, school location and telephone number, home address and phone number.

4. List of Medical Personnel (including addresses and telephone numbers): doctors, dentists, ambulance, school nurse, hospital.

5. Other Important Telephone Numbers: police department, fire department.

6. Injury Report Form: sample copy.

7. Insurance Brochure: sample forms to be used in making reports, prepared data on coverage, procedures, etc. (supplied by various companies).

8. Salary Schedule for Coaching: This is an optional item, depending upon the situation.

These items have been included as inserts for two main reasons. First, several of these are printed materials which will save time and effort in the organization of the handbook. Secondly, coaches may prefer to post certain lists rather than include them in the handbook proper. The posting is greatly facilitated where these lists are included as inserts. When changes in such information (such as in staff and phone numbers) are necessitated, it will not be necessary to revise the entire handbook.

The sturdier the handbook, the longer it will last. The sheets could be placed in a ring type notebook, a spiral form or in a binder, all of which will give the book more professional appearance. Many schools have facilities and equipment for binding such books. It would also be advisable to provide an attractive cover.

This format is offered simply as a guideline. The rules and regulations will naturally vary for individual schools, but we believe we have included all the information that is basic to all coaches.

Where all this information is readily available, the staff member will not have to run to the A.D. each time he requires an answer to a problem. The result will be a smoother more efficient organization.

THE COACH AND
THE ATHLETE

CHAPTER 33

THE VIOLENT WORLD OF THE ATHLETE

Sherwyn M. Woods*

WE LIVE IN AN ALL TOO VIOLENT world. War and territorial aggression on the international scene and violent crime and riot on the domestic front have become so commonplace that we have become at least partially inured to their presence. Indeed, the foremost danger may be that we become so desensitized to the violence around us that we fail to mobilize whatever individual and collective potentials we possess to minimize and eliminate it. The question, "Why violence?" has occupied the minds of some of the world's greatest thinkers in Philosophy, Sociology, Psychology and Psychiatry. From the psychoanalytic viewpoint, Freud believed it was the inborn and biologically derived sexual and aggressive instincts (drives) that most determined man's psychological and behavioral development and maturation. Violence was a manifestation of these basic instincts in man, insufficiently tamed by the ego structure.

Modern psychoanalytic thinking has focused considerably upon those drives in man which are primarily adaptative in purpose, nondestructive in intent, and aimed toward coping with the environment in an active, vigorous, discovering and creative way. Such activities will henceforth be referred to as *assertive.* This is in contrast to *aggression,* which refers to those activities which are hostile in intent, destructive in purpose and aim for elimination or removal of the perceived irritation or threat. Using Marmor's definitions, it is useful to further distinguish between *force* and *violence.* Force refers to the application of power to influence, restrain, or achieve mastery over an object, but with-

---

* Sherwyn M. Woods, "The Violent World of the Athlete, *Quest,* Vol. 16 (June 1971), pp. 55-60.

out necessarily destructive intent. Violence, on the other hand, is a specific form of force intended to injure or destroy. Thus, violence is intimately linked to aggression and force is usually associated with assertion. Capacity for violence, certainly innate in man, is not inevitable. Indeed, a society which aspires to non-violent relatedness does well wherever possible to encourage those developmental experiences which substitute force for violence and assertion for aggression.

Sports and athletics, particularly those of bodily contact, usually reside in the gray area between aggression and violence and assertion and force. As such, they have a powerful positive potential to assist growth toward maturity through helping the individual to tame his capacity for aggression and violence while developing capacities for the appropriate, skillful and sensitive application of assertive force that characterizes the effective and mature person. On the negative side is the potential for reinforcing adaptative patterns which rely on aggression and violence, using circumstances like athletics to disguise and to hide the destructive and hostile intent. Athletic competition provides ample opportunities to release "stored aggression" that may reside in a given participant, such stored aggression usually arising from sources and life experiences (developmental) very far from the athletic field. Under the guise of the athletic competition, the individual is freed from the anxiety, guilt and control which must normally be maintained in other life circumstances. When the quantity of stored aggression is massive, either consciously or unconsciously, the athletic situation may be exploited as a culturally approved vehicle for explosive discharge and, therefore, potential mayhem.

PERSONALITY DEVELOPMENT

To put the issue into perspective, it may be useful to trace the evolution of assertion and aggression in the course of human personality development. To do this, I will draw heavily upon the psychosocial theories of Erik Erikson. The infant enters the world helpless and dependent upon those caring for him, making his needs known and demanding his due by application of the force of his wails upon the parent figure around him.

This is a diffuse and disorganized "attack" on the environment, and soon gives rise to the more coordinated and purposeful self assertions associated with sucking, biting, grasping, walking and toilet training. With the advent of speech, "No" is a favorite word, even when not meant, for it assertively establishes autonomy, distinctiveness and separateness. Indeed, "yes" and "no" are important in accomplishing the separation-individuation which takes place early in infancy.

With the onset of play behavior, there is a mounting degree of initiative (self-assertion) evident in the exploring, searching and discovering of the world. Indeed, it is important for the parent to allow the infant or child the maximum freedom of which he is safely capable and failure to do so results in pathological dependency which at the extreme results in childhood psychosis. When crossed or impeded, the natural tendency is aggressively to lash out or to attempt to be rid of that which would interfere with one's desires or wishes. Parental punishment, controls, consistent education and the feared loss of love begin the task which will ultimately be reinforced by family, neighborhood, school and society. This is the task of taming and controlling assertion and aggression. Hopefully, this will not be merely repressive control, but will at the same time encourage increasing skillfulness and capacity for appropriate self-assertion and the skillful application of necessary force.

In learning to be a civilized human being, the process of identification and modeling is of tremendous importance, with parents the foremost but by no means the only models. School age brings teachers as secondary sources of modeling and, particularly for the boy, the athletic coach. The task of school age is primarily that of learning, but not merely academic studies. Equally important is solidification of sex role and social role. The boy realizes one day he will be a man (and the girl a woman) and begins the struggle to learn those skills and attributes which his culture states he must attain to achieve self esteem and the esteem of others. It is during this time that the identification process is particularly strong as evidenced by the profound struggles to be like mother or father and also like one's heroes. For the boy especially, those heroes are often athletes and sports are quickly identified with the strength, dominance, assertiveness and competitive skill that our society equates with masculinity. This is maximized in the struggles of adolescence which are primarily centered around the struggle to achieve and unify sexual, social and self-sufficient identity free from excessive dependency upon parents or parental figures. Breaking free of parents, when identification and independence are still being sought rather than established, means seeking new models for identification.

For the boy, the athletic coach is an exceptionally powerful influence and model. Athletic skills, physical strength and prowess are highly equated in our culture with the attributes of masculinity sought by the adolescent male and easily symbolized in the figure of the coach. With the extended adolescence present in our society, this certainly extends into college years, particularly for those who maintain involvement in athletics. The nature of masculinity and femininity is largely determined by cultural values which associate certain characteristics with one or the other. For each culture certain figures epitomize these qualities which arouse the envy of the developing child and therefore offer a powerful source of desire to imitate and model and identify.

ATHLETICS AS A SOCIAL INSTITUTION

Sports and the athletic competition are valuable social institutions which provide superb opportunities to develop and solidify many of those factors leading to the establishment of a sound identity and the capacity to enter the world in a healthy and effective fashion. These opportunities encompass both the personal and interpersonal aspects of development and will be discussed under four general headings:

1. Development of personal skills (self)
2. Development of coordinated skills (others, team)
3. Competition
4. Hidden agendas

Without question athletics provide superb opportunities for the individual to develop and refine a whole host of personal skills including strength, muscular coordination, agility, speed and the associated intellectual skills. All are important ingredients of self esteem and a self image as a competent and effective person. Bodily image is a major contributor to our overall self image, and adequacy for most includes a sense of at least reasonable capacity to meet those life circumstances calling for effective use of the body skills. As previously indicated, this is particularly true for the male where the whole issue of physical strength and ability becomes highly tied to the issue of masculinity in both a social and sexual sense. However, both men and women require sufficient physical strength and ability to have the sense of security that arises from competence to handle the ordinary life circumstances. Such abilities are in many circumstances a powerful antidote to fear.

Fear and panic have a strong ability to precipitate violence. In fact, persons probably are more often moved to violence by fear and panic than by "stored aggression." A reasonable sense of physical adequacy goes a long way in helping to prevent situations which only require assertive force from degenerating via panic into aggressive violence. All of the above is of course of special importance when dealing with children and adolescents for much of their personal growth and development rests upon their competently learning to use their developing bodies.

To live in our society effectively, it is essential that a person develop the coordinated skills and the capacity to *work with* that are embodied in team athletics. A major issue in maturation consists of the capacity to relinquish at times one's self interest to the interest of others. The child learns that a sense of pride and accomplishment can be obtained not merely from one's individual accomplishments, but also from the sense of being a contributor to a group effort and group accomplishment. The narcissism of man is exceedingly powerful and it is only with difficulty that we learn to live comfortably and happily with others. Effective teamwork requires assertion and force; and when this degenerates into aggression and violence, the individual is usually no longer functioning in a coordinated team fashion because he is too caught up in his own emotional discharge.

In addition, of course, team work and effort provide rich and important social interaction, not the least of which is a culturally acceptable way of engaging in close and intimate relationships with members of one's same sex. These shared athletic interests continue to be an important vehicle for such relationships throughout life, even when team participation itself is abandoned.

The third issue is that of competition, which shall be defined very simply as "to put oneself against and struggle to emerge victorious." With respect to developmental maturation and personality development, I submit that the important issue for the subject at hand is "triumph over" (assertion) versus "demolish and destroy" (aggression). In reality, few life situations call for the latter, though certainly a multitude of social, sexual and vocational circumstances call for the former. Indeed, an important task of personality development is to equip oneself with the physical, social and intellectual tools which are the *sine qua non* for success in our competitive world. Athletic competition is extraordinarily rich in providing opportunities to establish effective patterns of assertion, as well as providing comfort in using them.

A great deal of competitive failure arises from inhibitions in assertion which arise from failure to distinguish assertion from aggression, force and violence. When this occurs, the individual withdraws from life's competitive situations because he is filled with a sense of guilt or anxiety about injuring or destroying the other; or, conversely, he withdraws from competition because the failure to distinguish assertion from aggression gives rise to fantasies that via retaliation he will himself be seriously injured or destroyed. Competitive athletics can be a life experience for the child or adolescent which helps him to make that distinction and develops a sense of capacity and competence for realistic competition. The elements are extremely complex and certainly include such issues as finding one's limits as well as learning to exert one's physical or other forces short of injury or violence.

Equally important in the issue of competition is the opportunity to lose, to discover that one can lose without being destroyed by the other and without losing self-esteem or self-respect. The lesson that self-respect and self-esteem are as much a product of effort as of outcome is of inestimable value for the individual who is undoubtedly going to fall down many times in life and needs the capacity to do so with dignity and self-respect. Equally important is to get up and try again if that indeed is a reasonable thing to do. When a coach loses with such attitudes in mind, he teaches an important lesson to his team. What he says is of minimal importance compared to what he in fact does.

Hidden agendas are those issues present in the athletic competition which are generally not admitted to, and which are not readily apparent. I am primarily concerned here with the issue of relief from emotional tensions of various varieties. Physical exercise has long been associated with relief from general emotional tension, stored anger and aggression, and sexual tension. For most, athletics provide a reasonable outlet for such tensions and assist general life adaptation. For some, however, the nature of quantum of the tension is such that the athletic participation is mainly geared toward satisfaction of this inner psychological agenda. With respect to aggression, the varieties are limitless; but in psychiatric practice two types of individuals stand out. The first is the person who is filled with rage, resentment, anger and hostility by way of his life circumstances and experiences, and who uses the athletic competition to discharge these feelings which may be blocked from discharge elsewhere. He may be noted by teammates as seeming to derive pleasure from the injury or pain of others, and to exceed the limit of necessary force, to be "short fused" and quick to anger, or to be quick to move athletic competition to athletic battle. The second is the athlete with obsessive preoccupation with winning to the point where all else is seen as complete and utter failure. This person often lacks tolerance for himself in many ways, struggles to be a super-man and his value to himself as a human being is dependent upon winning. Most often this represents a desperate attempt to overcome an innate sense of worthlessness and failure or it may represent an attempt to overcome a sense of general inadequacy and worthlessness. Not infrequently such individuals have grave doubts about their masculine adequacy and hope to stifle their anxieties through winning. The desperation involved may lead the individual to aggression and violence because he perceives the event not really as an athletic contest but instead as a life and death battle. Other "hidden agendas" include athletes who have fused sexuality and aggression, so that physical combat is consciously or unconsciously erotic and often sadistic pleasure. Independent of his prowess and capacity and independent of whatever success he achieves, the athlete with a major hidden agenda is an emotionally troubled person who is often desperately in need of professional assistance.

THE HIGH SCHOOL AND COLLEGE COACH

As indicated earlier, the coach is one of the most potent objects for identification for the young male. He symbolizes the strength, competitive competence, independence and masculinity that the child and adolescent are so desperately struggling to attain. Further, he is not a "parent" from whom one has the task of separating and therefore whose ideas must often be rejected out of hand. In the best of all possible worlds, where rationality prevailed, he would certainly be evaluated and paid not by whether or not his teams won, but in terms of what kind of men he helped to build. As a model for identification his actions, views and values are highly potent forces for educational change. The way in which he handles his anger and potential for violence, his capacity for assertive force versus aggression and violence, the way in which he handles both winning and losing—all will be duly noted.

Again, in the best of all possible worlds and with the best of all possible educational systems we would certainly have a training program which included heavy emphases upon developmental psychology and social and group processes. In addition, we would certainly encourage every potential coach to resolve his own emotional conflicts, through professional psychotherapy if indicated, particularly when the conflicts are related to the kinds of issues discussed here. For a man with such an important social role, we can ill afford not to for the stakes are too high.

CHAPTER 34

ATHLETES ARE NOT INFERIOR STUDENTS

Walter E. Schafer* and J. Michael Armer

In two Midwestern high schools, the athletes had obtained higher grade-point averages than nonathletes.

DOES THE HEAVY EMPHASIS on sports evident in most of our high schools interfere with what is supposed to be the central purpose of all high schools—education? Does sports downgrade the value that students put on intellectual effort? Does it reduce the learning of the athletes themselves?

Fewer than one out of four high-school boys play in interscholastic sports. But if we consider the immense amount of time and money spent on stadiums and gymnasiums, on teams and on their equipment and training, and on pep rallies, marching bands, and cheerleading, it is easy to believe that athletics must seriously interfere with schooling. As James S. Coleman has observed, a stranger in an American high school could easily conclude that "more attention is paid to athletics by teenagers, both as athletes and as spectators, than to scholastic matters." To many observers, it has become a self-evident article of faith that athletics is overemphasized in our high schools, and that the effect of athletics is, overall, bad.

One of the difficulties with this belief, however, is that it is based on very little research. Studies that my colleagues and I have conducted strongly indicate that this belief is, in most respects, probably untrue. Not only does participation in sports generally seem to have little or no effect on a student's scholarship, but it seems to actually *help* certain students academically

* Walter E. Schafer and J. Michael Armer, "Athletes Are Not Inferior Students," *Transaction,* Vol. 6 (November 1968), pp. 21-26 and 61-62.

—especially those students from the poor and disadvantaged groups that usually have the most trouble in school.

The arguments of the critics run something like this:

Whatever athletics may contribute to a player's character development, sportsmanship, physical fitness, or to the pride and fame of the town, there are at least five different ways in which it interferes with the central academic objectives of a school:

1. An excessive amount of resources, personnel and facilities of the high school is diverted from more fruitful activities.

2. Although sports may get many parents and other adults apparently interested in school affairs, this interest is not in education itself but in a marginal activity—and therefore it may actually distract from any real educational involvement on their part.

3. Pep rallies, trips, attending games, floats, displays and all the other paraphernalia combine to draw students away from their studies.

4. Many potentially good students become discouraged about trying for academic excellence because the big rewards of popularity and status go to athletes and cheerleaders. Rather than being rewarded, the serious student may actually be ridiculed as a "square" and a "grind."

5. Sports demands so much time, energy and concentration from the athletes—and gives them so much prestige compared to their studies—that their school work must inevitably suffer.

The evidence so far accumulated that might shed light on these claims is sparse. By far the most important study, in scope and in recognition, has been reported by Coleman in *The Adolescent Society.* Therefore we can use it as representative.

Let us review the evidence, point by point:

Diversion of Resources

To our knowledge, no studies have been conducted on the extent to which the present allocation of resources, personnel and facilities to interscholastic sports in high school in fact creates a drain away from the school's academic mission. Clearly, such studies are needed. Clearly also, they would be extremely difficult to do, since no two schools or situations are alike.

Diversion of Parental Support

Coleman's investigation of teenage culture in ten Midwestern high schools focused mainly on the attitudes, values and norms of the students themselves. But a questionnaire was sent to parents, and they were asked this question: "If your son or daughter could be outstanding in high school in one of the three things listed below, which one would you want it to be?" The choices offered were "brilliant student," "athletic star" ("leader of activities" for girls), and "most popular." "Brilliant student" was chosen by more than three-fourths of the parents of boys and over half of the parents of girls, suggesting that most parents value scholarship far more highly than athletics.

A NOTE ON THE METHODOLOGY

During the summer of 1964, we examined the complete high-school records of 585 boys. These boys had been tenth-graders in 1961, attending two Midwestern senior high schools. By 1964, most had already graduated from high school.

One of the three-year high schools had an enrollment of 2,565 in the fall of 1963 and was situated in a predominantly middle-class university community of about 70,000 people. The other school had an enrollment of 1,272, and was situated in a nearby, predominantly working-class industrial community of about 20,000 people. For this study, the boys from both schools were treated as a single sample.

Of the 585 boys, we classified 164 (28%) as athletes. During the three years of high school, these boys had completed at least one full season in some interscholastic sport (varsity or junior varsity). Thirty percent of these athletes had completed one sports season during the three years; 34 percent had completed two or three seasons; 21 percent, four or five seasons; and 15 percent six to nine seasons. (Any boy could complete three seasons a year—for example, football, basketball, and track.)

What we did was to compare the grade-point averages and dropout rates of athletes with those of nonathletes. At first, no account was taken of possible differences between athletes and nonathletes in motivation, or ability, to get good grades or to stay in school. These factors were then taken into account by matching each athlete with a nonathlete on intelligence-test scores, occupations of fathers, curriculums, and G.P.A.s for the final semester of junior high school. Several studies of the grades and dropout rates of athletes had been made before, but this is the first one to reduce the effects of other influences, or to measure the relationships by the students' social background and amount and form of their participation in athletics.

Coleman points out, however, that "these values may not be those they express day by day to their children." In fact, the responses of the students themselves to a related set of questions suggest such a discrepancy. When each student was asked how his parents would feel if he were asked to be a biology assistant, 60.2 percent of the boys responded "both would be very proud of me," and 63.5 percent of the girls gave that response. When asked how their parents would react if their children unexpectedly made the basketball team (or cheerleading squad), 68.2 percent of the boys and 77.0 percent of the girls said both their parents would be very proud.

These data provide only very slight support, then, for the view that, in practice, parents' support of scholarship is undermined to some extent by their greater interest in athletic accomplishment.

Diversion of Energy Among Student Fans

To prove that support of school teams by the students interferes with their academic performance, one would have to demonstrate that, other things being equal, the greater the students' time and energy devoted to the support of athletics, the lower the students' academic achievement. Although such interference may well occur, there seems to be no evidence in the literature one way or the other, even in Coleman's research.

Discouragement of Scholarship

If popularity and prestige are most readily given to students for their athletic achievement, then *academic* achievement must be relatively unrewarded. A high scholastic performance may well bring about the student's exclusion, scorn or ridicule. Therefore, Coleman says, the students with the most intellectual ability will know better than to try for top grades.

But again the data are not conclusive. Coleman's own figures are not clear-cut in support of his thesis—and in some cases they actually work to refute it.

In short, schools that emphasize athletics do not necessarily do so at the expense of learning; the two may actually rise or fall together. In any case, Coleman's study says nothing about the extent to which athletics, as opposed to other factors, diverts students of high ability from trying for top grades.

Diversion of Athletes Away from Scholarship

Coleman's writings imply that an athlete's participation in sports tends to keep his scholarship down; and that athletics "recruits" many of the brightest boys and, in effect, keeps them from giving the energy and time they should to their studies. In the end, he maintains, society suffers: "Because high schools allow adolescent societies to divert energies into athletics, social activities, and the like, they recruit into adult intellectual activities many people with a rather mediocre level of ability, and fail to attract many with high levels of ability."

Yet Coleman presents no evidence about the percentage of boys with high I.Q.s who are in fact siphoned off this way. Moreover, studies by other researchers have showed that athletes tend, if anything, to have *better* grades than the average student.

Nevertheless, there are data and conclusions in *The Adolescent Society* that could support the view that, other things being equal, a student's participation in sports does hurt his school work. If it is true that (1) athletes do get greater social rewards (popularity, prestige, leadership) than good students; and (2) that most high-school athletes are boys; and (3) that boys value these informal rewards more than grades and promotions, or possible long-term gains (going to college, better jobs); then, true enough, boys can be expected to give as much time and energy as possible to athletics. If we further assume that time, energy and attention are limited resources, then it also follows that their studies must suffer if the boys invest these resources in athletics.

If these assumptions are stated as hypotheses, they can be put to an experimental test. For if these assumptions are true,

1. Athletes should not perform as well scholastically as nonathletes.

TABLE 34-I

MEAN GRADE-POINT AVERAGE FOR ATHLETES AND
ALL BOYS IN THEIR CLASS

	*Mean G.P.A.**	*Number*
Athletes**	2.35	164
All other boys	1.83	421

     * Grade-point averages are based on the following scale: A = 4, B = 3, C = 2, D = 1, F = 0. Each student's G.P.A. is based on his final marks in all major courses during the six semesters of his three-year high school. (Physical education is not included as a major course.) G.P.A.s may be based on anywhere from one to six semesters, depending on how long the student remained in school.

     ** Boys who completed at least one full season as a member of an interscholastic athletic team are classified as athletes.

2. The greater the student's participation in sports, the greater the detriment to his studies.

3. A student's participation in those sports that are given the greatest recognition and attention—generally, football and basketball—should harm his academic performance more than the minor sports that do not require so much time, or give as great social rewards.

Data have now been gathered from one medium-sized and one large senior high school to test each of these hypotheses. (See Table 34-I.)

In Table 34-I we have compared the grade-point averages (A = 4 = excellent, B = 3 = good, C = 2 = fair, D = 1 = passing, F = 0 = failure) of 585 boys in the two high schools, contrasting the athletes and nonathletes. Clearly, *the athletes obtained better*

TABLE 34-II

MEAN G.P.A. OF ATHLETES AND MATCHED NONATHLETES AND
PERCENTAGE OF ATHLETES WHO EXCEED
THEIR MATCHES IN G.P.A.

	Mean G.P.A.	*Percent of Athletes Higher Than Match*	*Number*
Athletes	2.35		152
		56.6	
Matched nonathletes	2.24		152

grades. The athletes, on the average, got over C, the nonathletes got less than C. There may, of course, be many reasons for this finding, apart from the students' participation in sports. Athletes could start high school with a greater potential or motivation, and get higher grades not because of but *despite* athletics, and so on. But even when we control for these initial differences, by match- ing athletes with nonathletes, we still find the athletes getting slightly higher grades. (See Table 34-II.)

Variation by Amount of Participation

What about the effects of *amount* of participation in sports? Dividing the athletes into those who completed one or two sea- sons on the one hand and those who completed three or more on the other, again we found that the results did not support the hypothesis. *The more the athletes participated in sports, the greater the positive gap between their grades and those of their matched nonathletes.* (See Table 34-III.) The difference between the grades of the less-active athletes and their matches was .03. Between more-active athletes and their matches, the difference was .18—six times as much.

Viewed another way, 51.5 percent of the less-active athletes ex- ceeded their matches, compared with 60.4 percent of the more- active athletes. Again, rather than eroding academic perform- ance, extensive participation in interscholastic sports seems to slightly increase a student's scholastic success.

Variation by Type of Sport

According to the prediction, playing football or basketball would hurt a student's grades more than playing in minor sports, such as track, swimming, wrestling and gymnastics, in which the rewards, effort and competition might be less. Table 34-IV clearly shows that, while participants in the two major sports have somewhat lower average G.P.A.s than participants in minor sports, those in major sports exceed their *matches* to a greater ex- tent than those in minor sports do. Therefore, the prediction does not hold up.

TABLE 34-III

PERCENTAGES OF ATHLETES WITH HIGHER, SAME, AND LOWER G.P.A.s THAN THEIR MATCHES, AND MEAN G.P.A.s OF BOTH GROUPS BY AMOUNT OF PARTICIPATION

| | Percentage of Athletes | | | | | | | Mean G.P.A. | |
| | With Higher G.P.A. | | With Same G.P.A. | With Lower G.P.A. | | | | | Matched |
Amount of Participation	.25 or more difference	.01 to .24 difference	-.01 to -.24 difference	-.01 to -.24 difference	-.25 or more difference	Total	Number of Pairs	Athletes	Non-athletes
Three or more seasons	48.8%	11.6%	1.2%	10.5%	27.9%	100%	86	2.45	2.24
Total	(60.4%)		(1.2%)	(38.4%)		(100%)			
One or two seasons	37.9%	13.6%	3.0%	9.1%	36.4%	100%	66	2.26	2.23
Total	(51.5%)		(3.0%)	(35.5%)		(100%)			

TABLE 34-IV

MEAN G.P.A. FOR ATHLETES AND MATCHED NONATHELETES, AND
PERCENTAGE OF ATHLETES WHO EXCEED THEIR MATCH IN
G.P.A., TYPE OF SPORT

Type of Sport	Mean G.P.A.	Percent of Athletes Higher Than Match	Number
Major Sport*			
Athlete	2.20		83
		60.2	
Matched nonathlete	2.02		83
Minor sport**			
Athlete	2.53		69
		52.1	
Matched nonathlete	2.50		69

* Major sports include football and basketball, according to our coding criteria. Participants in major sports sometimes participated in one or more minor sports also, but the reverse is never true, according to these criteria.
** Minor sports in both schools include baseball, track, cross-country, swimming, wrestling, tennis and golf; the larger school also fields teams in gymnastics and in hockey.

Variations Among Types of Boys

Having found no support so far for the various "interference" hypotheses, we can now legitimately ask whether the major prediction holds true among *any* of the boys. For instance, does participation in athletics have a greater positive effect on academic achievement among white-collar boys than among blue-collar boys? Among high-I.Q. boys than low-I.Q. boys? Among college-bound boys than work-bound boys? Or among high achievers than low achievers in junior high school?

The data in Table 34-V reveal two clear patterns. First, the slight positive association between athletics and scholarship persists in *all* subgroups. In no case is the relationship negative. More than half the athletes in each category exceed their matches and the average G.P.A.s of athletes is always higher than that of their matched nonathletes. Moreover, on father's occupation and curriculum, the gap is greater between athletes and their matches in the *lower* categories than in the higher. For example, greater percentages of blue-collar athletes than white-collar athletes exceed their matches in G.P.A.s (63.0% versus

TABLE 34-V

MEAN G.P.A. FOR ATHLETES AND MATCHED NONATHLETES, AND
PERCENTAGE OF ATHLETES WHO EXCEED THEIR MATCH IN
G.P.A., BY FATHER'S OCCUPATION, INTELLIGENCE-TEST
SCORE, CURRICULUM, AND G.P.A. FOR LAST
SEMESTER OF JUNIOR HIGH SCHOOL

Characteristic	Mean G.P.A.	Percent of Athletes Higher Than Match	Number
Father's occupation			
White Collar athlete	2.53		95
		53.7	
Matched nonathlete	2.48		95
Blue Collar athlete	2.05		54
		63.0	
Matched nonathlete	1.84		54
Intelligence-test scores			
Upper half of class			
athlete	2.64		94
		56.4	
Matched nonathlete	2.55		94
Lower half of class			
athlete	1.88		58
		56.9	
Matched nonathlete	1.74		58
Curriculum			
College preparatory athlete ...	2.47		123
		53.7	
Matched nonathlete	2.40		123
Noncollege preparatory			
athlete	1.85		29
		69.0	
Matched nonathlete	1.56		29
G.P.A. for last semester of junior high school			
Upper half of class			
athlete	2.82		78
		57.7	
Matched nonathlete	2.70		78
Lower half of class			
athlete	1.85		74
		55.4	
Matched nonathlete	1.75		74

53.7%). An even greater spread separates noncollege-preparatory
athletes from college-preparatory athletes (69.0% versus 53.7%).

In short, the boys who would usually have the most trouble in
school are precisely the ones who seem to benefit most from taking part in sports.

Interpretation

These findings, of course, do not tell us whether athletics diverts a high school's resources, staff manhours and facilities at the expense of the scholastic program; whether the support of parents is channeled away from education; whether the academic achievement of student fans suffers from their support of school teams; or whether potentially top students are discouraged from trying because social rewards go to athletes instead.

But these findings do bring into serious question the notion prevalent among many teachers, parents and social scientists that the supposed overemphasis on athletics in the American high school results in the lowering of academic achievement among athletes. At the very least, the data cast doubt on the validity of Jules Henry's irate judgment that "athletics, popularity, and mediocre grades go together with inarticulateness and poor grammar."

If there is in fact a positive effect of participation in athletics on grades, as the data suggest, why does it occur? Here we are forced to speculate.

1. Perhaps athletes are graded more leniently, because teachers see them as special or more deserving.

2. Perhaps exposure, in the sports subculture, to effort, hard work, persistence and winning spills over into nonathletic activities, such as schoolwork.

3. Perhaps the superior physical condition of athletes improves their mental performance.

4. Perhaps some athletes strive to get good grades to be eligible for certain sports.

5. Perhaps athletes make more efficient and effective use of their limited study time.

6. Perhaps the lure of a college career in sports motivates some athletes to strive for good grades.

7. Perhaps the high prestige that students obtain from sports gives them a better self-concept and higher aspirations in other activities, such as schoolwork.

8. Perhaps athletes benefit from more help in schoolwork from friends, teachers and parents.

Why does participation in athletics appear to have its greatest

positive effect on the academic performance of those boys with
blue-collar backgrounds and a noncollege-preparatory label? A
plausible interpretation of this finding is that, compared to nonathletes with the same characteristics, blue-collar and noncollege-
bound athletes are more likely to associate and identify with
white-collar and college-bound members of the school's leading
crowd. Illustrative cases are abundant of blue-collar boys who
were not at all academically-oriented or college-oriented until
they began to "make it" in sports and to be increasingly influenced by white-collar boys (and girls) with whom they would
not otherwise have associated or identified.

Another important type of educational achievement is graduation from high school. Does participation in interscholastic
sports keep boys in school? The data presented in Table 34-VI
strongly suggest a Yes answer. Whereas 9.2 percent of the
matched nonathletes dropped out of school before graduating,
less than one-fourth as many (2.0%) of the athletes failed to
finish. (These figures do not include boys who transferred to
another school.)

This finding suggests that athletics exerts a holding influence
on students, which might operate in four different ways. First,
the high prestige that athletes are likely to receive probably
makes them want to remain in school. Second, athletes who are
potential dropouts are likely to associate and identify with college-oriented (or at least graduation-oriented) boys more often
than are nonathletes who are potential dropouts. Third, some
athletes might stay in school simply to be able to participate in
high-school sports—or, later, college or professional sports.
Fourth, potential dropouts who are athletes are likely to get encouragement and counseling from coaches and others, while

TABLE 34-VI

PERCENTAGE OF ATHLETES AND MATCHED NONATHLETES
WHO DROPPED OUT OF SCHOOL BEFORE GRADUATION

	Percent	Number
Athletes	2.0	152
Matched nonathlete	9.2	152

nonathletic potential dropouts are likely to get much less encouragement, from anybody.

Whatever the reasons, it is clear that participation in athletics exerts a holding influence over some boys who might have otherwise dropped out. Of the nine matched nonathletes who dropped out with G.P.A.s of below 2.0, eight could be paired with athletes who ended up with equal or lower G.P.A.s but did *not* drop out. This finding provides limited support for Coleman's suggestion that "if it were not for interscholastic athletics . . . the rate of dropout might be far worse. . . ."

An assertion often heard, but little studied, is that competitive sports serve as an important vehicle for upward mobility. Numerous examples can be cited, of course, of college or professional athletes' having risen above their fathers in income and status solely or primarily because of athletic achievements.

We know of no prior systematic studies in the United States, however, to determine how often this is true. Yet information about the relationship between a student's participation in interscholastic athletics and his expectations of attending college is of interest for two reasons: It provides a basis for understanding the role of athletics in upward mobility, insofar as mobility is dependent on someone's attending and graduating from college; and it provides additional data about the extent to which athletics impedes or facilitates the attainment of one of high school's educational goals: to send a maximum number of youths to college.

Pertinent data on this point have been gathered from questionnaires filled out by 785 twelfth-grade boys in three public and three Catholic high schools in three middle-sized (50,000 to 100,000) Pennsylvania cities during the spring of 1965. (See "Participation in Interscholastic Athletics and College Expectations," Richard A. Rehberg and Walter E. Schafer, *The American Journal of Sociology*, LXXII, 1968.) Among other things, the boys were asked to name the extracurricular activities they participated in during their senior years, how far they expected to go in college, their fathers' education and occupation and how often their parents encouraged them to go to college. The

TABLE 34-VII

COLLEGE EXPECTATIONS OF ATHLETES AND ALL OTHER
BOYS IN THEIR CLASS

| | *Percent Who Expect to Complete ...* | | |
	At Least Two *Years of College*	*At Least Four* *Years of College*	*Number*
Athletes	82	62	284
All other boys	75	45	490

students' rank in their graduating classes was obtained from
school records.

Table 34-VII shows that, in comparison with nonathletes, athletes are slightly more likely to expect to complete at least two
years of college (82% versus 75%), and considerably more likely
to expect to complete at least four years of college (62% versus
45%). And if we hold the factors of background and early ability and aspirations about equal, we still get the same results. (See
Table 34-VIII.)

To what extent participation in athletics directly *causes* higher educational expectations is, of course, still open to question;
but there is little doubt that more athletes intend to go to college than matched nonathletes. Earlier, we noted that higher
scholastic achievement was especially marked among athletes who
were from working-class backgrounds and who were not college
bound. Are expectations of attending college, therefore, relatively more common among athletes who are less "earmarked" for
college? Our findings indicate that the answer is Yes. (See Table

TABLE 34-VIII

COLLEGE EXPECTATIONS OF ATHLETES AND ALL OTHER
BOYS IN THEIR CLASS—WITH CONTROLS

| | *Percent Who Expect to Complete ...* | | |
	At Least Two *Years of College*	*At Least Four* *Years of College*	*Number*
Athletes	80	61	284
All other boys	76	45	490

Note: Social status, the amount of encouragement from parents, and the students' rank in their graduating classes have been controlled for.

34-IX.) That is, a greater percentage of athletes than nonathletes expect to complete four years of college among working-class rather than middle-class boys; among boys with less, rather than more, parental encouragement; and among boys in the lower rather than the upper half of their graduating classes.

It would seem, then, that interscholastic athletics serves a democratizing or equalizing function. It represents a vehicle for upward mobility, especially of those otherwise not likely to complete college. And the data suggest that, at least as far as participants are concerned, athletics fosters rather than interferes with the educational goal of sending a maximum number of youth to college.

The question arises whether all of these findings apply to Negro boys. We know that sports is an important channel to success for many Negroes, but we do not know *how* important, or to

TABLE 34-IX

COLLEGE EXPECTATIONS OF ATHLETES AND ALL OTHER BOYS
IN THEIR CLASS, BY SOCIAL STATUS, PARENTAL EDUCATION
ENCOURAGEMENT, AND RANK IN GRADUATING CLASS

| | *Percent Who Expect to Complete . . .* | | |
| | *At Least Two* | *At Least Four* | |
Characteristic	*Years of College*	*Years of College*	*Number*
Social Status			
Middle			
Athletes	91	78	90
All other boys	89	67	144
Working			
Athletes	78	55	194
All other boys	69	36	346
Parental educational encouragement			
High			
Athletes	90	68	208
All other boys	88	56	298
Low			
Athletes	58	45	66
All other boys	55	26	164
Rank in graduating class			
High			
Athletes	94	85	116
All other boys	89	78	205
Low			
Athletes	74	46	164
All other boys	66	21	280

what extent it varies in time and place. Nor do we know how often Negro boys put all their hopes into becoming a Willie Mays, Wilt Chamberlain, or Boy Hayes in college or professional sports, but fail, and end up disillusioned and unprepared for more conventional routes of mobility.

In this article, we could not deal with the results of a student's relative *success* in sports. Obviously, athletics will effect the star and the substitute differently. Success means greater prestige; and this *might* mean higher self-regard, higher aspirations and higher academic performance. On the other hand, it might mean more praise and distraction than most teenage boys can handle and still do good school work.

It is a frequent claim of coaches, playground directors and Little League promoters that athletics deters students from deviance within the school and delinquency in the community. Over thirty years ago, Willard Waller noted that many teachers deliberately supported interscholastic sports because they felt that it "makes students more teachable because it drains off their surplus energies and leaves them less inclined to get into mischief. . . . Part of the technique, indeed, of those who handle difficult cases consists in getting those persons interested in . . . athletics." But we do not really know. Again, it seems that nobody has systematically investigated the problem.

A striking feature of varsity sports—college and high school— is the great authority of the coach in controlling the athletes' off-the-field behavior. The coach usually has the unquestioned authority to suspend or drop a boy from the team if he is caught smoking, drinking, staying out too late or violating a law. Some coaches even decide the hair styles, dress, friendship patterns and the language of their boys. A few "training rules," of course, are laid down for the sake of the athletes' physical conditioning and efficiency, but others can be understood only as part of the "moralism" associated with sports. The high-school athlete is supposed to be a "good American boy." A fascinating question for research, therefore, is: What are the long-term effects on the athlete from this rigid and often puritanical control by coaches? A related question: Do high-school sports really contribute to the "character development" that coaches so often claim?

Finally, what of the lifetime and career effects of a student's participation in athletics, after he has left high school and even college? Of course, many examples can be cited of individuals who have been successful through sports—either by staying in as players or coaches, or through the education or contacts that sports has made possible. But what of the others? And what are the direct and indirect factors and mechanisms involved?

These are all matters that call for careful and rigorous research. Clearly, interscholastic athletics is far more important in the American educational process—for good or ill—than most social scientists seem to want to recognize. And the extent of that importance cannot be determined by the unsupported rhetoric of those who have personal reasons to applaud, or denounce, high-school athletics.

SUGGESTED READINGS

Boyle, Robert H.: *Sport: Mirror of American Life*. Boston, Little, Brown and Co., 1963.

A journalistic account, abundant with sociological insights, of sport in America. Includes an excellent discussion of the Negro in sport.

Coleman, James S.: *The Adolescent Society*. New York, The Free Press of Glencoe Inc., 1961.

A large-scale study that describes the central place of athletics in the subculture of American adolescents.

McIntosh, Peter: *Sport and Society*. New York, International Publishing Service, 1963.

A comprehensive and suggestive work on a variety of sociological aspects of athletics.

Stone, Gregory P.: *Sport, Play and Leisure*. Indianapolis, The Bobbs-Merrill Publishing Co., forthcoming.

A series of essays, including a more extended version of this article, on topics ranging from the play of little children to the sociological dynamics of professional wrestling, the social determinants and consequences of baseball fandom, and the sociological implications of increasing leisure time.

CHAPTER 35

THE CULTURAL CRISIS IN AMERICAN SPORTS

Barry E. Stern*

Is it true that organized athletics in the United States serve the cause of political conservation? Are the Students for a Democratic Society right when they claim that school and university athletic programs frustrate cultural change and encourage proestablishment (things-the-way-they-are) attitudes? Does participation in school sports prevent an athlete from expressing his individuality? Is football really dehumanizing?

THIS ARTICLE ATTEMPTS to understand the cultural crisis in American sports. It emphasizes the changing coach-athlete relationship in educational institutions as the dimension of the dilemma which most accurately reveals the new directions which school and university athletics must take if they are to maintain their prominent place in American youth culture. Once the true dimensions and causes of this dilemma can be identified, it can be dealt with directly. Until the present, unfortunately, society has chosen to concern itself with the symptoms of the problem rather than eliminate the causes.

What, then, is the problem? The answer to this question depends on whom you ask. Most coaches perceive their dilemma with athletes in the same way that parents perceive their problems with their children. Some blame their misfortunes on permissive child-rearing practices and the subsequent lack of discipline in youth. Others cite the interracial strife which has gripped this country, or the war in Vietnam. In my own view, the nature of the dilemma transcends the race issue or the war issue,

---

* Barry E. Stern, "The Cultural Crisis in American Sports," *Journal of Health, Physical Education, and Recreation*, Vol. 43 (April 1972), pp. 42-44.

and the resolution of conflict between student athletes and coaches is more than a matter of strict versus permissive disciplinary action.

Simply put, the problem is that student athletes perceive a conflict between the sports culture in which they operate and the larger culture which values (or at least pays lip service to) the principles of participatory democracy and achievement on the basis of merit. Students raise questions concerning the limits of coaches' power and authority in governing sports competition. As in other areas of student life, students are requesting—in fact, demanding—greater voice and vote in making decisions which directly affect their lives. The fact that the "student power" movement affects so popular a part of student life as interscholastic and intercollegiate athletics should not surprise us. Considering the close relationship that coaches have traditionally had with students, athletes or not, it is somewhat surprising, however, that this movement has been resisted, if not ignored, by the great majority of coaches.

Perhaps the reason for their intransigence is that the basic assumptions made by the coaching profession about organized athletics are being challenged. Many coaches reason that if these assumptions are effectively challenged, their survival as coaches—moreover, the survival of organized athletics as they have organized them—is in jeopardy. In a way, they are right. The question remains, as it does for so many adult authority-figures in our society today, whether running scared to preserve the status quo is the answer, or whether the nature of coaching and athletics can be changed sufficiently to adapt to a changing society.

One assumption made by coaches that is being challenged is that team members must consider team loyalty above all else. Players and coaches are beginning to disagree more and more as to how much team loyalty is enough. Just what is a 100 percent commitment to an athletic team? Can one be committed to the team while he is committed to his manhood, the improvement of the human race, his studies, his girl friend? I interviewed one black player who said, "Look, I'm committed to a lot of things, not the least important of which is the survival of my race. If there's a late meeting of the black caucus and it's important that

I be there, I will go even though I know I might have to break curfew to attend. Now that's not a 100 percent commitment to football, but I feel I should play in the game if my 75 percent is better than someone else's 100 percent. Of course, if I really did not feel fit enough to contribute to a winning cause, I would feel obligated to tell the coach. He has the right to know if I was at an all-night meeting, as he would if I didn't get sufficient sleep because of a variety of other reasons."

What many coaches have failed to appreciate is that an increasing number of students, athletes or not, want to make their own choices, choosing among alternatives which they have created for themselves. Coaches are teachers (their athletes are merely advanced students of sport) and teachers should welcome this desire for autonomy and independence as a sign of emotional maturity and growth. If a student has loyalties and commitments which compete for his attention, all the coach can do is make his program as attractive as possible so that it will be given higher priority by these students. Moreover, both he and the players should agree on the kinds of competing loyalties and commitments which do not detract from one's performance on the team. Just as a classroom teacher should be willing to negotiate with his students to determine "what's fair," the coach must negotiate with his athletes.

In the name of developing a winning attitude in their charges, coaches over the years have seen fit to establish for players rules which govern a number of their outside-of-athletics activities. Some of these are training rules, e.g., refrain from smoking, drinking and consuming certain foods. Others refer to social life, e.g. when a player can go out on dates, and occasionally, who he can date and who he cannot. And still others refer to comportment in public, e.g. not to engage in loud or raucous behavior, to refrain from swearing, to abstain from associating with individuals who engage in, or who have been engaged in, delinquent acts, etc. Some coaches have even prohibited team members from joining political pressure groups, reasoning that this would somehow cause dissension amongst team members.

CULTURAL SENSITIVITY AND SOCIAL MATURITY

Obviously, some of these rules are reasonable and others are not. The point is that all should be considered negotiable. A boy of Latin American descent, for example, is oftentimes accustomed to drinking alcoholic beverages at a party. He does not necessarily get drunk and it will probably have no discernible effect on his athletic performance. Does the coach have the right to ask that boy to refrain from moderate drinking, or even to refrain from attending the party itself? Yes, he has the right to ask, to persuade and to suggest. Whether or not he has the right to demand abstinence from this kind of behavior is debatable. I would like to suggest that the rules regarding outside-of-school activities should accommodate rather than penalize team members from minority group backgrounds and that the coach make every effort to acquaint himself with the family and cultural background of each player. Being culturally sensitive helps a coach determine which rules are reasonable and which are not.

As always, "reasonable" depends on the context. What is right for a college athlete may not be appropriate for a professional. A high school student need not be treated as an elementary school child. Indeed, it seems to me that the most manly way for a coach to handle his team is to allow the players to help determine the rules by which they will live. Once coach and players alike have agreed what the rules shall be and what the consequences of breaking them will be, then all can be expected to abide by them. Participation in rule-making is a valuable lesson in growing up. If rule-making is the sole prerogative of the coach, the athlete becomes dependent on him for the development of his own moral ideology, hence delaying the achievement of social maturity. On the other hand, if an individual is encouraged to investigate the reasons for rules and is assured a voice in their development, he will be given a chance to grow and to obtain his independence. Developing social maturity in his players should be as much an objective of the coach as winning.

Coaches, for the most part, do not want to keep their players docile and dependent. On the contrary, the coach, perhaps more than any other professional working with youth, is actively attempting to facilitate social and emotional growth in them. Many, however, overreact to what appears to be rebellion against their authority by athletes. Many coaches perceive athletes' questions about the reasons for one team rule or another as personal attacks. They should instead understand that young people, for better or for worse, want more autonomy, a greater feeling of mastery over their environment and hence their lives. Young people are searching for good reasons for accepting the rules they are asked to live by. The pressure they are putting on coaches is no more and perhaps much less than the pressure applied to school and college administrators. Coaches have an excellent opportunity to channel this desire for increased participation into socially acceptable and responsible directions.

A noticeable result emerging from confrontations in athletics, however, is that *those students who choose not to conform are no longer choosing athletics as a form of self-expression. There* seems to be enough circumstantial evidence to postulate that nonconforming types do indeed shun athletics. In the San Francisco Bay Area, for example, it seems that the highly politicized high schools and universities (i.e. the ones with the greatest degree of student political activism) have the greatest student apathy toward athletics.

To be sure, many students regard athletics as one of the most important school activities and the father-figure coach is still admired and often worshipped by millions of our nation's young people. While the coach still serves as one of our society's ideal male role models, there is an increasing number of young people with whom he has not been able to establish any rapport whatsoever, particularly those from the radical, antiestablishment, longhaired and militant minority groups. In fact, the indifference to organized athletics found in many of these groups is beginning to change to outright hostility. What is ironic about this is that these turned off individuals are not turned off by the physical or nonverbal aspects of human experience. Indeed, many of these young nonconformists are seriously exploring such things as sensory or bodily awareness (something that the physical education profession has known about for years), and they really dig such things as hiking, camping and outdoor living. Why, then, are they not turned on by athletics?

The answer to this question could well be that these youngsters identify organized athletics with those elements of American "establishment" culture that they no longer respect. What are these elements?

NONCONFORMITY AND RELATIVE ACHIEVEMENT

For one thing, our nonconforming youth disagree with the notion that a person ought to be judged or evaluated on the basis of how he appears—his clothing, hairstyle, etc. Rather, they feel, an individual should be evaluated on the basis of what he can do and does. In most schools and colleges, however, athletes must conform to strict grooming regulations; naturally the nonconformist becomes less interested in athletics when the appearance issue becomes as important, if not more important, than the individual's measurable achievement. They perceive quite correctly that in athletics *especially* individuals should be evaluated on the basis of relative achievement.

Another cultural value which is being questioned by many young people is the principle of majority rule, especially when that rule is applied to such a degree that minority or culturally different groups become disenfranchised. While many segments of our society are beginning to accept the shift toward political as well as cultural pluralism (the right of different social, racial or ethnic groups to be different so long as they do not infringe upon the rights of other groups), the coaching profession has tended to "stand firm" against this change, demanding conformity, as it were, because the majority prefers conformity. Inasmuch as the nonconformist tends to agree that a shift toward pluralism is necessary (the "do-your-own-thing" philosophy), he is not likely to want to participate in a system (organized athletics) which still operates under the assumptions about democracy which are concomitant with too much majority rule.

DEMOCRACY VS. PLURALISM AND DISCIPLINE
VS. WINNING

Some coaches are perpetuating the myth that democracy and pluralism on the one hand and discipline and winning on the other are incompatible. Their notion of discipline has alienated a great number of students from athletics. In the name of discipline and preparing oneself to win, many coaches demand behavior on the part of athletes which denies them their individuality, even outside the team context. Why should individualism off the field mitigate effective teamwork on the field? This outlook is becoming obsolete; hopefully, coaches will modernize.

In microcosm, then, we see in the controversies over athletics many of the issues which confront our democracy today: pluralism vs. majority rule, student power vs. teacher power, selection on the basis of merit vs. selection on the basis of something else, individualism vs. conformity, etc. The forces which are bringing stress and strain to the coaching profession are the ones bringing stress to the society as a whole. Coaches are reacting in very different ways to their dilemma. Some are becoming more flexible in their approach to athletes and hence are putting up with more diversity and individualism than they have in the past. Many coaches, on the other hand, are saying that the more ground you give, the less chance you have of surviving.

Such statements, I feel, reveal a lack of understanding of what is happening in our society today. Anthropologists would call it "cultural lag," meaning that although the athletic programs in the United States were harmoniously integrated with the rest of our culture at one time in our history, these same programs are not accommodating themselves to the cultural change that our society is undergoing at present.

At this point, I am sure that many readers are taking sides for or against the so-called athletic establishment (i.e. the coaches, administrators, alumni and athletes who support the present system of organized athletics). But to take sides is to avoid the real issue, for organized athletics should have something to offer any student no matter what his political beliefs or behavior. *That* is the issue: whether or not present-day athletic programs can be made flexible enough to accommodate *all* students who desire to benefit from them.

What can be done to achieve this? First and foremost, a definite attempt should be made to limit and possibly reduce the power of the coaching establishment in the organization of school and particularly college athletics, ceding much of this power and authority to the group which presumably benefits the most from athletics, namely, the students (athletes).

Coaches are probably correct when they foresee a change in their role, but not all of their fears are well-founded. In spite of what some coaches say, no one is trying to tell them "how to coach" or "who to play at what position." In other words, no one is trying to usurp the professional tasks of the coach. Athletes invariably agree that the teaching and training tasks should be left to the coach. However, a significant number do resent the power which coaches have over the nonathletic aspects of their lives if they desire to participate on teams. Rather than striving for conformity—same haircuts, street clothing, social contacts, etc.—coaches should emphasize pulling together in such a way that common team goals can be achieved without sacrificing too much in the way of individuality. Perhaps the most salient advice for coaches who seek a solution to their dilemma with students and athletes is to become aware of the changing youth culture and its values and to modify their own behavior and programs accordingly.

REASONABLE RULES AND SOCIAL EQUALITY

More athletes, including competent athletes, will try out for athletic teams when they perceive the management of these teams to be governed by sensible and democratically arrived at rules. These athletes will be respected as persons as well as students. The coach will finally be allowed to be the professional teacher. As a result of the new status of the athlete, the coach can concentrate upon the physical skills, mental developments and teaching phases of the sport. He no longer need be the father, psychiatrist, minister and watchguard over the athlete. Finally, the greater participation of students and athletes in the governing of athletics will make the distasteful and often dishonest task of recruiting less necessary. The coach will become what any teacher ought to be—a human resource for the students who wish to take advantage of his expertise.

The greater social equality between the athlete and coach, as between student and teacher, will make for more honest and fruitful human relationships. Historically the coach, either through choice or circumstance, has been forced into roles with athletes which, in many instances, never should have been his responsibilities. The athlete too often has used the coach as a crutch for his whims and desires, for his failures and sometimes his successes. Now they will be in a position to respect each other as individuals both on and off the playing field.

The coaches' dilemma, in conclusion, reflects our country's social dilemma. If the issues raised here can be resolved effectively and ethically within the confines of organized athletics, perhaps the experience will serve as an example for the larger culture which must somehow reverse present trends toward social disorganization and alienation. Those of us involved in athletics have a very exciting opportunity to help lead our culture through peaceful change. We should be the first ones, not the last, to understand the youthful desire for increased participation.

CHAPTER 36

A STUDY OF SELECTED ASPECTS OF THE COACH'S INFLUENCE ON HIGH SCHOOL ATHLETES

ELDON E. SNYDER*

SOCIALIZATION, WITHIN SOCIOLOGY, is a major concept and field of study. The socialization process involves the learning of motives, feelings, skills, cognitive sets, and social norms and expectations. It embraces the informal acquisition of these attributes through peer groups and friendship relationship, as well as from formally designated socializing agents such as parents, teachers, ministers and others. The process incorporates both the development of the individual as well as transmitting cultural values and providing a means of securing potential consensus and social control in the collectivity or society.

Formal socialization occurs through the exercise of influence and control the socialization agents have over the socializee; recent studies by Campbell,[1] Clausen,[2] and Ellis and Lane[3] have documented this influence. Absent in the empirical research on socialization is the potential influence of the athletic coach on his players, though several investigators have noted the theoretical relevance of studying the coach's influence is socialization.

---

* Eldon E. Snyder, "A Study of Selected Aspects of the Coach's Influence on High School Athletes," *The Physical Educator*, Vol. 29 (May 1972), pp. 96-98.

1. E. Q. Campbell, "Adolescent Socialization," in D. Goslin (ed.), *Handbook of Socialization Theory and Research* (Chicago, Rand McNally and Company, 1969), pp. 827-833.

2. J. A. Clausen, "Perspectives on Childhood Socialization," in J. Clausen (ed.), *Socialization and Society* (Boston, Little, Brown and Company, 1969), pp. 132-181.

3. R. A. Ellis and C. Lane, "Structural Supports for Upward Mobility." *American Sociological Review*, Vol. 28 (1963), pp. 743-756.

For example, Strauss[4] considered the coaching role as a means of socialization, and more recently, Kenyon[5] pointed out the potential for studying aspects of directing the player into a target role was cited by Page when he noted,

> "When the kid who at fifteen or sixteen has tremendous promise, coaches are apt to think in career terms: 'you go to Michigan State, we have connections with such and such pro team.' In this way, coaches become career specialists."[6]

Further discussion was presented by Snyder[7] of several dimensions in the coach-player relationship that are important in the socialization process.

Research by Coleman[8] demonstrates that high social status is usually accorded to athletes in the high school structure and Schafer[9] has suggested a partial explanation for the importance of athletics rests with the school authorities who have apparently decided that athletics are important and should be supported because: (1) they feel athletics instill in the participants a number of educational benefits—primarily the development of personal attributes and social values, i.e. health, happiness, cooperation, competition, character and fair play, (2) athletics are thought to develop loyalty and interest in the school community, and (3) students are channelled into socially acceptable behavior by the social control mechanisms of sports. Athletes, as Matza has noted are:

---

4. A. Strauss, *Mirrors and Masks* (New York, The Free Press, 1959), pp. 100-118.

5. G. S. Kenyon, "Sociological Considerations," *Journal of Health, Physical Education, Recreation*, Vol. 39 (1968), pp. 31-33.

6. C. H. Page, "Symposium Summary, with Reflections upon the Sociology of Sport as a Research Field," in G. S. Kenyon (ed.), *Aspects of Contemporary Sport Sociology* (Chicago, The Athletic Institute, 1969), p. 200.

7. E. E. Snyder, "Aspects of Socialization in Sports and Physical Education," *Quest*, Vol. 14 (1970), pp. 1-7.

8. J. S. Coleman, *Adolescents in the Schools* (New York, Basic Books, 1965), pp. 35-51.

9. W. E. Schafer, "Some Social Sources and Consequences of Interscholastic Athletics: the Case and Participation and Delinquency." *International Review of Sport Sociology*, Vol. 4 (1968), pp. 65-68.

". . . enjoined to be 'in training'; they are to refrain from smoking, drinking, staying out late, and other forms of dissipation which violate the expectations of adult authority."[10]

Thus, athletics are promoted, at least in part, because of the presumed beneficial personal and social-cultural values. The present study provides empirical data on selected aspects of the coach's influence in this socialization process.

METHODOLOGY

In the spring of 1969, with the cooperation of the Ohio Association for Health, Physical Education and Recreation, this researcher drew a sample of 270 Ohio high schools that participate in basketball. This sample consisted of one-third of the high schools affiliated with the above association and was a representative cross-section of the schools by size classification that participate in the sport. A questionnaire was sent to the basketball coach and two varsity team members of each of the 270 schools. To maintain some uniformity in the ages of the players, the sample was randomly drawn from varsity team rosters after initially eliminating the younger members of the team from possible selection (96% of the players who returned their questionnaires were juniors or seniors). The response rate for the questionnaires was 64.5 percent for the coaches and 50 percent for the players.[11]

FINDINGS

To determine the players' perceptions of the extent and type of influence their basketball coaches had on them, they were asked: "Has your basketball coach been an important influence to you?" An open-ended follow-up question asked the type of influence. Only 11 percent of the players indicated the coach had been of little or no influence to them; 47 percent said the coach had been a great influence; and 42 percent said he had been of

10. D. Matza, "Position and Behavior Patterns of Youth," in R. Faris (ed.), *Handbook of Modern Sociology* (Chicago, Rand McNally and Company, 1964), pp. 191-216.

11. W. E. Schafer and J. M. Armer, "Athletes Are Not Inferior Students," *Trans-action*, Vol. 6 (1968), pp. 21-26 and 61-62.

some influence. The types of influence were then categorized. The most frequent responses indicated that 25 percent of the players felt the coach was influential in helping with personal problems; 19 percent cited his influence in developing basketball proficiency; 18 percent said the coach taught them pride, teamwork and sportsmanship; and 17 percent said he showed them the value of hard work. Only 3 percent of the respondents indicated the coach had influenced them negatively.

Data were also collected to determine the relative influence of reference persons in the athletes' educational and occupational plans. The findings show the parents were ranked first in importance, but the coach ranked immediately behind them as an influence in this area. Their peers, teachers, siblings, other relatives and ministers or priests all ranked considerably below the coach in this respect.

Since the guidance that people seek is likely to vary with the situation, two additional questions furnish data on the relative importance of reference persons in different situations. One question was,

> "If you were in trouble with the police over a traffic violation whom would you probably go to for advice?"

In this situation, trouble with the police, the coach is not likely to be readily consulted; the advice of parents, brothers and peers of the same sex are more likely to be consulted before the coach. Perhaps some players would prefer not to tell their coach about any trouble with the police for fear of jeopardizing their position on the team.

Another trouble situation, within an educational setting, was presented in the following question,

> If you were in trouble with the local officials because of a misunderstanding over a cheating incident whom would you probably go to for advice?"

In this situation, the coach ranks high, along with parents and classroom teacher, among persons the players would consult.

Data were also collected from the coaches to determine persons they felt were influential in their own educational and occupational plans. Their responses were tabulated to the following question,

> "When you were growing up, which of the following persons had the most influence on your thinking about getting an education and/or your future occupation?"

Their responses are similar to the players' responses to the same question except that their first choices showed a ranking of father, coach, and mother; in retrospect, the coaches perceive their own coaches as having been very influential in their decision to enter the coaching profession.

Schafer and Armer have raised the question of the great authority and influence of the coach in controlling the athletes' behavior beyond the context of the playing and practice area. For example, they pointed out that:

> The coach usually has the unquestioned authority to suspend or drop a boy from the team if he is caught smoking, drinking, staying out late, or violating the law. Some coaches even decide hair styles, dress, friendship patterns, and the language of their boys. A few 'training rules,' of course, are laid down for the sake of the athletes' physical conditioning and efficiency, but others can be understood only as part of the athlete is supposed to be a 'good American boy.' A fascinating question for research, therefore, is: What are the long term effects on the athlete from this rigid and often puritanical control by coaches? A related question: Do high school sports really contribute to the 'character development' that coaches so often claim?"

The present study does not provide data dealing directly with the questions raised by Schafer and Armer; however, data are available on advice given by coaches about the athletes' behavior beyond their actual participation in the sport itself.

There are important differences in the percentage of coaches and players who indicated that advice or suggestions were given on each category. Perhaps the coaches' perceptions are exaggerated regarding the extent of advice they give; inversely, the players' perceptions of the extent to which they have been given advice may be deflated. The differential perceptions, of course, may represent conflicting interpretations of statements made by the coach on these matters. Even with the probable differential perceptions, the Schafer-Armer position is supported regarding the coach's authority over the players' behavior beyond the immediate area of actual athletic participation.

An aspect of the coaches' potential influence in the quasi-religious and spiritual realm is the use of prayer at games. The present study revealed that 61 percent of the coaches said the team always or often had prayer before or during the basketball games; 16 percent sometimes; and 23 percent said they never had prayer. Players' responses indicated that 53 percent of their teams always or often had prayer; 13 percent sometimes; and 34 percent never. Once again the differential percentages between the coaches' and players' responses are interesting. However, the general pattern of extensive use of team prayers at the games in substantiated.

The influence of coaches does not necessarily cease when the players graduate. Many players continue to seek out their former coach for advice. Answers to the question, "Do you maintain contact with your former players?," disclosed that 51 percent of the coaches maintain regular contact; 47 percent sometimes; and only 2 percent do not continue these contacts. The coaches' responses to the question, "Do your former players come to you for advice or suggestions about personal problems?," showed 20 percent yes, regularly; 67 percent sometimes; and 12 percent seldom or never. The percentages of coaches who answered the question, "Do your former players come to you for advice or suggestions about educational and/or occupational plans?," were: yes, regularly 23 percent; 71 percent sometimes; and 6 percent seldom or never.

SUMMARY AND CONCLUSIONS

Research shows that participation in high school sports is an important status-granting activity. Thus most high school coaches are likely to have considerable influence over their players—especially the coach of a major sport such as basketball. When viewed from the theoretical perspective of the socialization process, the influence of the coach on his players contributes to both individual development and the transmission of cultural values and social expectations that contribute to the development of consensus and social control.

The present study provides empirical data that document several aspects of the coaches' influence over his players in the socialization process. A large majority of the players in the survey indicated that their basketball coach had been influential to them. A breakdown of the major types of influence included: helped with personal problems; development of basketball proficiency; taught pride, teamwork, sportsmanship and hard work. Several of these later traits reflect the manner in which sports are apparently transferring the values of the Protestant Ethic.

The data further demonstrate the important role of the coach in guidance and counselling of the players regarding their educational and occupational plans for the future. In general, the coaches ranked immediately behind the players' parents in this regard. Data collected from the coaches indicate that they also had been greatly influenced in the educational and occupational plans by their coaches. The influence of the reference persons and socialization agents does, however, vary with the situation. When faced with situations of trouble with the police and school authorities, the players indicated variations in their choice of persons they would consult for advice. Finally, the coach's influence as a socialization agent extends considerably beyond the behavior of players in the actual practice and participation in the game situation. Furthermore, the data shows that many former players continue to seek out their coaches for advice and suggestions.

This study illustrates the importance of additional research, preferably with a longitudinal dimension, to provide knowledge of the coach's importance in the socialization process. Continued research may illustrate variations in his influence, depending on such variables as the degree of player involvement, the coach's prestige, socioeconomic status, and/or ethnic group of the player.

CHAPTER 37

EVERYTHING THE ATHLETE ALWAYS WANTED TO KNOW ABOUT SELECTING A COLLEGE BUT WAS AFRAID TO ASK

WILLIAM F. STIER*

EACH YEAR THOUSANDS of high school student-athletes must cope with the problem of choosing the college that can best fulfill their academic and athletic aspirations. This task is seldom easy and is often viewed with more than just a little apprehension.

All too often the experience resolves into a hurried, high-pressured, and haphazard "Alice in Wonderland" excursion, instead of a systematic evaluation based upon predetermined criteria.

It is imperative for the college to be capable of providing meaningful academic, religious, athletic, social and cultural experiences—experiences that will enable the individual to develop his full potential.

When you consider the time, energy and care that are usually taken in selecting an automobile or a color TV set, it is amazing what little planning will go into the far more significant process of choosing a college. No wonder so many boys realize too late that their choice has failed to measure up to their expectations or meet their needs.

That is why it is so essential to plan most carefully. Though it is never too early to begin thinking about suitable colleges, it is probably wise to begin establishing a general plan of action sometime during the junior year in high school. By the fall of the senior year, at the very latest, the boy and his parents should

* William F. Stier, "Everything the Athlete Always Wanted to Know About Selecting a College but Was Afraid to Ask," *Scholastic Coach*, Vol. 43 (January 1974), pp. 80-81 and 94.

have established some specific guidelines to govern their dealings with college recruiters.

They must be cognizant of many general areas of concern about recruiting. The answers to the following questions should provide a frame of reference within which the student-athlete may compare various colleges and their athletic programs.

1. What type and size of institution am I seeking? Would I be happy in a large university with 25,000 or so students? A medium-size university with an enrollment possibly in the 8,000 to 12,000 range? Or would I be more comfortable in a smaller liberal arts college with an enrollment of 1,000 to 2,000? There are advantages and disadvantages to each and the student-athlete should be aware of them.

2. What about the location of the college? How far away from home do I wish to go? Is 200 miles acceptable? Would 1,000 or 2,000 miles be too far? Or is distance unimportant? Would I be able to get back home for vacations?

3. Do I want to commute to college or do I prefer the experience of living on campus? Would I be able to experience many more activities if I lived on campus?

4. What kind of town or city is the college located in? Is it a metropolitan area with thousands of residents and all the ills that accompany a densely populated area? Or is it a smaller community? How close to a major metropolitan area is the school?

5. What cultural, social and recreational opportunities are available within the college? In the community? How many of such activities are within driving distance of the school?

6. Do I desire a public or a private college? If the latter, would I prefer a school that is religiously affiliated or secular in nature?

7. Would I prefer a coeducational school to one for men only? If I prefer the latter, is there any nearby college with women students?

8. Is education my prime concern . . . to grow as a person while achieving competence in my chosen areas, thereby preparing for my life's work?

9. What type of academic discipline am I interested in pursuing? What is the reputation of the college? What is the reputa-

tion and status of the department in which I intend to major? Is the school progressive and innovative in its approach to higher education?

10. Is it the rule or the exception for athletes in this school to obtain their degrees within the usual four years?

11. What are the employment opportunities available to graduates in my proposed major field? Would a degree from this school increase such opportunities?

12. What are the general requirements of the college? How many semester hours of required courses are demanded? How many elective semester hours are allowed? What is the ratio between the number of semester hours in required and elective courses?

13. Do I possess the necessary skills and abilities to achieve, with hard work, some level of success in my proposed major field?

14. What are the opportunities for obtaining individual attention and assistance from faculty, administrators and counselors?

15. What is the structure of the academic calendar? Does the college operate on the traditional semester or quarter system? Or is one of the newer academic calendars in effect: the 3-3-3, 4-1-4, 4-4-1, or early semester calendar?

16. What type of food service is available to the student body? Is it a smorgasbord type of arrangement? Or are the students limited as to the amount and variety of food?

17. What about the residence hall situation? Are there rules (and are they enforced) governing quiet hours, etc., so that students attempting to study are not disturbed? Are all students required to live in campus facilities or are they allowed to live off campus? Are apartment style accommodations available to students, or are students limited to the more traditional dormitory style structures?

18. Are students allowed cars on campus as freshmen? As sophomores?

19. What is the attitude of the administration, faculty and students toward athletics in general and my sport in particular? Are athletics supported by the alumni and the community?

20. What is the relationship among all of the coaches of the various sports? Toward one another? Toward the entire athletic program? Is there bickering among them?

21. Is there harmony between the current squad members and the coaching staff?

22. How many athletes have quit the team during the past two or three years? Why? How many have been dismissed from the team within the same time period? Why?

23. If I am a member of a minority race, would I be comfortable in a situation where there are few or no minority students, faculty members or coaches? Is the institution cognizant of the needs of minority students? Are such needs being met?

24. Is there stability in the athletic program? Or has there been a great turnover of head and assistant coaches?

25. What type of facilities and equipment are available for academic, athletic and recreational pursuits? Are the facilities (football stadium, fieldhouse, ice hockey rink, baseball diamonds, wrestling rooms, etc.) and the equipment indicative of a first-class or a "bush" athletic program?

26. Is an athletic trainer available for the athletic squads? Is there a first-class training room?

27. What type of medical care is available to the athletes? What type of insurance program is provided? Who pays for the insurance program—the athlete or the school?

28. What are the specific goals of the athletic program, especially as they affect my sports?

29. What has been the past history, past accomplishments of the team in my sport?

30. What style of game would I prefer to play on the college level? For example, if I prefer fast-break basketball to the controlled style, would it be wise to reject the schools that favor the latter?

31. What is the caliber of the competition? Does the team compete in a strong league? What is the likelihood of post-season competition? Would a team have to win the conference or just finish in the top two to win a post-season bid?

32. How does the team travel? By private car, school car, bus or plane?

33. Has the college or coaching staff earned a reputation for mistreating or being dishonest with athletes?

34. How many players are usually retained on the squad? How many on the traveling squad? Does the school have a frosh team? A junior varsity team?

35. Does the coaching staff have a reputation for recruiting many junior college transfers?

36. How many freshmen are actually recruited each year?

37. Have I been promised a starting berth? How many other prospects have been told this by the coaching staff?

38. What are my chances of playing varsity ball during my four years? How many outstanding athletes will be ahead of me or competing with me for a specific position?

39. If I am promised or if I qualify for financial assistance, what exactly does such assistance provide? How should I evaluate and compare financial assistance among various schools? What is the difference (if any) between the financial assistance proffered and the total cost of attending the college each year? (A school providing $2,000 in financial aid while costing $4,500 per year requires the athlete to come up with $2,500, whereas a school providing only $1,500 in financial assistance but costing only $3,000 a year requires the student to pay only $1,500 to make up the difference.)

40. If the financial aid package involves work-study assistance, has the coach "promised" or indicated that such work will only be "token" and that someone will take care of crediting me with forty work hours for emptying a waste basket once or twice? If so, do I want to become involved in such a dishonest and unethical situation?

41. Has the coaching staff or anyone connected with the college or the athletic program offered any illegal or unethical situation?

41. Has the coaching staff or anyone connected with the college or the athletic program offered any illegal or unethical in-

ducements to me or my family? Can I trust the coach or staff who acts in such a manner to be honest with me in the future?

42. If I am to receive financial assistance, will it be continued if I am injured and cannot participate anymore?

43. If I am unable to earn the degree in four years, will I continue getting financial assistance in my fifth year? If I become academically ineligible, will I retain the financial assistance?

44. Will I be eligible to play for the college with my present academic credentials? Will I be able to remain eligible with an average amount of hard work?

45. Is the financial assistance guaranteed for one year, two, three or four years?

46. If the financial assistance is not guaranteed beyond a year, how is it renewed from year to year? Under what circumstances may it be rescinded or reduced?

47. What are the team rules with respect to dress, grooming, hours, training, etc.? Are the current rules compatible with my personal philosophy and life style? Would I feel more comfortable in a conservative or liberal atmosphere?

48. Is the coach and his staff interested in me as an individual or as merely a "tool" with which to win ball games? Does the staff recognize that the primary purpose of attending college is to earn a degree?

49. If I do not possess big-time potential, is it wiser to be a big fish in a small pond or a small fish in a big pond?

50. Does the head coach and his staff have a reputation for competency, honesty and integrity in all matters?

To obtain the answers to all these questions (and thus achieve greater insight into the college and its athletic program), it is necessary for the student-athlete to do his homework. He must consult with as many individuals and groups as possible.

The preliminary work should begin with the coaches, guidance counselors, and other faculty members at his high school. The boy should attempt to obtain as much specific information as possible about his ability and potential both in the classroom and on the playing field, as well as about the advantages and disadvantages of attending the schools he is interested in.

He would also do well to query other students and athletes who have attended or are currently attending these colleges. This will yield an additional insight into the type of life he might expect at these schools.

The key to obtaining the most from such consultations or visits lies in an intelligent and searching type of questioning. One should not make a major decision, such as the selection of a college, without first obtaining a clear and realistic idea of exactly what life at the college and on the athletic team will be like.

No discussion of student-athlete recruitment would be complete without mention of visitations. Both the boy and, if possible, his parents, should visit the schools that are seriously being considered.

They must remember that it is highly undesirable, if not downright unethical, to string along a coach or a school. The boy who expects to be treated honestly by coaches must be honest and frank with them. Whenever he eliminates a school, he should immediately inform the coach. He should not accept any ego or pleasure trips. He is not only taking unfair advantage of the coach and school but also stealing valuable time from his studies.

It is best to narrow the field down to three or five schools. Any number more than that brings on a confusing and cumbersome situation which only impedes the decision-making process.

Once the student-athlete decides on the colleges he wishes to visit, it is imperative to make his visitations meaningful. While on campus, he should visit potential professors (especially those in his major field), the academic dean, the dean of student affairs and even the president of the college, if the latter is available and willing to spend any time with him.

Admittedly, visitations with key personnel are often possible only on the smaller campuses, but the boy should try to see such people at the larger schools as well.

Some of the advantages traditionally claimed by the smaller liberal-arts institutions, such as greater individual attention, are not always the exclusive property of the "little" schools. They may exist in the largest of universities as well.

The student-athlete should also take advantage of the opportunity to eat on campus and stay in one of the residence halls overnight. This will give him an excellent opportunity to converse with a good cross-section of the student body. Of course a visit with the members of the team that he is being asked to join is also a necessity.

Without doubt these visitations are most valuable learning experiences which the individual should take advantage of.

What better way is there of obtaining a realistic concept of what is in store for him than by soliciting information, viewpoints and opinions from the individuals and groups who are currently involved with either the college and/or the team?

THE COACH AND
THE TEAM

CHAPTER 38

GROUP COHESION IN ATHLETICS

GARRY J. SMITH*

TEAM MORALE PLAYS a vital role in competition. It is a key ingredient in developing winning teams and the literature
teems with references attesting to this.

Bateman and Governali[1] claim that "Better morale is often
the factor responsible for victory of one team over another of
equal ability." McCracken[2] takes a similar stand when he states,
"The important factors that mean the difference between a great
ball club and an average one, even though the players are of
equal ability, are the unseen assets that must be developed by the
coach in his players." At the top of "unseen assets" are "team
spirit" or "morale."

Four other coaches corroborate this with almost identical statements: "The most important factor on the football squad is
morale." . . . "High morale is essential to team success." . . .
"Team success is contingent upon good team morale." . . . "Spirit
and morale are the guiding forces for the success of any team."

These statements are not scientifically grounded. They usually
stem from subjective evaluations based on many years of experience. The lack of a scientific approach does not necessarily mean
that the statements lack veracity. But it does make them suspect,
especially in view of the contradictory evidence uncovered by behavioral scientists examining the morale-productivity relationship.

Research-oriented physical educators have not concerned them-

* Garry J. Smith, "Group Cohesion in Athletics," *Scholastic Coach*, Vol. 39
(November 1969), pp. 52-53 and 79.

1. J. F. Bateman and P. V. Governali, *Football Fundamentals* (New York,
McGraw-Hill, 1957).

2. B. McCracken, *Indiana Basketball* (New York, Prentice-Hall, 1955).

selves greatly with human-relations problems in athletics. Graves[3] notes the insufficiency of material on team morale: "This par·ticular phase of the game . . . is the least discussed. There has been very little written about the subject, and almost no one has ever set up a particular guide to go by in this vital phase of the game."

The term, "morale," is used by coaches to describe an "all for one and one for all attitude." The terms, "team spirit" and "esprit de corps" are popular synonyms for morale.

Since the behavioral scientists prefer to use the term, "group cohesion," to describe the attraction of a group for its members, it will be emphasized in this paper.

A review of the literature reveals a schism. Some authors have found group cohesion beneficial to productivity, while others have found no significant relationship between the two variables. The studies traditionally have been carried out by sociologists and social psychologists, who have studied the concept of group cohesion primarily in an industrial context.

As mentioned previously, practically no scientific research on the concept of group cohesion has been carried out in a physical education or athletic context. The literature reveals only one truly scientific study.

In studying the effects of integration (or cohesion) and morale on the productivity of football teams, Stogdill[4] found: ". . . that a heavy investment of motivation effort and skill provided a condition under which positive correlations occurred between productivity integration and morale."

SUBJECTIVE OBSERVATIONS

The remainder of the writings by physical educators in this area are nonscientific in nature. They usually take the form of articles written by coaches on the benefits of high-level team spirit or morale. The views expressed are generally derived from subjective observations of various teams.

---

3. R. Graves, *Guide to Modern Football Defense* (West Nyack, N. Y., Parker Publishing Co., 1966).

4. R. M. Stogdill, *Team Achievement Under High Motivation* (Columbus, The Bureau of Business Research, College of Commerce and Administration, Ohio State University, 1963).

A study by Kaplan[5] typifies the physical educator's approach to group cohesion. The study consisted of a subjective analysis of the types of leadership exhibited on two informal volleyball teams. Kaplan found that group performance was highly related to group structural unity.

He reinforced this view with his description of a nonproductive team: "Morale deteriorates and the individuals unable to find satisfaction in the coordinated group seek personal satisfactions by nonpatterned idiosyncratic play."

Comments by Jackson[6] and Zeigler[7] serve to illustrate the kind of material traditionally offered by physical educators to explain the phenomenon of team spirit and its relationship to group performance.

Jackson claims: ". . . that teamwork and cooperation are absolutely essential for success in any group endeavor. Group spirit, subordination of the individual to the needs of the team, and self-sacrifice are all necessary for the best team performance."

Zeigler agrees with Jackson. He notes that "group effort means team effort . . . a team can best achieve its goal by unselfish cooperative play throughout the game."

Few coaches would deny that team spirit or morale is important in team success, yet little scholarly research has been produced to verify this belief.

A recent study by Mikalachki[8] appears to resolve much of the controversy and confusion surrounding the concept of group cohesion and its relationship to group productivity. Mikalachki developed a typology of group cohesion, breaking the concept

5. S. J. Kaplan, "Leadership and Group Structure in Volleyball: An Appraisal," *Journal of the Physical Education Association of Great Britain and Northern Ireland,* Vol. 53 (1961), p. 44.

6. C. O. Jackson, "What About Sportsmanship," *The Physical Educator,* Vol. 6 (1949), p. 13.

7. E. F. Zeigler, "The Case Method Approach to the Teaching of Human Relations and Administration in Physical Education," *The Physical Educator,* Vol. 18 (1958), p. 30.

8. A. Mikalachki, "Group Cohesion Reconsidered," Unpublished Doctoral Dissertation, School of Business Administration, University of Western Ontario, London, Ontario, 1964.

down into its various constituent dimensions. The two most important dimensions were labeled "task" and "social cohesion."

The difference between the two types of cohesion, according to Mikalachki, "revolves primarily around the focus of group integration. A task group's focus of integration is the task (that) the group is ostensibly organized to perform. A social group will focus on a social goal with develops spontaneously rather than on the specific goal or goals for which it was organized."

One of Mikalachki's major conclusions was that the level of production of the task cohesive groups would be high while that of the socially cohesive groups would be low.

This finding appears to have major implications for coaches, as high productivity is a major goal; and coaches with high-productivity goals obviously must develop, foster and maintain a high level of task cohesion.

The conditions which lead to the development of task cohesion have not been scientifically assayed and a great deal of speculation exists on what these ideal conditions might be.

One of the most important determinants in the formation of an extreme task cohesive group is the presence of a skillful leader. This type of leader must be imbued with a strong desire to succeed and must be able to instill this quality in the group members.

The leader must also possess personality and behavioral characteristics which will enable him to obtain the best possible performance from each individual and from the group as a whole.

Tannenbaum *et al.*[9] agree in listing as prime requisites for a leader the qualities of "social sensitivity" and "behavioral flexibility." Simply stated, social sensitivity refers to the leader's skill in diagnosing the behavioral phenomena within the group. Behavioral flexibility concerns the leader's capacity to react to his analysis of the group behavior.

The leader endowed with these human-relations qualities will be able to recognize and react to the various subtleties and nu-

---

9. F. Tannenbaum, I. R. Weschler and F. Massarik, *Leadership and Organization* (New York, McGraw-Hill, 1961).

ances inherent in group behavior. A good leader is thus essential in developing a high-level task cohesion.

It goes without saying that the leader must be technically competent. Poor athletes seldom become leaders. Also worthy of note is the point that although task cohesive groups must have skillful leadership, this leadership does not necessarily have to reside with the formal leader of the group. There may be joint leadership, where the group is led by the formal leader with assistance from a subordinate. An example of this would be the coach–quarterback leadership structure on football teams.

Wherever the formal leader is impotent and lacks group respect, the group can still continue to function in a task cohesive manner under the direction of an informal leader.

The implication that skillful leadership is a significant factor in group task cohesion points out a flaw in many physical education and coaching preparatory programs. Most professional courses strive to develop the individual's technical competence, but rarely emphasize his human-relations role.

Though other important determinants enter into the development of task cohesive groups, most of the authors feel that these hinge on the coach's ability to manipulate group conditions and climate.

This being the case it is extremely important for the coach to be cognizant of the significance of task cohesion and to know how to develop and maintain it.

SUGGESTED READINGS

Berkowitz, L.: "Group Standards, Cohesiveness and Productivity," *Human Relations,* 1954.

Faurot, D.: *Secrets of the Split T Formation.* Englewood Cliffs, Prentice-Hall, 1956.

Goodacre, D. M.: "Group Characteristics of Good and Poor Performing Combat Units," *Sociometry* 16:168-178, 1953.

Hayes, W.: *Football at Ohio State.* Columbus; Ohio State University Press, 1957.

Katchmer, G. A.: *How to Organize and Conduct Football Practices.* Englewood Cliffs, Prentice-Hall, 1962.

Katchmer, G. A.: *Pregame Football Preparation and Strategy.* Englewood Cliffs, Prentice-Hall, 1965.

Kraz, D., Maccoby, N., Gurin, G., and Floor, L. G.: *Productivity Supervision and Morale Among Railroad Workers.* Ann Arbor; Survey Research Center, 1951.

Krech, D., and Crutchfield, R. S.: *Theory and Problems of Social Psychology.* New York, McGraw-Hill, Vol. 6, 1963.

Mayo, E., and Lombard, G. F. F.: *Teamwork and Labor Turnover in the Aircraft Industry of Southern California.* Boston, Harvard Business School, 1944.

Schacter, S., Ellerston, N., McBride, D., and Gregory, W.: "An Experimental Study of Cohesiveness and Productivity," *Human Relations,* 4:229, 1951.

Seashore, S. E.: *Group Cohesiveness in the Industrial Work Group,* Ann Arbor, Survey Research Center, University of Michigan, 1954.

CHAPTER 39

THE COACH AS MANAGEMENT: ORGANIZATIONAL LEADERSHIP IN AMERICAN SPORT

George H. Sage*

L EADERSHIP IS THE PROCESS of influencing the activities of an organized group toward goal setting and goal achievement.[1] For most American sports teams the coach is the appointed leader. While it really is not known to what extent the success or failure of a team is due to the leadership competence of the coach, there is little doubt that it is an important factor in team performance and the coach, as the leader, is held responsible for the team's performance. Thus, the coach serves a function that is similar to management leaders in the business world.

Many aspects of our society are experiencing a transformation from traditional values of corporate organization and the Protestant Ethic to a new and different moral and ethical system. Accordingly, athletic coaches are being forced into reassessing their current beliefs concerning interpersonal relations, especially in a leadership context, and many are seeking ways of developing more effective personal relationships with the young athletes on their teams. Several recent critics from within and outside the sports setting have claimed that traditional sports practices and values are dehumanizing and brutalizing and that coaches are insensitive and autocratic.[2] They are calling for a counter-culture

* George H. Sage, "The Coach as Management: Organizational Leadership in American Sport," *Quest*, Vol. 19 (January 1973), pp. 35-40.

1. R. Stogdill, "Leadership, Membership, and Organization." *Psychological Bulletin*, Vol. 47 (1959), pp. 1-14.

2. D. Meggyesy, *Out of Their League* (New York, Ramparts Press, 1971).

J. Scott, *The Athletic Revolution* (New York, The Free Press, 1971).

B. C. Ogilvie and T. A. Tutko, Sport. If You Want to Build Character, Try Something Else, *Psychology Today*, Vol. 5 (October 1971), pp. 61-63.

in sport, based on individuality, human values, and self-actualization.

THE SCIENTIFIC MANAGEMENT AND LEADERSHIP STYLE

The fundamental complaint of those who attack athletic coaches is directed toward the leadership style which is employed by many coaches. Tutko and Richards[3] suggest that as leaders most coaches believe in strong discipline, rigidity of rules, extrinsic motivation and an impersonal attitude towards their athletes, and they characterize most coaches as being hard-nosed or authoritarian. This leadership strategy bears a strong resemblance to that employed by the so-called Scientific Management movement which emerged from the studies and writing of Frederick W. Taylor[4] in the early years of the 20th century, a time of population growth and industrial expansion. Taylor's managerial methods were based on cost efficiency. He suggested that an organization could achieve its production goals only when it could achieve an optimal cost-efficiency ratio. Taylor's primary propositions were, (1) Use time and methods study to find the one best way of performing a job. By the best way is meant the way that permits the largest average rate of production over the day. (2) Provide the employee with an incentive to perform the job in the best way and at good pace. In general, do this by giving him a specified bonus over regular rates if he meets the standard of production. (3) Use specialized experts to establish the various conditions surrounding the worker's task. Scientific Management treated man as a means by assuming that he would cooperate and work only when forced to do so. This arrangement reduced man to an instrument of the organization who functions under a hierachical authority relationship. The climate of interpersonal relationship under the Scientific Management approach was at a low level. Relations between leaders, or managers and workers

3. T. A. Tutko and J. W. Richards, *Psychology of Coaching* (Boston, Allyn and Bacon, 1971).

4. F. W. Taylor, *The Principles of Scientific Management* (New York, Harper and Row, 1911a).

F. W. Taylor, *Shop Management* (New York, Harper and Row, 1911b).

were closed and inflexible; there was little opportunity for change initiated by the workers.

The underlying notion implicit in the Scientific Management approach with regard to the nature of man is that he is bad, lazy and incentive orientated. This notion has firm historic roots. Machiavelli[5] in *The Prince*, suggested that man is by nature uncooperative and rebellious and must be ruthlessly controlled. He said: ". . . men in general . . . are ungrateful, voluble, dissemblers, anxious to avoid dangers, and covetous of gain." Hobbes, Darwin, Freud and more recently Ardrey have all held pessimistic assumptions about the nature of man.

American business enthusiastically adopted Taylor's approach to management leadership, and this leadership style has frequently been used by various nonbusiness organizations such as schools, the military and sports.[6] While research which began in the late 1920's and extended to the present has shown that the basic assumptions of Scientific Management with regard to worker performance has questionable validity, nevertheless some segments of American organizational life still adhere to the propositions and methods of Scientific Management.

One sphere of American organizational life in which this leadership style has traditionally been utilized is in athletic coaching.[7] With the rise of increasingly institutionalized and codified team organization, many coaches have tended to view team members as objects in a machine-like environment where emphasis is on instrumental rather than consummatory behaviors. Thus, the players become another man's (the coach) instru-

5. N. Machiavelli, *The Prince* (New York, Mentor Books, 1952), p. 98. Translation of the book first published in 1532.

6. R. E. Callahan, *Education and the Cult of Efficiency* (Chicago, The University of Chicago Press, 1962).

R. E. Callahan has argued that Scientific Management was one of the most important historic forces to shape the administration of public schools in America.

7. D. Riesman and R. Denny, Football in America: a Study of Cultural Diffusion. *American Quarterly*, Vol. 3 (1951), pp. 309-319.

Riesman and Denny in their classic paper on cultural diffusion and American football discuss the relation between Taylor's writings and the development of American football.

ment and are used to reach the objectives and goals of the organizational collectivity; they are reduced to cogs in the organization's machinery. Accordingly, coaches have structured coach-player relations along authoritarian lines; they have analyzed and structured sports team positions for precise specialization of the performers, and they have endeavored to control player behavior not only throughout practice and contest periods but also on a round-the-clock basis, e.g. grooming rules, training rules, dating behavior, etc. Furthermore, for incentives and rewards, a system of letter awards, newspaper stories, locker room posters, helmet decals, etc. have been used. An observer at many athletic team practice sessions might believe that he was viewing a factory assembly line work shift. Indeed, the coaches punctuate the air regularly with shouts of "work, work, work."

The organization in this case is the team and the players under this form of leadership are the instruments for the fulfillment of organizational goals. In most cases, they have not been consulted about the organizational goals (it is assumed that they want to be champions and that they are willing to pay the price to be winners). They have not been consulted about team membership, practice methods, team strategy, or any of the other dynamic functions of a team. The assumption has been made that they have nothing to contribute toward identifying group goals and the means for achieving them. Decisions are made by management (the coach), after a thorough cost efficiency analysis, and the players are expected to carry out the will of the coach for the accomplishment of organizational goals.

HUMAN RELATIONS MANAGEMENT AND LEADERSHIP STYLE

Over forty years ago social research began to throw serious doubt on the validity of Scientific Management versions of human nature and leadership functions. The research of Elton Mayo[8] at the Western Electric Company's plant in Chicago initiated what became known as the Human Relations school of

8. E. Mayo, *The Human Problem of an Industrial Civilization* (New York, The Macmillan Company, 1933).

management leadership. This was followed by the research of Kurt Lewin[9] in the 1930's and 1940's in social psychology; various writers and researchers built upon Lewin's work and by the 1960's McGregor[10] formulated a definitive work on leadership for executives which he called the Theory Y form of management. Finally, Abraham Maslow[11] indirectly contributed to Human Relations leadership theory through his writings in psychology which have fostered what has become known as Third Force Psychology. Mayo and his colleagues found in their studies at the Hawthorne plant of Western Electric in Chicago that formal and informal personal relations are critically important to productivity and job satisfaction. In *Human Problems of an Industrial Civilization,* Mayo concluded that his extensive research showed that workers do not respond as isolated individuals, but as members of a group. More specifically, he suggested that there is a social system consisting of established informal relationships between particular persons in any live organization and this system invariably has important consequences for achievement. Improvement of the organization's achievement will be either impossible or extremely difficult if informal relationships are not taken into account.

Building upon Mayo's work, Kurt Lewin, one of the most prominent social psychologists, suggested several implications of his research for organizational leadership. Most importantly he suggested that the willingness of a person to cooperate in a program of activities depends on his perception of the environment and his own place in it. Moreover, groups with a democratic atmosphere, whose members participate in determining their own

9. K. Lewin, *Dynamic Theory of Personality* (New York, McGraw-Hill, 1935).

K. Lewin, *Principles of Topological Psychology* (New York, McGraw-Hill, 1936).

K. Lewin and G. W. Allport (eds.), *Resolving Social Conflicts* (New York, Harper and Row, 1948).

10. D. McGregor, *The Human Side of Enterprise* (New York, McGraw-Hill, 1969).

11. A. Maslow, *Motivation and Personality* (New York, Harper and Row, 1954).

A. Maslow, *Eupsychion Management* (Homewood, Ill., Irwin-Dorsey, 1965).

goals, will have higher morale and more commitment to the organization than those directed by authoritarian leaders. Under some conditions, the amount of participation will determine the group's level of achievement.

Maslow developed an intriguing and persuasive theory of human motivation which touches on every aspect of human behavior. His theory challenged some of the basic premises that have dominated American social theory during the early 20th century. Maslow's theory is centered on man himself—his needs, his goals, his achievements and his success. He saw people as able to make their own decisions and deal with their own crises; he saw them as trustworthy, dependable and possessing a dignity and an integrity which must be respected; finally he held that people are capable of being creative, dynamic and active participants with their environments.

McGregor's work is in the tradition of the Human Relations approach and the Theory Y style of management which he proposed draws heavily from Mayo, Lewin and Maslow. The viewpoint underlying Theory Y is summarized by McGregor[12] as follows:

1. The expenditure of physical and mental effort in work is as natural as play or rest. The average human being does not inherently dislike work. Depending upon controllable conditions work may be a source of satisfaction.

2. External control and the threat of punishment are not the only means for bringing about effort toward organizational objectives. Man will exercise self-direction and self-control in the service of objectives to which he is committed.

3. Commitment to objectives is a function of the rewards associated with their achievement. The most significant of such rewards, e.g. the satisfaction of ego and self-actualization needs, can be direct products of effort directed toward organization objectives.

4. The average human being learns, under proper conditions, not only to accept but to seek responsibility. Avoidance of responsibility, lack of ambition and emphasis on security

12. McGregor, *op. cit.*, 1960, pp. 47-48.

are generally consequences of experience, not inherent characteristics.

5. The capacity to exercise a relatively high degree of imagination, ingenuity, and creativity in the solution of organizational problems is widely, not narrowly, distributed in the population.

6. Under the conditions of modern industrial life, the intellectual potentialities of the average human being are only partially utilized.

McGregor[13] suggests that if employees are lazy, indifferent, unwilling to take responsibility, intransigent, uncreative, uncooperative, their behavior is due to the traditional bureaucratic assumptions and methods of organization and control.

The Human Relations approach to leadership differs from Scientific Management in that it emphasizes men in contrast to positions; that is, it is deeply concerned with attitudes, values and emotional reactions of individual group members. This viewpoint sees man as only minimally controlled by the carrot and stick principle; instead effective control is viewed as developing from within the individual. External control will not motivate men to apply all of their talents in behalf of group goals. The emphasis is on nonauthoritarian styles of leadership, member participation in group decision making and encouragement of organization activities in the service of individual needs. In short, this approach permits individual autonomy, presumably maximizing task involvement and intrinsic motivation. Individual goals and organizational goals become the same.

The conceptions of human nature and personality are quite different within these two systems of thought. Scientific Management holds these assumptions about man: He is inherently self-centered, lacks ambition, dislikes responsibility, prefers to be led, is indifferent to group needs, resistant to change and is by nature an indolent creature who works as little as possible. Thus, strong leaders must be responsible for organizing the elements or goal accomplishments; they must direct, motivate and control

13. D. McGregor, "The Human Side of Enterprise," *Management Review*, Vol. 46 (1957), pp. 22-28 and 88-92.

the workers' actions, modifying their behavior to meet the needs of the organization. The leader's task is to persuade, reward, punish and control member behavior. The leader must get things done through the members. The Human Relations approach holds these assumptions about man: He is not by nature passive or resistant to group needs, he has become so as a result of experience in organizations; the motivation, the capacity for assuming responsibility and the readiness to direct behavior toward group goals are all present in people. This approach has as its foundation the notion that man's tendency toward good can be made to prevail, if given the opportunity, and that he can make sound decisions concerning himself and in cooperation with others engage in constructive and supportive performance. Accordingly, it is the responsibility of leaders to make it possible for people to recognize and develop their human characteristics for themselves. Leaders must arrange organizational conditions and procedures so that people can achieve their own goals best by directing their own efforts toward organizational objectives.

Organizational Leadership and the Coach

This second approach is more in keeping with contemporary values and ethics which emphasize individuality and freedom from capricious autocratic control. Today, the task of the coach is to enhance his players' potential and enable them to enjoy what they are doing, derive joy and satisfaction from their sports participation, and thus achieve self-fulfillment. In applying Human Relations leadership to sports, the coach will not assume without question that the total team program takes precedence over the needs and desires of team members. Preferences of the individual will be given equal consideration with those of the team. Team objectives and methods of reaching them will be accomplished by consultation with all team members. The coach will restrict his own authority to essentials, not imposing his arbitrary will upon the players. The old arrangement by which the athletes are instruments of the coach will give way to a mutuality in which each functions to the advantage of the other.

This is not to suggest that directive and dynamic leadership is to be abandoned to a form of obsequious equalitarianism. Many persons assume that strong, directive leadership is always bad, overlooking the fact that there are psychologically healthy leaders whose motives are for the good of their group members and the good of the organization. Indeed, in Maslow's opinion the great leader is one who has just the right combination of humility and flexibility while at the same time possessing the strength of character to stand alone when an important principle is involved. Maslow says: "The kind of person who must be loved by all probably will not make a good leader."[14] He implies that there are circumstances when the leader must say no, be firm, strong and courageous. But the excellent leader takes pleasure in seeing his group members grow and self-actualize under the necessary restraints of group membership. It is nonsense to suppose that every step in coaching can be democratic. It is obvious that in task oriented groups, such as one finds in sports, where decisions frequently have to be made quickly and on the basis of experience a pure democratic leadership system cannot effectively prevail. That a leader may have to unilaterally make decisions for the group does not necessarily diminish his sensitivity and humanism for the members.

The coach and athlete are in need of each other; team goals cannot be accomplished without both. The emphasis here is that coach and player need each other and benefit by mutual accommodation of objectives and goals. Leadership significantly affects the personal development of those who are led and it is often a critical factor in an individual's attitudes about the group and human relations in general. The coach needs to seek new ways of relating to players; he needs to become more aware and sensitive to other people. An increased sensitivity to others' unique humanness will enhance individual actualization and may lead to better performance. The coach can reflect in his leadership behavior a willingness to have confidence and trust in his players, for this creates a foundation for building individual confi-

---

14. Maslow, *op. cit.*, 1965, p. 130.

dence and security. In applying a leadership style of this kind the coach will be raising the level of interpersonal relations in the athletic world. Team membership will become inherently interesting and gratifying, and sports participation will become a genuine cooperative venture for coach and players and its rewards will be what Maslow calls "peak experiences" in personal-social living.

CHAPTER 40

ORGANIZATION BEGINS WITH THE COACH

DALE HANKS*

SINCE MOST COACHES agree that proper team organization is a prerequisite for success, it follows that before a coach can organize his team he must first organize himself. Of the former type of organization we hear frequently; of the latter type, so very seldom.

The ideas that follow certainly are not original, but rather techniques that have proved effective in industry and the armed forces.

The duties and functioning of a coach closely parallel those of a business executive or an armed forces officer. Either alone, or in conjunction with other people, the coach formulates certain plans. These plans, as pertaining to his department, are executed or put into effect by the coach.

Thus, he is in an executive capacity, being responsible for planning and carrying out these plans through the coordination of ideas, equipment, facilities and people working toward a common objective.

The coach who is forever looking for misplaced correspondence, forgetting important dates of events, and the like, is wasting considerable time and having his mind constantly cluttered with minor problems that could best be written down somewhere, thus freeing his mind for more important considerations.

First of all, if the coach is to properly organize himself, a definite need is an office or at least some area in which he can collect his varied paraphernalia along with his thoughts in an atmosphere of calm and quiet. Conducting administrative matters

---

* Dale Hanks, "Organization Begins With the Coach," *Scholastic Coach*, Vol. 29 (October 1959), pp. 66-68.

in study hall or by the water fountain too often leads to hap-hazard results.

On or near the coach's desk should be some type of device or structure commonly referred to as an "In Box." This device should contain at least three compartments of sufficient size to accommodate routine correspondence.

The first compartment should be marked "in." All incoming mail should be received and stored in this compartment while it awaits proper action. Correspondence to be sent out should be deposited in the second compartment labeled "out."

Arrangements should be made for some person, either the coach or some appointed individual, to collect all outgoing correspondence from this box at regular intervals and to see that it is properly distributed.

The third section should be marked "file," or "hold." This compartment should also be checked regularly and proper disposition made of the material therein.

In the vicinity of his desk the coach should maintain a current calendar. This should be of sufficient size and construction to allow written information to be annotated on the pertinent calendar dates. The calendar should be easy to read and permit the posting of new information which may become available from time to time.

If the coach is involved in travel with varsity teams, he will find it convenient to post a map of his travel area. This map, which should be of sufficient size to be easily read, is an invaluable aid in planning trip schedules.

In or near his desk the coach should maintain an ample supply of stationery. Preferably, this should bear the school or department letterhead, with, of course, a sufficient number of envelopes and stamps.

In addition to the stationery, there should be in a regular place an adequate supply of staples, paper clips, thumb tacks and other such devices. Although these are indeed minor items of equipment, they are often indispensable in helping keep things together and in the proper place.

If at all possible and/or practical, the coach's office should be equipped with a telephone. The amount of time and number of steps saved by having immediate access to this communication means will enable the coach to apply much more time and energy toward other necessary tasks. Generally speaking, the savings made here outweigh the expense many times over.

In regard to the maintenance of office files, the varsity coach in particular can benefit by emulating, to a degree, standard US Army procedure. In a sense, both coaching and army operations are very similar, with each sharing many common problems. With a minimum of planning, the coach can break his entire operation down into four phases:

1. Personnel (his own).
2. Intelligence (information of opponents).
3. Plans and Operations.
4. Supply.

In setting up his administrative files, the coach can divide the system into the four phases mentioned above. He can give each file a number as indicated. Where practical, it is best to have the four files completely separated. Within each filing compartment, material should be filed in standard manila folders which accommodate the normal 8½" by 11" sheets.

After dividing his system into the four general phases, it is an easy matter to place the file folders in simple alphabetical order for quick reference. In the "1" or Personnel file, for example, he would have readily available information on his squad, such as eligibility rosters, pictures and various information used by the press.

In the "2" or Intelligence file is kept all pertinent information regarding the various opponents on the schedule. It is advisable to maintain a complete folder for each opponent. Any information of the opponent such as scouting reports, eligibility lists, etc., can be safely stored in a systematic manner.

In the "3" or Operations file is kept all other material not dealt with specifically by the other three files. Any matter dealing with routine operations and plans is stored here. Since this file is referred to possibly more often than the others, it should be extremely well planned.

Operations File—Subdivisions

For example, the Operations file may be further subdivided into major units such as Football, Basketball, Track, Intramurals, etc. Within the football section would be, typically, signed contracts, schedule, list of officials, offensive plays, insurance matters, notes on future plans, pass patterns, defenses, rules, etc. The same type of file organization could naturally follow with regard to other areas of major interest.

In the "4" or Supply file should be kept all matters dealing with equipment, such as catalogs, orders, and repair. Each file— Personnel, Intelligence, Operations, and Supply—should contain a "suspense" folder. The purpose of the suspense file is to hold all matters requiring and awaiting further action.

In some cases it may be found more practical to include all suspense material in one folder. If so, this should be kept as a part of the Operations file. In either case, definite provisions should be made for suspense items dealing with all four phases. It must be remembered to check this file regularly for proper disposition of all suspense items.

Another expedient which makes for smoother administration is the utilization of standard forms; especially in high schools where students are used as managers and trainers and in the execution of other such tasks, the coach can increase efficiency with well-planned forms that serve as check lists.

A varsity manager or trainer, for example, in packing his equipment for an out-of-town game could ensure completeness in this task by checking off the many items he is responsible for on a simple, detailed form. There are other numerous instances where standard forms of this type can be employed to quite an advantage.

With standard forms used by students, it is advisable to include a place for the responsible student's signature upon completion of the task with which the form deals. It is indeed the exceptional high school student who functions effectively in a job without benefit of supervision and guide-posts.

By requiring the forms to be returned with signatures affixed certifying the job has been accomplished, the coach can be reasonably sure it has been done well.

It will be found convenient to store the blank forms in the "4" or Supply file for accessibility. By devising his own standard forms, the coach can easily obtain mimeographed copies, since most schools maintain this type of equipment. Dividends can be reaped many times over through proper use of standardized forms.

The final aid to greater administration efficiency is the bulletin board. Many boards are so ill-kept that they serve little or no purpose at all. Too often, the same material remains posted for so long that prospective viewers know what is there without looking and tend to eventually disregard the bulletin board completely.

The bulletin board must be appealing in order to attract attention. Some bulletin board material, by its very nature, may be of the permanent variety. Other material worthy of posting may be only of a temporary nature. Thus, a desirable feature of the bulletin board would be a division into two sections, aptly designated as "Permanent," and "Temporary" or "Current."

In order to be effective, though, the temporary section must be changed with frequent regularity or else the entire effort will be of little avail. If no material is on hand that merits posting, it is better to leave the bulletin board vacant rather than clutter it with meaningless triviality. A well-kept bulletin board can be an important asset in dispensing information and a subtle medium for planting ideas and molding opinions.

By way of summary, one could say that team organization, which is so essential to success, begins with coach organization. Coaches on any level can gain valuable tips on administrative techniques from two highly organized American institutions—industry and the armed forces.

Specifically, the coach can implement or improve his own organizational campaign by arranging his desk in an orderly and business-like fashion. He should maintain a simple filing system that will enable him to have immediate and easy access to records which are pertinent to any phase of his operation.

He should develop a set of standard forms that are consistent with his situation and which are especially helpful in delegating duties to students. He should maintain for his squad an attractive and up-to-date bulletin board through which he can disseminate much information.

By having himself properly coordinated in administrative matters, the coach will generate an atmosphere of organization that will surely be reflected by his players on the "fields of friendly strife."

CHAPTER 41

RACIAL EMPATHY AND
THE WHITE COACH

ROD PAIGE*

A MERICA HAS ALWAYS REGARDED athletics as bastions of racial equality and has held up its interracial teams as symbols of racial harmony—and then came the late 1960s.

Events at Wyoming, Washington, Indiana and Syracuse ripped off the cover and exposed "the awful truth"—that racial prejudice is as common in athletics as in other walks of life.

Facing a problem is the first step toward its solution. Those of us in leadership positions must accept the responsibility of seeking out the causes of racial problems and of correcting them. The athletic world is no longer the sacrosanct area it was in years past. It is now open to the same scrutiny as other institutions. The alternative to solving our own problems is having them solved for us by people outside of athletics.

Whenever a coach has a racial problem on his team, he believes that it stems from someone else, more often than not the black athletes. The black athletes usually feel that the problem stems from the coach or other athletic leaders.

It is rarely that simple. Neither group is always blameless. But the writer suggests that the racial empathy of the coaches is *the* most important determinant of racial harmony on a team.

Many coaches believe that the elimination of formal discriminatory policies constitutes the extent of their responsibility to black athletes. They are unable to identify with the problems of these athletes. They do not seem to realize that racial problems are caused not from the wording of a policy but from the practice of it.

---

* Rod Paige, "Racial Empathy and the White Coach," *Scholastic Coach*, Vol. 41 (October 1971), pp. 56-58 and 62-64.

In order to practice fair and equal treatment for all athletes, the coach must be able to identify with the needs and problems of everyone. Policies and practices must be evaluated in terms of their impact on all. To achieve racial harmony, the coach must develop a racial empathy that will move him to search out and eliminate conditions which can lead to racial tension.

Empathy is the intellectual identification with or vicarious experiencing of the feelings, thoughts or attitudes of another. By being aware of the feelings, thoughts and attitudes of his athletes, the empathetic coach will be able to predict how they will feel, think and act in a wide variety of situations. The coach will not always be right, but the better his predictive ability the better his chances will be to establish harmonious relationships with the athletes.

Vital point: The coach's understanding of each player must encompass such factors as his background, his customs and folkways, his life style and his general view of the world.

Therein lies the source of many racial conflicts. The coach, a product of white experience, could have this predictive understanding of white players (although he often does not), but he may have to develop it with respect to black players.

Unfortunately, many coaches are unwilling to exert the time and effort this requires. It is much simpler to ignore the differences between black and white players and to expect the blacks to fit into the white mold from which the coach's values were shaped.

By contrast, the racially empathetic coach is aware of the importance of racial experiences in the shaping of the players' thinking, beliefs, feelings and concept of self.

After studying the background of racial conflicts at several major universities, the writer is convinced that coaches and administrators can alleviate racial tensions by making a greater effort to understand the modern athlete in general and the black athlete in particular. The person who expects to benefit from the talents of black athletes is obliged to become sensitive to their problems, needs and feelings.

The leader whose racial sensitivities have been blunted by

stereotyped concepts has little understanding of the depth of the modern black athlete. His insensitivity makes him incapable of recognizing potential problems and, consequently, he can expect increased conflict.

When a racial conflict explodes on the athletic field, more often than not the causes have manifested themselves in racial incidents long before the eruption. Each of these lead-up incidents offers the administrator an opportunity to head off the conflict. Unfortunately, his racial empathy often is so shallow that he will disregard the potentially explosive incidents or consider them relatively unimportant.

There are two types of racially insensitive leaders: those who suffer from prejudice and those who are not prejudiced but who have not tried to understand the nature of their black athletes. Both types are equally dangerous, the difference being that there is hope for the latter.

The danger of the bigot is exemplified by an incident at a Midwestern university during the 1968 football season. One Monday following a big game, several of the black players told an assistant coach that one of their white teammates had continually directed racial insults at one of the opposing black players. They explained that all of them felt that if their white teammate could refer to a black opponent as "nigger bastard" "black s.o.b." and "coon," then he obviously had little respect for his black teammates. They wanted the coach to consider some type of disciplinary action.

When the head coach learned of the situation, he confronted the white player with the charges. The player admitted that he had yelled insults, but that he had only been trying to make the player angry, feeling that the anger would somehow reduce his efficiency.

The coach suggested that the player apologize to the team in general and to the black players in particular. The player chose to quit the team rather than make the apology. At a team meeting the head coach explained what had happened and asked that everyone forget the incident and bind together for "the good of the team."

One of the assistant coaches spoke about "togetherness" and the sacrifices that individuals must make for the good of the team. Another coach also had a few words to say on "the good of the team." A third coach, who felt that he had rapport with his men, told the black players that they must be bigger than the petty insults and that accepting such abuse proves that they are bigger than the person dishing it out.

He went on to explain that he had worked at a university at the time it had recruited its first black player, and how the player had had to accept certain insults at first but that as he kept working hard and turned out to be an outstanding halfback, the white players began to respect him.

Although the sincerity of these coaches was genuine, their speeches reflected their inability to empathize with the young black athlete. First, their corrective measures were aimed primarily at the black athletes. Secondly, what they really had said was: "It's clear that you have been subjected to some verbal insults from a teammate, but you should sublimate personal feelings to the more lofty goal of 'the good of the team.'"

They were asking the athletes to adopt the kind of approach that Jackie Robinson had used in integrating baseball years ago. Their appeal for team unity might have been more successful had they made it unequivocally clear *to the whole team* that racial insults would not be tolerated.

The coaches' approach held little promise of success because, first, athletes are not likely to make any sacrifices for "the good of the team" unless they feel that *the team is prepared to make adjustments for the good of the individual. Second*ly, athletes know that outstanding performance should not be a prerequisite for humane treatment.

Fifteen, maybe ten, years ago you might have tried to tell a black athlete that he was showing character and courage by not retaliating when he was abused. The modern Black has no patience with this kind of plea. Whereas the former Black had to swallow his feelings of anger and frustration, the modern Black usually feels that sometimes personal safety must be hazarded to protect his concept of self and dignity.

RACIAL DIFFERENCES

The well-meaning coach can do much to enhance his racial empathy. Probably the first thing he can do is recognize the differences in his players' racial backgrounds. One well-meaning coach was heard to say, "On my team I don't have black players and white players, only football players."

As a manifesto of fair treatment, regardless of race, this type of attitude is laudatory. As a philosophical truism—that when a group of young men put on their football equipment and run on the field, they become more alike than they are off the field—it could not be more wrong.

The "all-alike attitude" should apply to concepts of equality of opportunity and fairness. But it does not relieve the coach of the responsibility for recognizing the differences in his players' backgrounds and, consequently, outlooks on life. A black man in football uniform does not cease to be a black man. He becomes a black football player.

This concept is not radical. We know that no two people are alike. Educators emphasize individual differences and just as there are differences between individuals, so are there differences between groups.

The black man encounters problems that are unique to his race. Of course the young white man has problems, too, but the black college man has all the difficulties of any other college student *plus* those presented to him by society, college life and athletics because of his blackness.

For an example of how this difference is expressed in terms of attitude and behavior, we have only to notice how the two groups respond to the term "boy."

To the black man, manhood is a goal that has been systematically denied him through the years. He has heard his grandfather referred to as "boy" by young whites a fourth his age. The American ideal of manhood is clear to all of us. We know the traits associated with manhood: aggressiveness, self-assertion and self-confidence. Young blacks also know that these are the very same traits that white society dislikes most in black males.

Grier and Cobbs state it this way:

"For the black man in this country, it is not so much a matter of
acquiring manhood as it is a struggle to feel it his own. Whereas
the white man regards his manhood as an ordained right, the black
man is engaged in a never-ending battle for its possession. For the
black man, attaining any portion of manhood is an active process.
He must penetrate barriers and overcome opposition in order to assume a masculine posture. For the inner psychological obstacles to
manhood are never so formidable as the impediments woven into
the American society. By contrast, for a white man in this country,
the rudiments of manhood are settled at birth by the possession of
a penis and a white skin. This biological affirmation of masculinity
and identity as master is enough to insure that, whatever his individual limitations, this society will not systematically erect obstruc-
tions to his achievement."

The black youth knows that no matter how similar his environment, abilities and skills are to that of his white counterpart, he has one unique attribute that will cause society to treat
him differently—his blackness. He has come to learn that he has
a history, a culture and a future greatly distinct from that of
his white counterpart and his coach will do well to discover this.

The white coach can increase his racial empathy by learning
more about the history, culture and folkways of the black people. The inability of coaches to understand the racial differences
between athletes is usually related to his inability to detect the
differences in athletes in general.

Coaches must realize that the modern young black man is
quite different from his brother of a few years ago. Coaches
who are unable to accept this difference will find themselves trying to handle today's problems with yesterday's solutions.

The modern black man is more likely to accept his blackness
with individual and group pride. He is more likely to verbalize
and dramatize his resentment toward injustice, especially racial
injustice. He knows that he will always be black, so he is not as
easily molded into white patterns. In other words, he will strive
to keep his personal identity, and that identity is a black identity.

At one time the Negro, when faced with discrimination which
impeded his progress, coped with it by working harder, being
more persevering and trying harder to prove himself worthy of

admittance to the white world. The modern Black is more apt to confront the discrimination, as he does not feel he has to prove anything.

At the 1969 American Football Coaches Association meeting, a coach related that he told an educator in his school: "Maybe things in your world have changed, but the ingredients that went into the making of the first football players at Rutgers 100 years ago are the same ingredients that make up the football player of today."

Though coaches will agree that the basic ingredients of winning athletes have not changed, the perceptive individual realizes that the athletes themselves have changed. We admit that modern athletes are bigger, stronger, faster. It is time to notice that they have changed in other ways as well, and that the men we coach on the field are the same men the professors teach in the classroom.

"MILITANT" ATHLETES

A college recruiter was questioning a high school coach about a black athlete. After asking the standard questions about height, weight, speed, test scores and class rank, the recruiter found it necessary to add: "Is he militant?"

What did the recruiter mean by "militant"? It was clear that he inferred a negative behavioral trait that was undesirable in athletes. No one should write off spirited athletes as troublemakers or bad eggs. We must accept the fact that increasing numbers of black athletes are exercising more self-assertion, refusing to accept unquestioningly the values and social attitudes prescribed as model conduct for Blacks, developing more pro-black attitudes, developing a genuine pride in their black heritage, and learning that white is not synonymous with right.

Too many coaches continue to stereotype black athletes as "good ones" and "bad ones." What these coaches must learn is that an athlete's silence on racial matters does not necessarily indicate satisfaction with his racial plight. Nor does a pro-black attitude and overt pride necessarily indicate anti-white feelings.

They must learn that all black men are dissatisfied with their racial plight in America. Grier and Cobbs wrote:

". . . all blacks are angry. White America seems not to recognize it. They seem to think that all the trouble is caused by a few 'extremists.' They ought to know better."

Does this mean that the situation is hopeless? Not in the writer's opinion. It just means that in order to alleviate racial tension a coach must:

1. Acknowledge the existence of race as a factor in the lives of *all* black men.

2. Recognize such slogans as "black is beautiful" and "right on, brother" as gestures of racial pride rather than racial threats.

3. Not ask an athlete to reject his heritage in order to be acceptable.

4. Be able to deal with racial matters calmly and factually.

5. Be able to distinguish between discipline, discrimination and self-assertion.

Included in the coach's racial empathy should be recognition of the new unity among black people. More and more Blacks are rejecting the class concept in favor of the ideology of Black communality. It is becoming increasingly clear to Blacks that regardless of their educational achievement, economic status or social standing, all black people belong to one class set apart by an unchangeable trait—their blackness.

The reference of one black man to another as "brother" is not a casual thing. It reflects a feeling of close kinship between people who share the experience of racism. Edwards says that "from their (racists) perspective the only difference between the black man shining shoes in the ghetto and the champion black sprinter is that the shoeshine man is a nigger and the sprinter is a fast nigger."

The coach who understands this knows that in order to achieve or maintain racial harmony on his team, it is essential to protect even the lowest black scrub from racial abuse by his teammates and coaches. He cannot give the black stars the royal treatment and allow the scrubs to be racially abused. The stars are certain to regard racial injustice to any black athlete as injustice to all.

Although charges of racial discrimination are not always justified, the empathetic coach will concern himself with the athletes' reaction as well as the reality of the situation. Because race is such an influencing factor in his life, the black athlete is likely to view problem situations in terms of race.

The coach must, therefore, not only make sure that all his athletes receive fair and equal treatment, but that they *know* they are going to be treated fairly. Remember, what the athlete *believes* to be true influences his behavior more strongly than what *is* true.

PLAN OF ACTION

Racial differences need not predispose to conflict. Although we differ in racial heritage, we share a common humanity. Unity does not require uniformity and mutual respect can be achieved.

The following plan is suggested for white coaches who feel a need for greater racial empathy:

1. *Make an honest appraisal of your racial attitude.* "Know thyself." Really research your racial feelings. When you are a able to identify, admit and accept your racial attitudes, you are in good position to handle your problems.

2. *Rid yourself of stereotyped and shopworn racial concepts.* Educators have proven that a teacher's expectation from and attitude toward his pupil greatly influence the pupil's response to him. Develop enough objectivity to be able to relate to a player's actual rather than expected behavior.

3. *Develop a fair and open-minded posture* that will encourage players to talk out racial problems. Players will discuss their problems if they feel you are interested in their well-being. Each time a player brings a problem to you for discussion, he presents you with a fine opportunity to gain a greater insight into him.

4. *Deal with every racial incident calmly and factually as soon as it develops.* Close examination of racial conflicts suggests that they are usually caused not by a single incident, but by a culmination of many unsolved racial incidents over a period of years.

5. *Initiate informal discussions with black players and really listen to them.* To really hear what someone is saying, you must resist the urge to think your own thoughts and you must concentrate on the speaker.

6. *Respect the feelings of the black athletes.* Intense emotional feelings are powerful determinants of behavior. You must be able to accept sincere expressions of strong feelings without criticism. It is a good idea to respect anyone whose respect you desire.

7. *Exert a sincere effort to learn more about the history, culture, customs and folkways of black youth.*

There undoubtedly are many other things that a coach can do to intensify his racial empathy, but the best plan of action is still the Golden Rule: "Do unto others as you would have them do unto you."

We hope the reader understands that we are not blaming our school officials for all the racial conflicts that occur in sports. Nor that we are suggesting preferential treatment for black athletes. Our black athletes must, like everyone else, assume responsibility for their behavior.

What we are trying to say is that a coach no longer can expect to play black athletes without making himself responsive to their problems, needs and feelings. The coach who hopes to have racial harmony on his team cannot ignore the reality of racial factors in our society.

THE COACH AND PSYCHOLOGY

MOTIVATIONAL PSYCHOLOGY IN COACHING

Joseph M. Goldfarb[*]

IN RESEARCHING THE LITERATURE on the psychology of coaching, one is struck by the fact that many coaches are putting the ends before the means.

They speak at great length about the motivated and nonmotivated athletes and the traits of each. They also offer numerous definitions of words such as "fight," "mental resolve," "superhuman effort," etc.; but few of them mention the basic force behind a psychologically motivated athlete or team—*the self-motivated and motivating coach*. The highly-motivated coach represents the *means* for producing highly motivated athletes; his motivating influence can be contagious.

According to the dictionary, the word "motivate" means to move, impel, induce; to stimulate interest through appeal to associated interests or by special devices. Psychology entails the study or treatment of the mind. Hence, in athletic terms, a highly-motivated and motivating coach can stimulate, induce and incite the mental processes of an athlete or team to the point where he or they performs to maximum capability.

The writer feels strongly that an athlete's psychological motivation must come largely from the coach. This does not mean that a motivated coach is the only requirement for a successful program. On the contrary, each link in the following formula must be present for maximum results:

Highly motivated and motivating coach *plus* highly motivated and motivating team captain *equals* highly motivated athletes,

---

* Joseph M. Goldfarb, "Motivational Psychology in Coaching," *Scholastic Coach*, Vol. 37 (February 1968), pp. 54-57.

which, in turn, *equals* a psychologically superior team with a superior performance level.

In effect, if a coach can either control the individual athlete psychologically or teach the athlete to control himself psychologically, the athlete will surpass all his previous performance.

Many coaches and athletes feel that if the body is physically and physiologically conditioned to the maximum, it follows that the athlete's performance will be superior.

What part does psychological conditioning play in performance? Can a physical or physiological response be elicited from a psychological stimulus?

Any person will feel and act in accordance with what he believes is true about himself and his environment. If a good hypnotic subject is told that he is at the North Pole, for example, he will immediately begin shivering and actually raise goose pimples.

A similar physical and physiological reaction to a psychological stimulus has been demonstrated on wide-awake college students. After they were asked to imagine that they had one hand immersed in ice water, the "immersed" hand showed a drop in temperature!

In another instance, a hypnotized subject was told that the hypnotist's finger was a red-hot piece of metal. The subject not only grimaced in pain when the hypnotist's finger touched him, but his lymphatic and cardiovascular systems also became inflamed and even produced a *blister* on the skin!

When wide-awake college students have been told to imagine that a spot on their head was extremely hot, the skin temperature at that spot showed an increase!

These cases show that an individual may, to some extent, control himself or be controlled psychologically.

A more common example of how psychological attitudes can alter your physical feelings: You wake up one morning. The sky is blue and the sun is shining. You put on new clothes, and you look and feel "like a million." Not only your psychological attitude but your physical feelings are changed. You stand a little straighter, wear a bigger smile and greet others warmly. Those little mistakes bother you less and you are more relaxed.

But what if you wake up and it is raining? Your clothes just do not look right and your hair stands up straight. The effect has to be detrimental to your psychological attitude and physical feelings.

These are but a few of the situations that seem to prove that psychological control—or the lack of it—can make a difference in physical actions and mental attitudes. Can't we conclude then that psychological control can make a difference in an athlete's performance?

Dr. James E. Counsilman, swimming coach at Indiana, who coached the 1964 Olympic team, stated that before Don Schollander competed in the 100-meter freestyle, his pulse rate was a near normal eighty beats per minute. Yet trackman Gerry Lindgren's pulse rate was well over one hundred fifteen beats per minute after a meal a few days prior to his competition.

We know that prior to competition the blood sugar level, which is controlled by the adrenal gland, rises. This action of the adrenal gland is affected by the emotionalism engendered by a close race. If the blood sugar level remains high for several days in succession, it can lead to physical exhaustion and inferior performance.

In general, a championship performance requires a maximum effort that approaches the physiological capacity of the human organism at a specific time. This physiological capacity can be restricted by the individual's mental attitude. Self-doubt or emotionalism, for example, can set a psychological limit on performance long before the athlete approaches his physiological capacity.

The fact that Schollander did so well and Lindgren so poorly seems to substantiate the point that psychological control can indeed affect the body's physical and physiological functions and, hence, the athlete's performance level.

Next we must consider the factors which make psychological control difficult or impossible to achieve. Among the more general detriments are such internal restricting factors as thoughts of the pain and stress which must be endured in order to achieve a maximum effort.

Internal factors produced by overprotective or underprotective parents can lead to what Pavlov calls "internal inhibition." Parents or coaches who condition an athlete to be careful, "don't hurt yourself," etc., are more specifically detrimental to maximum performance.

However, Pavlov stated that while internal inhibition is constant, it is not as stable (strong) as some types of external stimulation. It is possible, therefore, to overcome these internal inhibiting factors. In an experiment involving a pistol shot (external), Drs. Steinhaus and Ikai found that noise produced greater effort.

Humans have used external stimulation to conquer internal inhibition for centuries. The "Rebel Yell" of the Civil War, the paratroopers' "Geronimo!" of World War II and the Egyptian weightlifters' cry of "Allah!" are all psychological controls designed to suppress anything which might interfere with maximum performance.

Any factor which prevents the physically and physiologically conditioned athlete from achieving maximum performance may be termed a "stress factor." A common cold can "stress" an athlete much the same as a social, emotional or psychological problem.

All of these stress factors must be suppressed or removed prior to competition. The responsibility for this lies with the coach. As stated earlier, the superior coach will either control his athletes psychologically or teach them to control themselves. By "controlling the athletes," we mean seeing that the athlete's problems, worries, fears or uncertainties are either suppressed or eliminated before competition.

ALL-OUT EFFORT

Competition requires 100 percent of the athlete's physical and mental energy. Any problem which he brings with him into competition may be a detriment to his achievement.

Experimentation with rats showed that under a single stress factor—heat, cold, intense exercise or noise—the rat tended to adapt without much effort. When more than one stress factor was introduced at the same time, however, the rat tended to exhibit an overstressed adaptation.

Hans Selye refers to this as the "triad response." These over-stressed responses decrease proficiency in both physical and mental performance.

The coach must realize that the athlete is under a continuous physical, physiological and emotional stress throughout the season—the stress of training and competition. If the athlete is burdened with any other major stress factor, his physical performance may be impaired.

The coach must do several things to eliminate these undesirable factors. First, he must not allow any stress factor of his *own* to influence his attitude toward an individual or the team.

Second, the coach should understand his athletes: their likes and dislikes, their ambitions and their academic goals. He must also know how his athletes discipline themselves in their academic and social environment. He must earn their respect to the point where they will feel free to bring him their problems before they develop into stress factors.

The coach must also maintain good communication with the boys' parents, girl friends and other associates. Often, these people outside the athletic "world" are indispensable in resolving a potential stress factor.

In the last few years, many coaches have been administering personality tests in the hope of obtaining a more specific understanding of their athletes' motivation and outlook on life. Hunnicutt and Iverson, for example, found that whereas the introverted subject responded to praise with increased effort, the extroverted subject responded to praise with decreased effort but responded to criticism with increased effort.

The athlete usually feels that unless he can mentally gird himself for a contest, the whole thing will come off badly. A superior coach can recognize and understand basic individual differences and utilize them to extract maximum performance from each athlete.

Now let us discuss specifics. What can a coach do to help motivate the athlete to a truly maximum performance? The writer feels that the superior coach should follow the seven steps of the "success-type" personality: sense of direction, understanding, courage, charity, esteem, self-confidence and self-acceptance.

Sense of direction—the ability of the coach to define mutually agreed upon goals for each athlete, based on what the athlete desires from the athletic situation.

Understanding involves good communication between coach and athlete. Most failures in human relations are due to "misunderstandings." Given a set of facts or circumstances, we expect others to react, respond and come to the same conclusions as we do.

The coach must understand that the athlete's response often may differ from the coach's. The coach should always ask himself: "How does this situation appear to the boy? How will the athlete interpret the situation?" By understanding why the athlete acts as he does, the coach can establish a good relationship with him.

Courage to act is the next step in the "success sequence." The superior coach must imbue the athlete with the courage to act, for only by actions can goals, desires and beliefs be transformed into realities.

All problems become smaller when you face them squarely. Touch a thistle timidly and it pricks you; grab it boldly and its spines crumble. The athlete must have the courage to make a few mistakes and suffer much pain to get what he wants.

The coach must convince the athlete not to sell himself short. "Most people," says General R. E. Chambers, chief of the Army's Psychiatry and Neurology Consultant Division, "don't know how brave they really are. In fact, many potential heroes, both men and women, live out their lives in self doubt. If they only knew they had these deep resources, it would help give them the self-reliance to meet most problems, even a big crisis."

QUALITY OF CHARITY

Charity also plays a part in the success-type personality. The coach should endeavor to develop within the athlete a genuine appreciation for other people, not only teammates and other athletes and coaches, but also locker room attendants, managers and custodians. The athlete should take the trouble to stop and think of other person's feelings, viewpoints, desires and needs.

He should also make it plain that other people are important and treat them accordingly. Remember, the coach, by his example, provides a tremendous motivating influence.

Esteem plays a major role in the "success sequence." The coach must not allow his athletes to picture themselves as defeated, worthless persons. He must constantly remind them of their assets and values so they will stop derogating themselves.

The hardest lesson for a coach to teach a defeated or nonproficient athlete is that self-pity wastes valuable time and energy which could be spent more profitably in improving skills.

Self-confidence is built upon successful experiences. Success breeds success. Boxing managers carefully build up their fighters' confidence with a progressive series of successful experiences. The coach, similarly, must provide success for his athletes.

Many coaches do this by scheduling teams they are certain they can beat. Other coaches schedule weaker teams early in the season, then progressively point toward the "tougher" teams. More specifically, a coach may insure success by purposely misreading the stopwatch during a time-trial, telling the athlete that he performed faster than he actually did.

There is much disagreement on the methods for developing successful experiences. Each coach must determine for himself the best methods for his own boys.

Another common problem is restoring an athlete's self-confidence. Dr. Winfred Overholser, Superintendent of St. Elizabeth's Hospital, said that a boy's belief in himself can be restored by recalling past triumphs. The superior coach will make certain that his athletes do not dwell on bad experiences which might affect their self-confidence.

FINAL FACTOR

Self-acceptance is the final factor in the "success sequence." The coach must convince the athletes that they matter as individuals. Too many persons say to themselves, "Because I'm too skinny (fat, short, tall, etc.), I am nothing." The coach must convince his athletes that although they are not perfect, they are something. He should challenge them to make the most of that something.

How can a coach do all of these things? With a smile or a frown; with an arm around the shoulder or a kick in the seat of the pants; with a kind word or constructive criticism; with a firm handshake or an irritated shrug of his shoulders. There are countless methods for motivating the athlete.

The difficult task is to apply the correct motivational ingredient at precisely the right time. This is the real challenge.

The importance of the motivated and motivating coach can best be illustrated by this simple line: "He who would kindle another must glow himself."

SUGGESTED READINGS

Counsilman, James E.: Classroom Lecture, Indiana Univ., July 20, 1966.

Griffith, Coleman Robert: *Psychology and Athletics.* N. Y., Charles Scribner and Sons, 1928.

Gross, Nancy E.: *Living with Stress.* N. Y., McGraw-Hill Book Co., 1958, p. 16.

Hunnicut, C. W. and W. J. Iverson (Eds.): *Research in the Three R's.* N. Y.; Harper, 1958.

Journal of Applied Psychology, Vol. 16. No. 1, Jan. 1961.

Krumdick, Victor F.: "Mental Attitude and Athletic Performance." *Swimming World Magazine,* Feb. 1966.

Maltz, Maxwell: *Psycho-Cybernetics.* Hollywood; Wilshire Book Co., 1960.

Nichols, Williams: *Words to Live By.* N. Y., Simon and Schuster.

CHAPTER 43

THE LEARNING PROCESS AS APPLIED TO COACHING

GEORGE D. SMALL*

A NUMBER OF YEARS AGO, when football was still in its infancy, the late Pop Warner had an assistant at the famous Carlisle Indian School by the name of Bunny Larkin. Bunny, operating on the theory that the Indian boys found it difficult to master the fundamentals of the game, developed his own unique methods of teaching which were a model of brevity.

At the beginning of each season he lined up his boys, showed them a football and then in a few well-chosen words explained what the game was all about. "When the white man has the ball," he explained, "get him. When the Indian has the ball, knock the white man down."

Football has made a great deal of progress since the early days of Pop Warner and Bunny Larkin. It is no longer that easy to explain the fundamentals of the game to a group of boys. Today a team must learn a great many complicated and difficult patterns of offensive and defensive play. What makes the game even more complicated for the individual player is that coaches now insist that their players not only master their own assignments but those of their teammates as well. This means that each player must learn upward of one hundred or more assignments.

What has been said of football can also be said of many other sports. From this brief analysis it is easy to see that the good coach must be a master teacher, employing the same sound methods and techniques used by any good teacher in any other com-

* George D. Small, "The Learning Process as Applied to Coaching," *Athletic Journal*, Vol. 36 (February 1956), pp. 28-42.

plicated field of learning. Above everything else, the good coach in any sport should be thoroughly familiar with what psychologists have called the principles and laws of learning and how these principles and laws can be applied and modified to meet the conditions which he faces in teaching the players who come under his jurisdiction on the athletic field.

It should be understood that every field of human endeavor has its own peculiar conditions which produce particular methods and techniques of teaching and learning. In athletics, for instance, the coach can and often does utter a few swear words as a matter of emphasis. These words may be familiar to the classroom teacher but the latter dare not use them. The coach may also publicly *eat out* one of his players to a point where it must be humiliating and embarrassing not only to the player who is on the receiving end but to anyone who hears it. The hard-boiled, energetic, driving, vitriolic coach is as much a tradition in athletics as the hard-boiled sergeant is in the Marine Corps. In fact, they have become so much a part of the athletic tradition that some coaches feel they must act out the part of the hard-boiled taskmaster whether it is a natural role or not.

But, judged by any standards, sarcasm, ranting, neurotic raving and swearing are not marks of a good coach. They may be marks of inferiority used only because the coach has not been able to develop sufficient emotional stability. Such actions on the part of the coach violate every law of good learning practice. They are not good coaches because they employ these techniques but in spite of them. They would be better coaches if they learned sounder techniques. A coach does not have to be the hard-boiled taskmaster in order to be firm in the handling of his boys.

What then are the most important principles and laws of learning which the coach can apply effectively to situations which he faces on the athletic field?

1. The players will learn more readily and retain what they learn over a longer period of time when the coach instills in them a firm desire to learn. The psychologist is aware that learning is often a matter of mind set or attitude on the part of the

player. If the player is ready to learn or willing to learn, coaching will be a much easier job. Not every boy who comes out for an athletic team has the right mind set to become an outstanding player. At least, the coach can never take this quality for granted.

Every observing coach is familiar with the type of boy who has all the physical and mental equipment to be an outstanding performer in his particular field but who never quite makes the grade. One reason, of course, is that he has not been motivated to put forth his best effort. He may be satisfied just to make the team and earn his letter. He is not interested in going all-out and becoming a star. We speak of him as a player who does not have the heart or who does not bear down in the clutches. As a result, he does just what he has to do and no more. The only time he extends himself is when he is aroused emotionally. That is why some coaches try to get a particularly phlegmatic player angry before an important game. A coach should also recognize that the disinterested player only half listens to the instructions he is given and, very naturally, makes many mistakes. Part of his problem may be traced to the fact that this type of player will not discipline himself to achieve extra effort.

Getting players in the right attitude and instilling in them the desire to learn are the most important single factors in learning. There are of course, many ways of getting this maximum effort from players. The enthusiasm and drive of the coach, if it is a natural quality, will overcome a great deal of player inertia. Some players are also motivated by the all-out efforts of other players. Nearly every youngster worth his salt will want to carry at least his share of the load and will extend himself in proportion to the extent that other members of the squad are extending themselves. Therefore, keeping key players going at top speed is one of the details to which the wise coach give full attention.

Giving players an individually acceptable incentive will also prove effective in many instances. Breaking school, conference or national records in the various sports is always potent medicine. Squad talks will also bring further results. Few coaches take full advantage of this important technique. For instance, one coach used the last five minutes of all squad meetings, which he held once or twice a week, to get across messages which he felt would be helpful in motivating his players to give their best efforts. In these talks he usually pointed out what extending themselves to their best efforts could mean to them in personal dividends of character building.

The importance of this step should not be overlooked. William James, one of America's greatest psychologists, once said, "It is extremely doubtful if a single individual living today has ever reached a point where he uses more than 40 percent of his potential abilities." Think of what it would mean if a coach could get even 10 percent greater effort over and above what he now considers the maximum effort of his players to be. Getting this plus effort could be the difference in many of those close ball games.

However, the best results will be obtained through personal interviews with squad members. Here is a story to illustrate the point. When Bernie Wietucki brought Marvin Matuszak to Tulsa he weighed only 180 pounds but had a burning desire to make the team at guard. He made the freshman squad and put on an extra 15 pounds. When he left school at the end of his freshman year, Bernie, an assistant to Coach Brothers at the time, called Marvin into his office for an interview.

"Marvin, you have succeeded in making the freshman squad here at Tulsa this year, what do you want to accomplish next year?"

The reply from the blonde South Bend youngster was instantaneous. "I want to make the varsity squad."

Bernie then pointed out what it would take to realize this goal. The next year Marvin succeeded in making the varsity squad. Again Bernie followed his formula by calling Marvin in before he left for his summer vacation.

Now Marvin's reply was spontaneous. "I'm going to make all-conference."

He succeeded so well this time that he not only made all-conference but All-American as well. Bernie did not let the boy coast even at this stage. At the end of his junior year he called Marv in again.

"What's for next year, Marv?"

Almost in a whisper the boy gave his reply. "I'm going to try to be the best lineman in America." He made all-conference and All-American for the second year in a row and there are many coaches who will tell you that he realized his first ambition as well.

Purpose, backed by sound attainable goals is the greatest motivating force in the world, either on or off the athletic field. Getting the players to outline their own goals and purposes creates a bond that can be satisfied only by an all-out effort on the past of both the player and the coach. It is one of the best ways of getting maximum effort that the psychologist knows.

2. The players will learn faster and are more likely to retain what they learn when they see clearly in their own minds the reason or purpose of what the coach wants them to learn. It is not enough for the coach to have the idea, reason or purpose why he wants his players to learn something or to learn it in a particular way. He must get his ideas, reasons and purposes into the minds of his players as well.

The coach who says: "Tom on play 69 you always take the tackle to the outside," invariably takes too much for granted. If Tom knows why he should always take the tackle to the outside he will probably not make the same mistake again after being corrected by his coach. But, if he does not know why, he may make the mistake over again at a strategic point in an important ball game no matter how many times he has been drilled to do it differently. The very fact that the coach had to correct him is good evidence that he does not know why. Telling a player why the coach wants him to do a thing a particular way is the follow-up of teaching and every coach knows how important follow-up or follow-through is in all phases of athletics.

The coach should say: "Tom on play 69 you always take the tackle to the outside. Do you know why?" It may take more time but it is always best to let the player analyze the play for himself. If he knows the answer, it will give both the coach and the boy satisfaction. It is also the coach's only way of knowing for sure whether he is getting his points across. If the player does not know the answer, it is up to the coach to give him a clear, concise reason.

Recently we heard a hard-boiled Texas League manager call across the diamond to a young college player who was working out with his team. "Jim, cut down that stride." That was all. The youngster automatically and in response to the manager's command shortened his stride. He kept it shortened for exactly three swings at the ball and then dropped back into doing it his own way. Shortly after the manager remarked to one of the players:

"The boy is hopeless. He can't take coaching." The youngster had not heard this remark but he knew that the manager was displeased with him. After his turn in the batter's box he went up to one of the older players on the team who had a great deal of baseball knowledge and said: "I don't seem to be able to shorten my stride up there at the plate and get any power in my hitting. Why did the skipper tell me to do it?"

The veteran took him to one side where he would not be embarrassed and where they would not be disturbed. "Look Jim, the skipper has been up here a long time. To his way of thinking there is just a right way and a wrong way to do things. When he tells you to do something, chances are that he is right about it. If you ask him he might not be able to tell you right off. For instance, he once told me to keep the toe of my front foot pointed out toward the pitcher when I took my stride. I asked him why and I thought he was going to have apoplexy. He never did give me an answer, but I did what he told me on the theory that he knew best and after a time I figured that it was because I could follow through on my swing more effectively."

The veteran paused for a moment and then continued. "After you've been here for awhile you study good hitters and see that nearly all of them do certain things alike. This way becomes the right way and that is what managers pass on to their players. The reason—call it experience.

"Now he told you to shorten your stride when you stepped

into the ball. If you noticed, you were hitting a great many pop-ups when he called to you. To the skipper this meant that you were overstriding and missing your timing, or it meant that your timing was off and you were overstriding because of this fact. If you had shortened your stride and still popped up, he probably would have followed through on your timing."

When the youngster stepped up to the plate for his next turn at bat he still popped-up although he had shortened his stride and sure enough the skipper bellowed out another order: "Don't start your swing so soon. Watch the ball right up to the bat."

This time the youngster smiled and followed instructions to the letter. Once the intelligent player gains faith in the coaching he is receiving, the coach will find that the boy will follow instructions and seek answers on his own. However, until this time arrives it is necessary to give him reasons. It may seem tedious at the start but it will save time in the long run. The better the player understands what the coach want him to do, and why he feels it is the best way, the more rapidly he will learn.

3. The players will learn more readily when a coach can demonstrate just what it is they are to learn. This is the reason why taking pictures of games pays such large dividends. With an action picture of the game before them coaches are able to point out to the players both the good and bad techniques in their play. Pictures are particularly valuable if the coaches have demonstrated the assignments by running through them on a slow-motion basis in practice sessions or have sketched them out in detail in skull sessions.

It should be pointed out that it is seldom good learning technique to embarrass a player in public. For the benefit of the team, individual mistakes may have to be pointed out in front of the rest of the team. Particularly glaring mistakes should be pointed out in a private showing of the film.

Films are not the only means by which the various assignments in the different sports can be demonstrated. Still pictures can also be used to demonstrate good techniques as can individual instruction when the players can see the execution of a particular method and then demonstrate and practice it on each other.

Every visual aid device that the coach can find or invent should be used in teaching the subject matter. Mimeographed copies of plays and individual assignments, slides, loop films, large cardboard strategy maps and even toy football players that can be moved about over a miniature field are used by many coaches to demonstrate correct techniques to their players.

4. Players will learn more readily when they can visualize what the coach wants them to learn in its entirety before it is broken down into parts. This is probably due to the fact that almost all coaches are always looking for short-cut methods or they assume that their players are actually farther advanced than they really are.

The whole-part theory of learning operates on the assumption that the learner reacts more intelligently to whole situations or total patterns than he does to isolated or abstracted parts of situations or patterns. When the learning experiences or situations are organized into systems or total patterns they are less likely to be forgotten. It also follows that isolated and fragmentary items are soon forgotten. This latter fact may explain why players in almost any sport frequently forget fundamentals. Chances are they have been taught the fundamentals as isolated items and without seeing their relationship to the whole. As a result, many of the fundamentals which the coach stresses so thoroughly have little meaning or purpose to the players.

There are three steps in the whole-part learning process with which the coach should be familiar.

First, we have the description. In basketball, football and baseball, the game in itself is the whole, while blocking, tackling, passing, punting, etc., are the parts in football. Passing, dribbling, catching, shooting, pivoting, etc., are examples of the parts in basketball. Hitting, fielding, throwing, sliding, etc., are the parts in baseball. Offensive and defensive patterns and assignments for each sport are smaller wholes.

The determination of the size of the whole to be learned will depend to a large extent upon the degree of individual skill which the players have attained in their particular sport. In any case what is to be learned will be much more meaningful if the players can visualize the total situation. Thus, in addition to the individual skills they will be called upon to learn in the part learning situations, they will be able to visualize total strategy, timing and teamwork which cannot be developed or visualized in the part learning situation. These last three factors can be learned only by integrating all the parts into the whole. This is the reason why psychologists maintain that the whole is always equal to more than the sum of the parts.

As an example, let us use the initiation of a new offensive assignment in football. In describing the assignment to his players the coach describes its similarity to other assignments. In the early stages of any new assignment, accuracy of execution is emphasized above speed. It is well to diagram the play in its entirety on the blackboard, showing what the play is designed to accomplish, when it can be most effectively used, how it differs in purpose from other plays, and the individual assignments of each member of the squad. When this procedure is followed each squad member will see his own assignment in relation to the assignment of every other member of the team and at the same time see the significance of timing, team effort and total strategy. If pictures are available, the squad can be shown just what the play looks like when it is executed properly.

The second point to be considered is demonstration. When the team goes to the practice field the new play should be run through in slow-motion with the offensive and defensive units in their positions so that each player can again visualize what his assignment is in relation to that of every other man on the squad. When the play reaches a point where each man can be shown to be carrying out his assignment, the coach should call a halt to the proceedings so that each man can see how the play has developed and determine how his particular assignment fits into the pattern of the play as a whole.

Drill is the third point. At this stage the squad can be broken down into smaller units for individual drill. After a prolonged drill period the squad should be reassembled into whole units and emphasis should be placed upon speed as well as accuracy. General Bob Neyland said that Tennessee never put a play in operation in a regular game until it had been rehearsed at least five hundred times.

5. The learning process and its products are conditioned by heredity and environment. For athletics the hereditary factors are: A plastic nervous system, which determines the player's ability to adjust to new situations; his mental ability, which determines his aptitude for learning the game; the various physiological factors such as the player's glandular balance, bone structure, chemical composition and secretions, visual acuity, dexterity, and muscular co-ordination, which determine his general physical fitness and physical tone; his organic drives which will determine the player's interest pattern, energy and fatigue level, and his competitive drive.

The environmental factors important in athletics are the player's cultural heritage. These include the social mores which conditioned his early training, customs and institutions he had come in contact with, pressures of many kinds, economic status, informal educational influences and the school system. All of these factors determine whether he participates in athletics, the type of athletic participation, the degree of sanction given the game, the competitive pressures placed upon him to excel and whether to continue or not to continue participation, the traditions entertained about the game as well as the experience level, and background attained.

All of these factors, both hereditary and environmental, should be studied by the coach to determine the player's qualifications and readiness for the level of competition in the sport in which he seeks to participate. While such a detailed study may seem too tedious to undertake, the more the coach knows about these details, the better will be his insight and understanding of his players.

We are listing other brief principles and laws of learning which the coach can make use of in handling his boys.

1. The learning process and the acquisition of learning are materially affected by individual differences.

2. The learning process and its products are affected by the level of maturity of the learner as indicated by the chronological, mental, emotional, physiological and social age of the player

CHAPTER 44

GET MORE FROM PRACTICE

PHILIP R. COPPAGE*

SUCCESS IN THE COACHING FIELD depends greatly upon what transpires during practice. From eighty to eighty-five percent of a season is spent in practice where a player develops the necessary skills, attitudes and other game requirements. There are many different skills to be mastered—both team and individual. Does a player, when attempting to learn a new skill, have to begin at the lowest level, or with the simplest fundamental, or does previous knowledge and experience enhance and expedite development of proficiency? Are there factors to be considered by the coach in selecting or designing drills so that maximum benefit can be obtained and so that what is learned in practice will transfer to the game situation?

The coach, in preparing for the season, breaks his particular sport into component parts for it is impossible to teach a complex game as an entity. This breakdown of the game is done with the assumption that the experiences of the practice sessions will transfer to the game situation and that the parts will become an integrated, complex whole. How can the coach be better assured that the greatest amount of transfer, if any, will occur? What principles and knowledge should the coach be aware of so that he may conduct and design drills to maximize transfer? An understanding of motor learning transfer will certainly aid in planning practice sessions in order that players will "get more" from them.

THEORIES OF TRANSFER

Transfer, when dealing with motor learning, may be defined as the effect that practice or previous learning has upon perform-

---

* Philip R. Coppage, "Get More from Practice," *The Physical Educator*, Vol. 30 (December 1973), pp. 197-200.

ance at a later time. Transfer is not limited solely to individual physical or mechanical skills, but includes game situations and conditions, i.e. transfer of learning from the practice field to the actual game. Does what one learns in practice transfer 100 percent to the game?

There are several theories that attempt to explain transfer, but the most popular two deal with identical and general elements. The identical elements theory postulates that transfer may take place only when the skill components involved are similar. In other words, skills and drills will transfer to the extent that the responses made by a player to different stimuli or situations are identical; transfer will occur when the same neural responses are involved when performing in practice and in the game. For this reason practice should include skills to be used in the game and drills should be as gamelike as possible. Games should not present new situations to players—the coach should simulate all individual and game skills in practice exactly as they will be performed in competition.

The general elements theory emphasizes that general instructions, basic laws and principles influence transfer, which may be an unconscious transfer of learning from one situation to another. In view of this, one might expect transfer to exist between all racket games, between all hitting skills and between catching skills. Transfer exists with the above mentioned skills because there are certain principles and basic laws common to each group.

Transfer should occur when an understanding of the relationships that exist between situations and conditions are apparent to the learner. This transfer is not limited to stimulus-response experiences, or unconscious transfer, but is an understanding of principles and relationships that will enable one to transfer to a wide range of experiences. If a player has a thorough knowledge and understanding of the principles involved in learning skills, and the purposes of drills, then transfer will occur.

Basketball goal shooting may be used to exemplify the above mentioned theories. The identical elements theory infers that transfer will occur between the different types of shots to the extent that identical neural responses exist, i.e. the ball leaving the finger tips. The general theory says that transfer will occur between the different types of shots because factors are common to all of them—that of giving impetus to the ball, understanding trajectory of flight patterns, ball spin and rebound angles if the backboard is used.

CHARACTERISTICS OF TRANSFER

Transfer has been defined as the effect that prior or past learning has upon future learning or performance. One might assume that transfer has a single distinct influence of enhancing performance, but what one learns may help or hinder, or transfer may be positive or negative.

Positive transfer is said to exist when the practice of a skill, or a learned skill will aid, enhance, or facilitate a later performance. If what one learns in practice is carried over to the game then the drills must have been worthwhile for the desired outcome has been accomplished. If a player reacts to a similar or new situation with a previously learned response, transfer has occurred and the coach has prevailed in his design of drills and teaching techniques.

Negative transfer exists when the practice or learning of a skill interferes with a later performance. If a player reacts to a game situation with a response learned in practice but the response is not appropriate, or is incorrect, then negative transfer exists. A basketball drill that has all the earmarks of transferring negatively is a rebound drill in which a player rebounds the ball and, while in the air, returns the ball to a player on the other side of the basket by passing it off the backboard and over the basket. This skill of passing the ball over the basket is not compatible to the game of basketball. If a player, during a game, overshoots the basket with an offensive rebound, the coach could possibly look to the rebound drill as a factor contributing to the missed shot.

Another characteristic of motor learning that a coach should be aware of is negative influences on previously acquired skills by newly learned skills, or retroactive transfer. A player, for example, who is skilled in badminton and learns to play tennis may have difficulty in regaining the proper badminton stroke because of the difference in stroke technique. Total arm movement is involved in hitting the ball in tennis while the badminton stroke emphasizes a wrist snap with lower-arm rotation.

In competition, a team prepares for the game by trying to counteract the opponent's strategy from an individual and team point-of-view. For example, a team's pass coverage for a specific game may differ somewhat from the defensive principles taught earlier in the season, thus necessitating a new set or type of coverage. The new pass coverages may retroactively interfere with the execution of the original pass defense principles, so the players have to relearn the earlier taught coverage. Although the players may have learned the original pass coverage well, a coach has to cover the defensive strategy for each game—pass coverage for one opponent may not be applicable for another opponent, so the practice situation should be used to eradicate the effects of "new" learning if the "old" set of skills are desired for the game at hand.

The desirability of a coach understanding motor transfer is a requisite of successful coaching. Those skills and drills of practice that do not transfer positively should be deleted or modified. Drills should be constantly evaluated to make sure that maximum benefit is obtained—that they contain the characteristics which will better enhance positive transfer.

CONDITIONS INFLUENCING TRANSFER

Coaches should be greatly concerned with drill design and their relationship to transfer. Drills should be constructed and conducted so that maximum positive transfer will result. There are several factors that can be controlled with regard to transfer and the practice situation. These factors are the similarity between drills and the actual game situation, the amount of practice or learning, the method of teaching and the awareness of the intent of transfer.

Similarity is one of the most important considerations in determining the degree of transfer and should be emphasized in gaining optimum transfer of drills. Coaches should design and use only those drills in practice that highly replicate the game. Drills and skills should be executed in practice exactly as they will be reproduced in the game; drills should be as gamelike as possible.

The relationship between the degree of similarity and the amount of transfer does not correlate directly. When conditions are very similar, transfer is very high; when slightly similar, negative transfer could result and when they are highly dissimilar, there is no transfer. Drills not identical to game conditions and those that do not contain some game skill have minimum transfer benefit for the player, so they should be excluded from the practice agenda.

Transfer is effected by the amount of practice. Generally, if a small amount of learning has taken place, then little transfer will result. A small amount of transfer infers that general aspects of the skill have transferred. If a high level of proficiency has been attained, then more transfer will take place in the form of specific, precise and accurate skill performance.

Mistakes should be expected of players if thorough teaching is not done and responsibilities are partially learned. Coaches cannot leave any aspect of the game to chance or verbal instruction, nor should they make drastic changes during the course of a game or season because of the difficulty of adapting to new game conditions. Players should be drilled to the extent that reactions to game conditions and situations are automatic responses instead of thought actions. If a player has to think what to do— if his reactions are not habitual—then he has not learned his assignments well enough.

The method of teaching is still another factor in transfer. Of the several methods of teaching that are acceptable, no conclusion has yet been reached as to which is best for maximum efficiency of learning and transfer. Generally, the best method depends upon the activity and the learner.

Methods of instruction deal with the terms "part" and "whole." A "whole" may be defined as any unit of instruction that is logical, meaningful and directly related to a final objective; it is an integral part that can stand alone. In coaching it is necessary that the game be broken down into "wholes" for it is very difficult and often impossible to learn complex skills in a game situation, so to facilitate learning, components of complicated games have to be considered.

Briefly, the methods of teaching are the whole method—learn by the game situation; the whole-part method—learn by the game situation and revert back to practice of particular parts; the part-whole-part method—learn by practicing skills, participating in the total activity, and then returning to skill practice; and the progressive-part method—learning by the gradual accumulation and combination of distinct parts of the game or activity.

Which method of instruction should a coach be concerned with if maximum transfer is to be gained from practice? Research has shown that the highest transfer potential is realized if the largest "whole" is practiced, i.e. break the game into the largest components that the players can handle intellectually and skillfully.

The progressive-part method of teaching (coaching) results in significant transfer also. This means that drills should be designed so players can progressively learn an increasing number of fundamentals from a single drill. For example, a drill in basketball might initially be designed to teach dribbling, then modified to include shooting and dribbling, and with time, include numerous fundamentals until actual game conditions exist. Another example is to begin with two-man situations, progress to three-man, and finally to five-man or team situations.

Most authorities agree that the amount of transfer can be increased if teaching is done with transfer as an objective. If the coach indicates, when explaining a drill, that certain elements are common to several activities, then learning will be enhanced if the players have had past experiences in any of the activities.

The objective and purpose of drills and how they fit into the game should be explained. If a player understands what he is supposed to realize from a drill, then learning will be facilitated and the parts can be more easily fitted together. A coach should teach for transfer to the total activity or game. A drill is not an end itself; it is a means to an end—the understanding of the total game.

SUMMARY

Transfer is not automatic, it has to be taught. The individual has to be aware of relationships—whether specific or general—between practice drills and game situations.

The more meaningful a drill is to the individual, the more likely transfer will result. Generalizations and principles should be pointed out to the player and then practice should be provided applying these common factors. If an old or learned response occurs in a new situation, transfer has occurred.

When breaking the game down into drills for the practice session, care should be taken not to design drills that teach a minute part of the game. A player learns the game from drills; the larger the parts, the easier the understanding of the whole.

Drills can be progressive in design also. Begin with a simple skill and add other game components until the whole picture is achieved. Explain the purpose and objective of all drills—this gives meaning and understanding by the player and a better chance of transfer of what is learned in the drill to the game.

SUGGESTED READINGS

Cratty, Bryant J.: *Movement Behavior and Motor Learning.* Second Edition. Philadelphia, Lea and Febiger, 1967, 367 pp.

Cratty, Bryant J.: *Psychology and Physical Activity.* Englewood Cliffs, Prentice-Hall, Inc., 1968, 214 pp.

Lawther, John D.: *The Learning of Physical Skills.* Englewood Cliffs, Prentice-Hall, Inc., 1968, 150 pp.

Oxendine, Joseph B.: *Psychology of Motor Learning.* New York, Appleton-Century-Crofts, 1968, 366 pp.

Singer, Robert N.: *Motor Learning and Human Performance.* New York, Macmillan Co., 1968, 354 pp.

CHAPTER 45

PRAISE OR PUNISHMENT?

Don Veller[*]

A N INDIVIDUAL'S DEEPEST EMOTIONAL needs all of his life are for recognition or approval, a feeling of importance. The most effective way to arouse enthusiasm is through appreciation and encouragement.

With rare exception in coaching much more can be accomplished privately by persuasion and encouragement than by yelling at candidates in the presence of other squad members. The temptation to shout at and deride players is so great, that most coaches would have to restrain themselves voluntarily to overcome the tendency.

A boy must be left with his dignity intact. Some, for various reasons, are more sensitive than others to public reprimand. We know a young athlete who had been orphaned early in life and was left to be reared by an older sister. They had a pretty tough time financially and this boy was denied many of the things his peers possessed. While growing up he became more or less bitter, adopting the attitude that the world and everyone in it was against him. Because of a fumble in practice one day his coach derided him before the other squad members. Because of this incident he was *down* and performed far below his potential for two or three weeks.

Some might say he was spoiled, a baby. No, he merely needed to be handled in a different manner—taken aside for friendly instruction or admonition.

Then there is the boy who is doing his best all the time. Admittedly there are few enough in this mold, but they do exist.

---

[*] Don Veller, "Praise or Punishment?" *Athletic Journal*, Vol. 48 (February 1968), pp. 78-81.

He will respond unfavorably to a tongue lashing in front of the group, especially if there is the slightest hint that his error was caused by lack of effort. We saw a scrapping 163-pound college fullback, who was a star the year before, gradually have the fight taken out of him by a new, not so smart coach who screamed at him (and others) incessantly. The constant yelling implied that the boy was not trying hard enough. At 163 pounds, how else could a boy be a star college fullback without a lot of *the old college try?*

The late Jock Sutherland, of Pittsburgh fame, said a coach who constantly goads his players is unsure of himself. John Bridgers, of Baylor University, has an admirable rule that no coach ever raises his voice at a player.

An athlete who has received a dressing down in the presence of the squad will often resort to making excuses, or blaming others. The complications here are obvious.

Therefore, nagging and sarcasm should be avoided, especially in front of the candidate's peers. This is not to say that a player never deserves a reprimand or a little prodding, but care should be taken in the selection of the individual toward which it is directed. Occasionally a conceited athlete can perhaps be helped by a sharp barb from the coach. The danger here, however, is that many of our apparently severe cases of egotism are really cover-ups for an inferiority complex. Yelling at such a fellow will make him worse.

Whether it is with players, faculty, principals or what have you, problems can be settled quicker and more efficiently in private. Then, too, shouting frequently reaches the ears of news media, parents and other outsiders.

Calling the boy aside and talking quietly with him can get the job done more effectively 99 percent of the time. A highly recommended method for dealing with an erring or slumping player, is to ask him privately to drop by the coach's office. It is truly amazing how a player will level with a coach behind the closed doors of an office where just the two of them are face to face. He will reveal things that could never be elicited in front of squad members. The slumping performer very often has prob-

lems, either real or apparent, which affect his play. Frequently
he and the coach can work them out in these private sessions. He
may then not only become a better performer, but also a better
citizen and the coach will concomitantly become a better coach.

It is not uncommon in one of these private talks to see mature
boys—yes, even in college—break down and cry while pouring
out their problems. How else can a coach help a boy without getting his side of the story?

It is sometimes best to say nothing to the lad who has made a
mistake, especially if it is quite obvious that he is already painfully aware of his error. Take the case of the quarterback—
with his team ahead 24-21, thirty seconds to go, throws a flat pass
squarely into the hands of the opponent's fastest back, who
sprints unmolested for a touchdown. A prudent coach said nothing to him, and would not have, even if he had not come out of
the game with big tears in his eyes.

Following is a quotation from an anonymous professional
football player, which points up another way in how not to reprimand a player: "I do not think I could take another season of
playing under him. He is the type of guy who chews you out
publicly—in a meeting or through the newspapers—but when
you get him face-to-face, he shies away from you. I do not respect a man like that, and do not want to play for him."

The following interesting and significant commentary comes
from another professional football player and is directed towards Allie Sherman, coach of the New York Giants, who had
coached this player in the Pro Bowl Game in Los Angeles. "You
get a lift playing for him. The guy I played for during the season, all I got from him was a growl if I blew an assignment.
When I came off the field in the Pro Bowl after making a good
block, Allie made a point of coming over and saying something
good. And if I made a mistake, he discussed it and he did not
cuss me. I wanted to play for him. It was different." Sherman is
quoted as saying: "The only inventory you have in this business
is human beings. Almost anyone can draw the circles and Xs on
the boards. But you have to learn that the circles and Xs are people and you have to operate within their limitations."

Military type punishment, disciplining the entire squad for the transgressions of one individual, should be used sparingly and as a last resort. Woody Hayes said: "One pressure we shall never use. We will never penalize the team for an individual infraction. We simply do not believe that is fair, and if it is not fair, it cannot contribute to the ultimate good. Also, we do not set one player up and discipline him as an example, for this not only creates resentment on his part, but usually develops resentment on the part of the balance of the squad. The player has definite rights. He has the right to be treated fairly and individually."[1]

One of the most effective methods of dispensing punishment is to let the squad make the decisions. Carefully oriented and operated through the captain, a set of rules and/or standards are drawn up, and when there is a violation, the squad members judge the case and mete out their own punishment. This method was spelled out in more detail in another article.[2]

Another method which has proved successful is to set up a grievance committee, usually composed of seniors. The idea here is that each player is pledged to report his own shortcomings or violations to the coach. If he does not report himself, then the committee is obligated to do so.

Giving boys the silent treatment can be an effective type of punishment and correction. This is a planned procedure wherein the other players are let in on the scheme to shun an individual who is not measuring up. The player will soon realize something is up and will make inquiry as to what is wrong. The opportunity for improvement has been revealed. Fear of social disapproval is a strong motivating factor. The cold-shoulder treatment is quite a jolt.

A somewhat similar treatment is one in which the coach, by innuendo, transmits the word of dissatisfaction through another player, perhaps a friend of the transgressor.

1. Woody Hayes, *Football at Ohio State* (Columbus, Ohio, The Ohio State University Press, 1957).

2. Don Veller, "Getting Them to Train," *Athletic Journal* (February 1967), p. 60.

When larger numbers are involved, such as desultory team performance, the novel method can be used effectively. This involves planting a rumor, so to speak, among the group through the captain or one of the players. In industry this is called the grapevine method. For example, the coach may want to get it around that he is going to make some changes in the lineup if the team does not show marked improvement.

Special gimmicks have been used effectively to punish or snap boys out of wrongdoing or poor performance. Occasionally such a gimmick will backfire. There is the case of a basketball team which was an overwhelming favorite, but which had not been performing quite as well as the coach expected. Attempting a little psychological punishment, he started the second team. The underdog team quickly forged well ahead. Then the coach entered his first team and the score mounted even more in favor of the other team. Everything his regulars did was wrong and the underdogs had a good night, winning in a big upset.

The coach decided to try another gimmick to snap them out of it. He passed the word that he was ashamed to ride home with them on the bus, leaving them in charge of an assistant. The team members, strongly believing the loss was the coach's fault, were almost mutinous. The affair finally culminated with the coach's apologizing to the squad, admitting he was largely to blame for the debacle.

There are many varieties of more or less minor punishments, such as trips around the goal posts or floor, early morning workouts, running up the stadium steps or extra push-ups. Each coach has his pet type.

Among the more common punishments, however, is *benching,* a procedure which has operated effectively for many years. The question, however, is whether or not the coach might be punishing the other (innocent) members of the team. He could be precluding their most efficient performance by holding out one of the good players. For instance, his play might be the difference between victory and defeat.

Benching sometimes occurs as the result of a coach's getting mad at a player. Even though it is difficult for him not to become provoked on occasions, staying sore at a player is not in itself a valid reason for keeping him on the bench. Again, it might hurt the other players, and then it becomes major punishment.

Even a more important point than severity, perhaps, is that the coach be consistent with his punishments. He must also make certain the punishment is related to the violation.

An excessive amount of threats creates an unfavorable atmosphere. To reduce the necessity for punishment do not say, "If you do such and such, I will do this." Better say, "I do not want this done."

Another admonishment, especially in the case of an inexperienced coach—be careful about predetermining or stating exactly what the punishment will be for a particular violation. Once a coach declares himself, he either has to stick to it, or lose face.

One very successful coach says when he has been particularly tough on a boy, he always makes it a point to talk with him before he leaves the locker room. "Never let a boy go home with a bad taste in his mouth," he says.

Woody Hayes, speaking on fairness said: "We find that a youngster is open to criticism and will accept it in the right manner as long as he is left with his dignity intact. If he still realizes that we have a very strong interest in him, our corrective measures can be quite severe, but we must leave him with his sense of importance to the squad."[3]

He goes on to say: "We coaches are not perfect and are apt to make mistakes just like anyone else. For that reason if a youngster feels that he has been unfairly dealt with, he has every right to come to the head coach and discuss it man-to-man without any threat of disciplinary action. If this involves some other coach on the staff then the player must first go to the other coach on the staff, and bring him to the head coach. The one promise we make to our players is this—we will make every effort to deal with his problem fairly. The final decision must rest with the head coach, but it is our promise that we will do everything we can to look out for that individual's welfare."

Although praise is important and necessary, it is sometimes

---

3. Hayes, *op. cit.*

more difficult to apply than punishment. Like punishment, it loses its effectiveness when administered too often. Choosing the time and the person for it is the real problem. The coach who praises everybody and everything is not going to accomplish very much, because when a genuine praiseworthy act occurs, further accolades will have very little meaning.

Coaches must be careful, too, about praising an isolated case, such as a good block, a circus catch or a long basket. When he praises one boy for making a good play, and then misses (does not see) another one, then the one who has been missed will probably feel slighted. Make a special note of this, because it happens too often, inadvertently, perhaps, most of the time, but still too often.

It is possible, yes probable, that boys will be praised too prolifically after a pleasant victory. Here again, it is easy to heap praise on the boys who carried the ball or hit the most baskets and neglect the blocks and passes which really made victory possible.

Whether or not we like to admit it, all of us have our favorites. It is highly probable that when praise is dispensed these favorites will get more than their share, even though we may not be aware of our partiality. Be on guard for this.

Even though some varieties or methods of praise have shortcomings, it remains one of the great motivating devices for inducing top performance. A testimonial to the powerful effect of praise as a motivator is exemplified through a well-validated experiment by a research specialist who used members of a large math class as subjects. After dividing the class into three equated groups, he pretested them. He then gave praise by name to group one, criticism by name to group two and ignored group three. Upon retesting it was discovered that group one improved twice as much as group two, which had improved slightly. Group three showed no deviation from the first testing. If, through more self-confidence, boys will compete better, it is possible that praise of performance, even though a mediocre one, might improve upon future accomplishments. All boys want recognition in some manner. Recognition by the coach may eventually bring recognition by the school and possibly the community. The person does not exist who will not do a better job after he gets a pat on the back.

In conclusion, may we say that there is no more obvious truism than that which says you can catch more flies with honey than with vinegar. To rephrase it, much more can be accomplished through praise than through punishment.

In any cross-section of our society (including the area of athletics) some punishment seems inevitable. However, the prudent coach will emphasize the positive (praise), not the negative (punishment).

An athlete (or anybody else) is happier and will perform better when his basic needs are satisfied. Among these are the need for acceptance, status, security, success, love and for strengthening his self image.

No prescription works more effectively to satisfy these basic needs than praise.

So praise them, coach, but wisely.

VERBAL CONDITIONING IN SELECTING
SKILLS

BOB BROUGHTON AND DALE O. NELSON*

SUCCESSFUL COACHES with such diverse personalities as Connie Mack and Paul Bryant have testified that there are relatively few great "natural" athletes. Many of our colleges and pro athletes possess about the same amount of physical ability. The degree of success they achieve depends primarily upon their mental attitude.

Now, if you agree that mental attitude can be changed either positively or negatively by the spoken word, it would appear that our coaches would do well to investigate the art of verbal conditioning.

As S. I. Hayakawa writes in *Language in Thought and Action,* "If meaningless noises will move the audience, meaningless noises must be made; if facts move them, facts must be given; if noble ideals move them, we must make our proposals appear noble; if they will respond only to fear, we must scare them stiff."

We know that people respond strongly to verbal stimuli. Consequently, the right word or expression can help tremendously in producing the desired result. Every coach should understand that *what* he says and *how* he says it can greatly affect his players' attitude and performance.

Though most of us know that verbal conditioning can produce amazing results, there is little scientific information available to go on. Having always been interested in this subject, we

* Bob Broughton and Dale O. Nelson, "Verbal Conditioning in Selected Skills," *Scholastic Coach,* Vol. 37 (November 1967), pp. 38-40 and 44-47.

decided to investigate the effects of certain words and phraseology on selected measurable physical skills.

Our first problem was to arrange an objective battery of tests. Though we understood that the basic ingredients of performance cannot always be isolated, we felt that such components as speed, reaction time, strength and endurance are consistently applicable. We therefore selected three tests that abounded in these qualities.

Our subjects consisted of sixteen members of the Utah State football and wrestling teams. Each subject took each of the three tests under four different conditions—one in which no words were used (control) and the others in which positive, negative and neutral terms were used.

The subject, alone in the laboratory with the experimenter, took five trials in each verbal category, with the experimenter employing the following phraseology, accenting the italicized words.

Test One: Grip Strength

This was measured with a hand grip dynamometer whose face was turned down so that the subject could not read the dial.

NEUTRAL TERMS. As the subject came into the lab, the experimenter said, "Let's get started." After the first trial, the experimenter said "O.K." After two trials, "A little more strength on it." After three trials, "O.K." After four trials, "One more to do."

POSITIVE TERMS. As the subject came in, "You look as if you are *Full of Strength* and ready to go." After one trial, "Good." After two, "That score was *best of all*." After three, "That's a *mighty fine score*." After four, "Your total score is going to be an *extremely good one*."

NEGATIVE TERMS. When subject came in, "*Wake up* and let's get started." After one, "*Not too good*." After two, "A *cold* try." After three, "*Bad*." After four, "That try was in *vain*."

Test Two: Starting and Running Six Feet

A plumb bob was used to set the subject at the starting line (in an upright position) so that he ran exactly six feet each time. An athletic performance analyzer was activated automatically as a horn sounded in the timing device.

The subject was commanded to "Get ready," at which time the device was activated. The command of execution (horn) sounded from one to two seconds later, and was varied each time so that the subject could not guess the timing of the horn.

A cord from the timing device was clipped to the rear of the subject's trunks. At the end of six feet, the cord was pulled from the timing device, thus stopping the timer and giving us an accurate timing. The timing, to the nearest 1/100 second, measured a combination of reaction time and the time it took to move a very short distance (six feet).

NEUTRAL TERMS. After subject completed grip test, "We'll begin now." After trial one, "That's about normal." After two, "You need to keep your feet going forward." After three, "Work on your feet action." After four, "Last time."

POSITIVE TERMS. After completing grip test, "Let's see if you can do as *well* in your starts." After trial one, "An *outstanding* effort." After two, "You look as *fast* as Bob Hayes." After three, "*Excellent* quickness." After four, "You've had some *fine* tries; let's make this the best one."

NEGATIVE TERMS. After grip test, "Let's get the *lead out* on the start." After one, "*Disappointing.*" After two, "You looked like Grandma on that one." After three, "*Terrible.*" After four, "*Poor* score."

Test Three: 60-Second All-Out Ride on a Bicycle Ergometer Against a Ten-Pound Resistance

This was used for testing leg strength and as a reflection of endurance. Scores were in terms of revolutions, with the verbal communications given at 12-second intervals.

NEUTRAL TERMS. After the running test, "Last exercise." After 12 seconds, "O.K." After 24 seconds, "The last person did well on this one." After 36 seconds, "Your leg work counts here." After 48 seconds, "Let's get finished."

POSITIVE TERMS. After running test, "Keep the *good work* going on the bicycle too." After 12 seconds, *Outstanding ef-*

fort." After 24 seconds, *"Great* work." After 36 seconds, "It's going to be a *phenomenal* ride." After 48 seconds, "O.K., now finish as if you're in the Olympics and riding for a gold medal."

NEGATIVE TERMS. After running test, "Pick it up now." After 12 seconds, "You act *tired."* After 24 seconds, *"Slow."* After 36 seconds, "You look *exhausted."* After 48 seconds, "You might as well finish."

Results

The data were treated statictically with analysis of variance procedure. The grip strength and the starting and running tests were found to be significantly different at the .01 level of probability, while the bicycle ergometer scores were found to be non-significant, although a consistent trend was apparent.

The accompanying table shows that for Grip Strength, the response to the positive terms (137.96 lbs.) was significantly better than the other scores. Though the three other scores were not deemed significant, it should be noted that the negative terms produced the poorest mean score (130.98 lbs.). The score for the control, or no-words, condition came next (132.58 lbs.), followed by the score for the neutral terms (133.21 lbs.).

The Starting and Running test also recorded a significantly better score (1.145 sec.) for the positive terms, as well as a significantly low score (1.200 sec.) for the neutral terms.

Although the scores on the Bicycle Ergometer were not deemed significant, it should be noted that the best score (300.56 revolutions) was produced in response to the positive terms, while the poorest scores were produced in response to the neutral (281.44) and the negative (282.88) terms.

TABLE 46-I

MEAN SCORES FOR THE PHYSICAL TESTS

| | Verbal Conditioning Terms | | | |
	Positive	Negative	Control	Neutral
Bicycle ergometer (revolutions) ..	300.56	282.88	286.55	281.44
Grip strength (pounds)	137.96	130.98	132.58	133.21
Starting and running (seconds) ..	1.145	1.176	1.181	1.200

The pattern of performance on all three tests showed that the positive terms produced the best responses (highest scores).

We all know that most people respond favorably to a positive verbal approach; it seems to motivate them, build confidence and inflate the ego. Though our subjects were not familiarized with the procedure beforehand, they seemed to become aware of our purpose early in the study. It has been demonstrated that knowledge will affect a person's performance.

The response to the negative terms was of particular interest. On several occasions, the subject became aggravated enough to stalk out of the laboratory—so angry, in fact, that he had to be persuaded to return the next day to complete the testing.

Asked why they had lost control, the subjects would reply that though they knew what was happening, they just could not help becoming angry. Oddly enough, it was the subjects who most understood our purpose who reacted the most violently to the negative terms.

Every athlete requires confidence in order to achieve top performance and this is a factor which can be manipulated by the coach through proper verbal conditioning.

The results of this study, though exploratory in nature, produced the expected results. They lent validity to the value of positive terminology in dealing with athletes. Obviously, the proper selection of words and the proper emphasis on them can enhance performance.

The task is to discover and apply the best positive terms in teaching physical skills.

CHAPTER 47

COACH'S DILEMMA

HARRY H. HOITSMA*

How can the coach help the player overcome the psychological problems involved in changing a skill technique? Understanding the pitfalls of the transitional stage of learning is the key.

HOW MANY TIMES has a coach made what he considers a constructive suggestion encouraging his player to alter his batting stance or add a new pitch to his repertoire only to find that his well-intended advice produces results directly opposite to those desired?

The coach who must make recommendations for a drastic change in the execution of a skill by one of his players faces a perplexing problem for himself as well as the player.

Regardless of the sport involved, the serious effects of change for the athlete are often manifested in discouragement, disillusionment, confusion and ultimately failure to perform to maximum capacity. A change in batting style, a different way to execute the jump shot, a new procedure for throwing the forward pass—all of these changes are not without a learning problem for the coach and the athlete alike. Attempts to change often bring poorer execution of the skill and a loss of confidence for the athlete, leading to reduced caliber of team performance and, of course, additional anxiety for the coach. What are the underlying reasons for this collapse? How can the coach still teach and yet avoid these pitfalls?

Part of the answer lies in recognizing the existence of a "transitional stage." While learning a new or different technique or

---

* Harry H. Hoitsma, "Coach's Dilemma," *Journal of Health, Physical Education, and Recreation,* Vol. 32 (December 1961), pp. 25 and 58.

procedure in the execution of a skill, the player oftentimes reaches what can be called the transitional stage of learning. This term refers to a period when the player is no longer able to execute the skill as he had prior to the coach's suggestion and still has not reached the state of mastering the new technique or procedure. As a result, the player is trapped in a predicament of drastic consequences almost always manifested in a reduction in the skill. No longer able to perform the skill in his comfortable, familiar manner, yet not at ease or confident in his newly developing technique, the player becomes disheartened by his failure to perform at a level equal to his past performances—which may have been quite poor, at best. Disillusionment and loss of confidence result, and the player performs worse than ever. The net result may be his removal from the line-up and relegation to a bench-sitting role as the forgotten man of the team.

The coach is left in a state of severe frustration or consternation. But there are several things a coach may do to prevent this problem, or at least mollify its effect.

In guiding an athlete toward the development of a different technique or procedure to execute a skill in any sport, the coach should:

1. Make certain that his suggestions are sound, based on methods that have been proven successful in practice, and that they are applicable to the particular athlete involved.

2. Be aware, and make certain that the player is also aware, of the problems that must be faced during the transitional stage of learning.

3. Be positive in his approach to the player, encouraging him whenever possible, offering suggestions that serve as an incentive for learning.

4. Emphasize correct movements, stimulating a serious, meaningful practice under favorable conditions.

The coach who knows through personal participation, careful analysis and objective consideration that his method of executing a skill is sound and that it has been proven successful is most likely to instill confidence in himself on the part of his players.

This confidence aids in the player's desire to master the skill according to techniques and procedures suggested by the coach.

The importance of acknowledging that many successful athletes, even at the professional level, often violate sound principles of execution must be realized. Superior native ability makes this possible for the exceptional athlete. This is hardly an indication that any method of execution is correct, but the coach may have difficulty convincing the athlete that this is true.

Probably the most important consideration in teaching a new technique or procedure is that both the coach and the player must understand the pitfalls of the transitional stage of learning. This awareness on the part of the player and coach will aid significantly in reducing hazards. The seeping panic that fills the mind of the athlete, who finds that he cannot execute a skill as well as he once did (however poorly that may have been) and has not mastered the techniques that are foreign to him, may be eliminated entirely if the coach and the player are both alerted to this danger. A realistic approach enables the athlete to focus his full attention on learning; it reduces the psychological burden of excessive anxiety and unnecessary concern over a problem that he can and will overcome with studied application on his part—and with the encouragement, understanding and patience of the coach.

Understanding the implications of the transitional stage of learning will also serve to reduce the athlete's natural desire for immediate results when employing a new procedure, thereby helping to eliminate another psychological problem. The desire for speedy perfection and the loss of interest which follows when this desire remains unmet is another serious pitfall that can be avoided. The more likely occurrence is that the athlete making change will get worse before he gets better. Obviously, an awareness of this perplexing situation is the first step in making adjustments to overcome it.

During the transitional stage, the athlete needs encouragement as much as he needs suggestions and advice for mechanical improvement. The coach must exhibit extreme patience during this period, coordinating his suggestions for mechanical improvement with a sincere understanding of the athlete's psychological state.

Unawareness of the problem of the transitional stage of learning and an inability to cope with it if discovered, will only serve to compound the innumerable problems of the coach and to produce discouragement and failure with all its negatively concomitant ramifications for the athlete. Understanding, encouragement, constructive criticism, patience, praise when deserved and sincerity of purpose are the requirements for the coach who looks for beneficial results from a change in technique.

CHAPTER 48

EMOTIONAL UPSET AND PSYCHOSOMATIC PROBLEMS IN COACHING

Warren R. Johnson*

THE PURPOSE OF THIS ARTICLE is to alert present and future coaches to a hazard which has quite needlessly driven good men out of coaching and has made coaching unpleasant and quite possibly dangerous to a great many others. This is the hazard of prolonged emotional stress—the type of stress which may aggravate numerous physical and mental disturbances and may lead eventually to any of a variety of temporary or chronic psychosomatic symptoms such as ulcers, indigestion, skin disorders, headaches and circulatory disturbances. Coaching need not be dangerous, but it may be unless the hazards are understood and precautions against them are taken.

High school and college coaching seems to be one of the most attractive challenges for men in the field of education. Because of the opportunity to work on intimate terms with comparatively small groups of talented boys, a great many teachers welcome an opportunity to add coaching to their other duties, even though extra compensation may be insignificant or not provided at all.

Research in physical education has revealed to us what athletic sports participation does for young men; but what does coaching do *to* coaches? This question has not been studied extensively, in spite of the fact that the welfare of a large number of individuals is concerned.

Coaching is more or less strenuous from a purely physical point of view. In addition, most coaching responsibilities in-

---

* Warren R. Johnson, "Emotional Upset and Psychosomatic Problems in Coaching," *Athletic Journal*, Vol. 37 (February 1957), pp. 44-46.

volve pressure and in many cases tension. For example, what about the matters of budget, money raising, getting along with administrators, game scheduling, public relations, securing and caring for equipment, planning and supervising trips, attending to discipline, dealing with the public and alumni groups and seeing that the contract is renewed. There is also the matter of coaching and the usual teaching job must be done before coaching begins.

Briefly, the coach's life is full of activities which, in combination and in terms of the exacting personal relations involved, are likely to keep his nervous system and endocrine glands jumping overtime.

Of course, some men take to the high-speed movement, routine and adjustments of the coach, just as some fighter pilots seem to thrive on combat flying. However, at the other extreme, physicians have held coaching responsible for severe illness and even death at comparatively early ages. H. C. Carlson, physician and basketball coach at the University of Pittsburgh, wrote us that he considers coaching a very real threat to health and reported that he has compiled a list of well-known men who are presumed to have died because of coaching or who have left this work because of illness or other evidences of severe emotional stress. Clearly, those individuals whose success as a coach is measured entirely in terms of the scoreboard and whose positions and security depend upon this kind of criterion are in a particularly hazardous position health-wise. The educational growth of the athlete is not likely to be of prime importance to the individual who must coach under these conditions.

We have studied the emotional reactions of coaches in a limited way. One technique used was that of studying emotional arousal by way of some physiological indicators such as pulse rate, blood pressure and galvanic skin response before, during and after local competition and regional tournaments. We found that some of the coaches became as upset, as indicated by pulse rate, as does the average athlete whom we had studied previously. Pulse rates of one hundred thirty beats per minute were not uncommon for men whose normal was below eighty. Blood

pressure of the coaches was also definitely up, but not as much
as that of athletes such as wrestlers and boxers.

The emotional state of athletes, while often intense before
competition, tends to decline when the contest begins and is usually normal a relatively short time after the contest. In other
words, the tension of the mind and body of the athlete may be
said to find relief in physical action. This seems to be a point of
great importance because the human organism is well prepared
to handle intense emotional excitation for a short period of
time and, indeed, may well be *supercharged* by it. However, prolonged emotional stress that is maintained for considerable periods, even though it is less intense, is quite another matter and is
more likely to be damaging. It is this prolonged though low intensity stress which is held responsible for the majority of psychosomatic ailments that plague an incredible number of our
population.

The coach must contend with emotional stress of the latter
type. Apart from the pressure involved in the routine business
of coaching, we have found that the coach's pre-contest emotional excitation frequently begins early, continues throughout the
contest and lingers afterwards. We have known coaches whose
pulse rates did not drop below one hundred for hours after
competition. One wrestling coach expressed part of this problem
aptly when he said: "The wrestlers are lucky. They only have to
wrestle one man, but I have to wrestle the whole team." Consequently, coaches describe themselves as being *worn out, washed
out* or *beat* when a contest is over.

Our second means of studying the emotional upset of coaches
was through the questionnaire technique. In one study a group
of outstanding American coaches gave us some information on
this subject. The following were named by them as common
coaching experiences which are manifestations of emotional upset: 1) unable to sleep well the night before contests; 2) have
trouble sleeping the night after contests; 3) feel irritable or upset as competition approaches; 4) feel quite fatigued when it is
all over; 5) lose appetite on the day of matches; 6) feel deeply
upset over losses; and 7) have the feeling that coaching takes a

good deal out of a person. Of course, not all of the coaches specified all of these reactions.[1]

At a coaches' clinic held in the spring of 1956, Mr. Julian L. Dyke, a Maryland high school coach, distributed a questionnaire to fifty-one coaches in attendance. The following questions were asked and responses are indicated under *yes* and *no*.

		Yes	*No*
1.	Are you able to sleep before a game?	38	13
2.	Do you have trouble sleeping the night after contests?	19	32
3.	Do you feel fatigued after it is all over?	47	4
4.	Do you feel irritable and upset as the game approaches?	20	31
5.	Do you lose your appetite on the day of a game?	5	46
6.	Do you feel deeply upset over losses?	51	0
7.	Do you have the feeling that coaching takes a great deal out of you?	51	0
8.	Do you remain seated on the bench during games?	7	44
9.	Are you considering leaving coaching?	13	38
10.	If you were in college now, would you still plan to enter coaching?	34	17

11. Do you experience any physical or nervous reaction as the game nears, as it is played or after it is over? Some responses to this question were: "I break into a sweat; sometimes I'm cold when it's really warm." "Sometimes during games I itch." "I just might be pessimistic but I imagine everything bad can happen to my team. I just worry the whole game." "After the game is over, I relax by taking it easy. By the time the game is over I'm beat." "As game time approaches, I grow sleepy and depressed. I feel tired in every muscle and would like to and possibly could sleep. On occasion players and coaches have asked me if I felt all right because I looked pale and according to some had a far-away look in my eyes."

When considering the intensity and length of emotional stress, it is also necessary to consider that after a few years a coach's youthful resiliency tends to fade gradually. As a rule, the young coach is very nearly on a par with his athletes in regard to vital-

---

1. A. W. Umbach and W. R. Johnson, *Successful Wrestling* (St. Louis, C. V. Mosby Co., 1953), Chap. 5.

ity and fitness. But as time passes he tends to become less well conditioned, less fit and less able to carry the load lightly. He tends to accumulate flesh and to deprive himself of rest and sleep because of the demands of his work. In a word, he tends to become less able to stand up under the demands of coaching and the pressures of emotional stress. Then there is every likelihood that coaching can become a serious hazard to his health.

As a matter of fact, if heart or circulatory disturbances, unusual nervousness or other conditions which are known to be aggravated by emotional excitation are acquired, it may well be wise to give up coaching. An alternative choice for those who love to work with youth and who feel that they have an important service to render is to switch from varsity level coaching to intramurals, recreation programs and athletic club or neighborhood youth programs where qualified leadership is needed desperately and where emotional stress is much easier to avoid.

Coaches and would-be coaches might well give serious consideration to the following suggestions:

1. *Physical Examination.* Before going into the kind of work, either on a part-time or a full-time basis, the prospective coach should have a thorough physical examination with special attention given to the circulatory system. This check-up is especially important if the individual has lapsed into middle-aged inactivity and careless eating and overeating. Conceivably, the examination may show that coaching is really not a safe occupation for him.

2. *Medical Check-ups.* The coach should continue to have periodic medical check-ups, particularly before and after his sport season. In other words, he should take as good care of himself as he does of his athletes.

3. *Care of Himself.* Such things as nervousness and lingering bodily pain should be taken seriously, especially if they persist and increase in intensity as time passes. If they do, the coach should consult a doctor about them.

4. *Modification of Habits.* In the course of his coaching, if he discovers that he has acquired a chronic or incipient illness, or if he finds that this work is taking too much out of him, in

addition to having a medical examination, the coach should study his method of coaching for habits which may be putting undue strain on him. Modification of these habits may make leaving the coaching field unnecessary. For example, many of the details pertaining to equipment, keeping records, making preparations for home contests or trips, etc., can be handled well by athletes and other student help. Such chores amount to a tremendous mass of detail for one man to carry and, incidentally, they often interfere with the more important business of coaching.

A coach may also find that he is permitting himself to be carried away by his emotions before and during contests. A more realistic philosophy of athletic competition and a little self-control may be all that are needed to make coaching pleasant and safe. By exercising self-control he will probably set a better example of mature behavior for his team and other students.

It is important to realize that undesirable emotional behavior can be modified. We are slaves to our emotions only when we permit ourselves to be. Over the years we have had quite a number of graduate students who took these suggestions seriously and found that coaching does not have to be the nerve-jarring, emotional trauma they had permitted it to become. For example, one coach used to have a startling assortment of psychosomatic symptoms, including actual hives, indigestion, and sleeplessness, occur before and after his team's contests—simply because as an athlete he had associated competition with intense emotional arousal and had continued this association into his coaching. His coaching days were definitely numbered and he had received medical warnings to this effect. But when he realized that things do not have to work this way, he changed his behavior. In a short time he was enjoying coaching more than ever before, was free of symptoms and was confident that the change had made him a better coach and surely a healthier influence on his athletes and students.

5. *Preparation for the Sports Season.* The coach should view his sports season as a period of considerable physical and emotional stress and prepare for it accordingly just as his athletes do.

It is essential that he adopt a living regime which will provide for adequate rest and sleep. A diet that is well balanced but light should be selected. Heavy eating, which is often more common when men are under emotional stress, and overweight tend to put additional strain on the heart and blood vessels, thus cutting efficiency and increasing possible danger. It is important for the coach to get himself into physical shape. He should start slowly and follow a graded program of exercises until he reaches a satisfactory level of fitness and then hold that level. Although most coaches will probably not attempt to stay with the exercise regime of their athletes, they can usually use part of the conditioning time for their own lighter routine and should do so throughout the season.

If exercise is done properly and is accompanied by a good moderate diet and adequate rest, the organism is brought to the point where it can do a bigger job with greater ease, a greater sense of well-being and a decreased likelihood of *going to pieces* under the physical and emotional stresses of coaching.